Individualized Reading:
Readings

Compiled by

Sam Duker

The Scarecrow Press, Inc.
Metuchen, N.J.   1969

This Book is Dedicated
to
Guy A. Lackey, Professor Emeritus at
Oklahoma State University. Treasured
friend, inspired teacher, and warm
human being.

Table of Contents

	Page
Introduction	9
Acknowledgments	11
1. The Nature of Individualized Reading	19
Using Paperbacks. Jonathan Kozol...	21
Criteria for an Individualized Reading Program and Their Rationales, San Diego County Department of Education	24
What Is Independent Reading Like? Alexander Frazier...	29
Are Skills Neglected in an Individualized Reading Program? Lyman C. Hunt, Jr. ...	33
2. Individualized Reading in the Primary Grades	40
How Individualized Reading Was Used in One First Grade. Elizabeth A. Senderling...	41
Individualized Reading in a Combination First and Second Grade Classroom. Sylvia W. Roston...	58
How 189 Third Grade Teachers Provided for Individual Differences. Janie K. Bollinger...	67
3. Individualized Reading in the Intermediate Grades	72
Individualized Reading Procedures in a Fourth Grade. Carol H. Peters...	73
A Fifth Grade Individualized Reading Program. Glenda A. Gray...	76
The Individualized Approach to the Teaching of Reading in a Fifth Grade. Floy Utz...	80
The Use of Individualized Reading in Another Fifth Grade. Marguerite P. Caliver...	85
How Individualized Reading Worked in a Sixth Grade. Hazel S. Webb...	94
4. Individualizing Reading Practices	99
A Longitudinal Study of Individualized Reading. Frances V. Cyrog...	101

5

Individualizing Reading Practices
    A Survey of Individualized Reading Practices.
      Beverly M. Dernbach...   105
    Teachers' Problems in Using Individualized
      Reading. Donna Delph...   118
    Survey of Teaching Practices in Individualized
      Reading on a County-Wide Basis. Baltimore
      County Board of Education...   136
    How 78 Teachers Employed Individualized
      Reading in Their Classrooms. Anna M. Rix... 146
    Difficulties Faced by Individualized Reading
      Teachers. Patrick J. Groff...   150
    Survey of 150 Classroom Teachers Combining
      Individualized Reading with Basal Reading.
      Beverly L. McKay...   155

5. Orientation to Individualized Reading   161
    How Does a Teacher Prepare Himself to Use
      Individualized Reading? Patrick J. Groff...   162
    How a Fifth Grade Class was Introduced to
      Individualized Reading. Glenda A. Gray...   167
    The Effectiveness of an Individualized Reading
      Program. Phyliss S. Adams...   169

6. Individualized Reading Procedures   207
  Teacher-Pupil Conferences
    How 47 Teachers Used Teacher-Pupil
      Conferences in Their Individualized
      Reading Programs. Gertrude M. Sullivan...   209
    A Checklist for Teacher-Pupil Conferences.
      Sylvia W. Roston...   215
    Using Teacher-Pupil Conferences to Develop
      Reading Skills. Doris D. Roettger...   217
    How One Teacher Kept Records on Her
      Conferences with Pupils. Anna M. Hune...   218
  Sharing
    Fifty Ways of Sharing in an Individualized
      Reading Class. Amy E. Jensen...   221
    How Children Can Share Their Reading
      Experiences. Auline L. Bailey...   229
  Record Keeping
    Record Keeping in an Individualized Reading
      Program. Dorothy L. Donahue...   232
  Combining Programs
    Should Individualized Reading and Basal Reading
      be Combined? Gudelia Fox and
      Raymond B. Fox...   235

7. Individual Differences and Individualized Reading   237
    ⋁How Children Differ from Each Other.
        Edgar S. Farley...   238
    Principles of Individualization of Instruction.
        Roy P. Wahle...   242
    Individualized Reading and the Disadvantaged
        Child. Beverly M. Keener...   246

8. Books! Books! and More Books!   249
    Using Children's Literature Effectively.
        Charlotte S. Huck...   250
    How One Teacher Prepared Reading Guides.
        Robert G. Delisle...   258

9. The Teacher of Individualized Reading   267
    A Teacher Inventory. San Diego County
        Department of Education...   268
    Training Individualized Reading Teachers
        Through the Use of Films.
        Lyman C. Hunt, Jr. ...   288

10. The Librarian's Role in Individualized Reading   297
    How the Librarian Can Help the Individualized
        Reading Teacher. Patrick J. Groff...   298
    A Librarian Views Individualized Reading.
        Marguerite P. Archer...   302
    Another Librarian's View of Individualized
        Reading. Jean E. Lowrie...   307

11. Reactions of Pupils and Their Parents   313
    Inventory of Reading Attitudes. San Diego
        County, Department of Education...   315
    Asking Children About Their Reading
        Experiences. Doris D. Roettger...   321
    Some Features Children Like About Individualized
        Reading. Rose A. Arkley...   323
    How Parents Feel About Individualized Reading.
        Auline L. Bailey...   325
    ⋁ Children's Feelings About Individualized
        Reading. Anna M. Hune...   327
    A Survey of Children's Attitudes Toward
        Individualized Reading. Glenda A. Gray...   330
    A "Book Motivation Scale." Sylvia W. Roston...   333
    Pupil Reaction to Individualized Reading.
        Auline L. Bailey...   336
    What Parents Can Do. Amy E. Jensen...   339

7

12. Evaluation and Results   341
    How Does a Child Read? Doris D. Roettger... 343
    A Chart for Measuring Progress in Reading
        Skills. Marjorie R. Anderson...   348
    Guidelines for Teachers Planning to Use
        Individualized Reading at the First Grade
        Level. Phylliss S. Adams...   352
    Test Results. Doris D. Roettger...   359
    How Children Using Individualized Reading
        Performed on Reading Tests. Rose A.
        Arkley...   365
    Reading Gains in Individualized Reading as
        Measured by Standardized Tests. Anna
        M. Hune...   370
    Reading Test Scores of Children Taught by
        the Individualized Reading Approach.
        Frances V. Cyrog...   372
    Desirable Outcomes of a Reading Program.
        Amy E. Jensen...   374

13. History of Individualized Reading   376
    Breaking the Lockstep. Frederic Burk...   377
    Individual Instruction. Frederic Burk...   383
    Development of the Individualized Reading
        Movement. Frances M. Seeber...   387
    History of the Teaching of Reading. Jane
        A. Goode...   412

14. Research   423
    A Plan for Research. San Diego County
        Department of Education...   424
    Needed Research. Sam Duker...   446

15. Summary   456

Index of Names   458

Subject Index   462

Introduction

The teaching of reading in the elementary school and elsewhere presents extraordinary challenges. There are many approaches to this task but no panaceas. One such approach is the use of individualized reading instruction. Proponents of this approach tend to be highly enthusiastic about its use, while opponents are sceptical about its effectiveness.

Recently I compiled a bibliography of the material that has been written about individualized reading. This was published in July 1968 by the Scarecrow Press.[1] In that work a lengthy introduction presents a description of individualized reading procedures and of the arguments offered for and against its use. Since this is readily available, a similar description will not be included in this introduction.

It is very difficult to make a selection of material that could most profitably be included in a book of readings. One always regrets the necessary omission of some material. While a small portion of the contents of this book has appeared in well-known journals and is therefore generally available, the major portion of this book is made up of selections from unpublished materials such as academic theses and other reports of research which generally are not conveniently available. The aim has been to select passages which tell about actual procedures used in individual reading rather than passages giving opinions for or against individualized reading.

Almost all of the items included have been abridged to avoid duplication. To reduce the bulk of this book, bibliographical and footnote references have been abbreviated by using the entry number of the item in my bibliography when it is to be found there.

Note

1. Duker, Sam <u>Individualized Reading: An Annotated Bibliography</u>. Metuchen, N. J. Scarecrow Press, 1968.

Acknowledgments

My interest in the individualized reading approach to the teaching of reading goes back many years. When I used this approach as an elementary school teacher, I did not know that it had a name or that so many others were also using this approach.

A book of readings, I feel, should be more useful at this time than a book written by any one person. I have selected material which is recent, not previously re-published, and factual rather than opinionated. This book should be of value to the classroom teacher as well as to the student in teacher training.

To prepare myself for making the selection of materials to be included in this book I was helped by many individuals. First of all I should thank my pupils at Hawkins School in Grady County, Oklahoma; then my student teachers at Brooklyn College who worked so hard to make individualized reading effective in the classes to which they were assigned; last, but not least those many people from whom I gained ideas about this approach to reading instruction. It is not possible to list all the names of persons falling into the last category but I must mention Dr. May Lazar in particular.

I am also greatly indebted to the Brooklyn College Library and its staff for their cooperation in securing materials on interlibrary loans and for many other services.

Most of all, I acknowledge my obligation to the kind and gracious authors of the material included in this volume. The formal acknowledgments which follow this paragraph do not begin to adequately thank them for their contribution.

Excerpts from the article by Jonathan Kozol entitled, "Life at an Early Age," which appeared in The New York Times Book Review, February 25, 1968, are used with the kind permission of the author and of The New York Times. Copyright (c) 1968.

11

Excerpts from the 1964 Ohio State University master's thesis entitled, A Comparative Study of Two Methods of Teaching Reading at the Fifth Grade Level are used with the kind permission of the author, Marguerite P. Caliver.

Excerpts from the 1963 Ohio State University master's thesis entitled, A Comparative Study of Two Approaches to the Teaching of Reading at the Sixth Grade Level are used with the kind permission of the author, Hazel S. Webb.

Excerpts from the 1964 Claremont Graduate School master's thesis entitled, A Longitudinal Study of an Individualized Program in Reading are used with the kind permission of the author, Frances V. Cyrog.

Excerpts from the 1965 DePaul University master's thesis entitled, Approaches Toward the Individualized Reading Program in Selected School Districts in Cook and DuPage Counties, Illinois are used with the kind permission of the author, Beverly M. Dernbach.

Excerpts from the 1963 Ball State Teachers College master's thesis entitled, An Investigation of Problems in Individualized Reading Felt by Selected Elementary Teachers in the Public Schools of Hammond, Indiana are used with the kind permission of the author, Donna Delph.

Excerpts from A Pilot Study of Individualized Reading in Baltimore County Public Elementary Schools, 1957-1958 are used with the kind permission of the Baltimore County Board of Education.

Excerpts from the 1962 Kutztown State College master's thesis entitled, A Survey of Individualized Reading as Practiced by Teachers in Several Elementary Schools in Pennsylvania are used with the kind permission of the author, Anna M. Rix.

Excerpts from the article by Patrick J. Groff entitled, "A Check on Individualized Reading," which appeared in Education 84:397-401, March 1964, are used with the kind permission of the author and of the Bobbs-Merrill Company, publishers of Education. Copyright (c) 1964.

Excerpts from the 1964 Drake University master's thesis entitled, Individualized Reading as Part of an Eclectic Reading Program are used with the kind permission of the author, Beverly L. McKay.

13

Excerpts from the article by Patrick J. Groff entitled, "Helping Teachers Begin Individualized Reading," which appeared in National Elementary Principal 43(4):47-50, February 1964, are used with the kind permission of the author and of the Department of Elementary School Principals, N. E. A.

Excerpts from the 1965 Marshall University master's thesis entitled, A Study of the Individualized Reaching Program at Holy Elementary School, Charleston, West Virginia are used with the kind permission of the author, Glenda A. Gray.

Excerpts from the 1962 University of Denver doctoral dissertation entitled, An Investigation of an Individualized Reading Program and a Modified Basal Reading Program in First Grade are used with the kind permission of the author, Phylliss S. Adams.

Excerpts from the 1966 Rhode Island College master's thesis entitled, A Study of The Conference Technique in Reading Instruction Among Elementary Teachers of Rhode Island are used with the kind permission of the author, Gertrude M. Sullivan.

Excerpts from the 1962 National College of Education master's thesis entitled, An Individualized Reading Program in a First and Second Grade are used with the kind permission of the author, Sylvia W. Roston. Copyright (c) 1964.

Excerpts from the 1964 University of Tennessee master's thesis entitled, The Effectiveness of an Individualized Reading Program in Developing Reading Skills and Interest in Reading are used with the kind permission of the author, Doris D. Roettger.

Excerpts from the 1959 Ohio State University master's thesis entitled, The Organization, Implementation and Evaluation of an Individualized Reading Program in an Upper Socio-Economic Community are used with the kind permission of the author, Anna M. Hune.

Excerpts from the article by Amy E. Jensen entitled, "Attracting Children to Books," which appeared in Elementary English 33:332-39, October 1956, are used with the kind permission of the author and of the National Council of Teachers of English.

Program in Grade Six are used with the kind permission of the author, Robert G. Delisle.

Excerpts from An Experimental Project Appraising the Effectiveness of a Program Series on Reading Instruction Using Open-Circuit Television, a report on grant number 736059.00 N. D. E. A., are used with the kind permission of the author, Lyman C. Hunt, Jr.

Excerpts from the article by Patrick J. Groff entitled, "The Librarian and Individualized Reading," which appeared in The Wilson Library Bulletin 36:359-61, January 1960, are used with the kind permission of the author and of the Wilson Library Bulletin.

Excerpts from the article by Marguerite P. Archer entitled, "Individualized Reading," which appeared in the Library Journal 86:3609-11, October 15, 1961, are used with the kind permission of the author and of the Library Journal. Copyright (c) R. R. Bowker, 1961.

Excerpts from the article by Jean E. Lowrie entitled, "Elementary School Libraries Today," which appeared in The Library Quarterly 30:27-36, January 1960, are used with the kind permission of the author and of the University of Chicago Press. Copyright (c) 1960.

Excerpts from the 1961 University of Washington master's thesis entitled, The Analysis and Evaluation of an Individualized Reading Program for Third Graders Based on Contemporary Children's Literature are used with the kind permission of the author, Rose A. Arkley.

Excerpts from the 1964 Willimantic State College master's thesis entitled, A Study of Individualized Reading in an Ability Grouped Sixth Grade Class at The Bolton Elementary School are used with the kind permission of the author, Marjorie R. Anderson.

Excerpts from the article by Frederic Burk entitled, "Breaking the Lock-Step," which appeared in the N. E. A. Journal 13:123-24, April 1924, are used with the kind permission of the National Education Association.

Excerpts from the 1965 University of Kansas master's thesis entitled, An Evaluation of Two Methods of Meeting Individual Differences in Teaching First Grade Reading are used with the kind permission of the author, Frances M. Seeber.

16

Excerpts from the 1965 Baylor University master's thesis entitled, A Historical Study of Reading Instruction in the Elementary Schools of the United States, 1880-1963, are used with the kind permission of the author, Jane A. Goode.

The article, "Needed Research on Individualized Reading" by Sam Duker, which appeared in Elementary English 43:220-25+, March 1966, is used with the kind permission of the National Council of Teachers of English.

Chapter 1

The Nature of Individualized Reading

It is the essence of individualized reading that there is no one single, best way to employ this approach. No two teachers are likely to use identical procedures. No one teacher is likely to employ identical ways of conducting his class from one year to the next. Teaching methods are adapted to the teacher as well as to the pupil. Obviously there are certain common elements in the various applications of individualized reading procedures but the common essential is in the spirit of adjusting to individual differences.

Jonathan Kozol, author of Death at an Early Age, in which he describes his painful experiences as a teacher in the Boston Public Schools, has probably never used the term "individualized reading" but he captures the essence of the spirit of this approach in his description of the use of paperbacks in his classroom.

The common elements binding all individualized reading programs together are set forth in a monograph by the San Diego County Department of Education's professional staff. One need not accept all the criteria given, nor need one accept all the rationales listed but this presentation will certainly contribute to the reader's thinking about individualized reading.

Alexander Frazier of Ohio State University has long experience with individualization of instruction in reading. His description of the nature of independent reading activities is the third selection excerpted in this chapter.

The final selection is written by Lyman C. Hunt, Jr. of the University of Vermont who has long been in the forefront of those advocating and explaining the use of individualized reading. One of the most common fears expressed about individualized reading is that the teaching of reading skills will be neglected. In the passage by Professor Hunt this issue is frankly faced and discussed.

Using Paper Backs

by

Jonathan Kozol

(This material is excerpted from the author's
article, "Life at an Early Age," which appeared in the New York Times Book Review
on February 25, 1968. Copyright (c) 1968.)

The classroom is quiet. It is 9:15 on Monday morning. The fifth-grade students are putting away their mathematics books and getting set for reading.

A visitor in the doorway watches for a while, then
turns to the classroom teacher and asks her what chapter in
the reader they are going to be doing. The words are hardly out of her mouth before it occurs to her that it was a
foolish question. There are no readers--not in the children's
hands, not on the tables. Instead of that uniform array of
imposing and expected hardback volumes--instead of the assigned chapter, instead of the sheet of written questions--
there is appearing all over the classrooms (from desks, from
pockets, lunchboxes and purses) a lively little battalion of
multi-colored paperbacks. Some are familiar classics; others
are new novels, biographies and science fiction. The teacher
does not make a move to start the lesson. She does not say
a word or put instructions on the blackboard. The children
settle into desk-chairs. Some go off and camp out in the
corners. A group of three monopolize a striped cushion by
the window. The visitor watches.

"Where are the readers?" she at last cannot help asking.

"Over there----" replies the teacher, pointing to a
glassed-in closet. Behind a door, which looks to be well
shut and fastened, there stand the rows of official fifth-grade
"readers," crisp and handsome, costly and unspoiled, where

21

no one disturbs or touches them. They are supposed to last
for five years, but they will probably last for fifty--books
can last for a long time when nobody is reading them.   In
this classroom, as in an increasingly large number of other
innovative classrooms in many sections of the country, the
hardcover readers are receiving the restful sleep and peace
that belong to old and tired people.   The paperbacks have
taken over.

It is--curiously--a hopeful phenomenon of change which
school officials and school systems seem uneager to recognize.   In the minds of school committees there is still something a little suspect and "unprofessional" about paperbacks;
and many of the school systems have had long and friendly
relations with the hardback publishers and still feel loyal to
them.

Children, asked to explain what they like about the
books, comment first on the obvious fact that the paperbacks
are inexpensive.   They like the idea that they can buy a book
and take it home, dog-ear the pages, make comments in the
margin, pass it on to someone else, keep it at their bed-
side, or--if they don't happen to like it--throw it in the gar-
bage.   The cheapness of the books, and the fact that the pupils themselves select and buy them, tend as well to lead to
a spirit of literary independence and irreverence.   More frequently than ever before, children now tend to say just what
they think about a book and they do this without bothering to
invite adult approval: "Madame Curie is a good book because it has suspense... Follow My Leader is the stinkiest
book I've ever read... Call of the Wild is one of the best
... It had tragic, happy and sad parts, no comic parts.
That's what I like."

Teachers, especially at the elementary level, used to
feel compelled to psyche out the whole area of reading for
their pupils and would tell their children, sometimes gently,
sometimes remorselessly, exactly what they ought to like and
where they should be heading.   Now, in classrooms flooded
by the lists of paperbacks, teachers are prevented from
carrying out this unattractive function and children are permitted, by necessity if not by enlightenment, to advise and
inform and instruct each other about their tastes and preferences.

Sometimes a child is even in the position nowadays
of being able to tell his teacher about a book before the

teacher knows about it. Some teachers consider such a turn-
about almost an act of insurrection, but the children seem
to find the switch exciting, and I know for my own part that
I owe to such a reversal the discovery of some of the best
children's books I've read.

Criteria for an Individualized Reading
Program and Their Rationales

by

San Diego County Department of Education

(This material is excerpted from A Description
of Three Approaches to the Teaching of Reading.
Reading Instruction, Monograph No. 2, 1961.)

The major objective of the Individualized Approach is
to provide opportunities for each pupil, progressing at his
own rate of growth, to gain experience in a variety of reading situations. This approach is based upon the child's own
desire to discover, explore, and react to stimuli in his environment. Guided by his own motivation to learn, his reaction to those stimuli which he selects enables him to develop meanings which are essential to behavioral change.
Basic to this approach is the principle of learning theory
which recognizes that each individual learner is most genu-
inely motivated in terms of his own needs, and that when
provided with the appropriate environment, guidance, and materials he will tend to choose materials most suitable to his
maturity, ability, and interests.

The major functions of the teacher using this approach are these: to provide a balance of reading materials,
to evaluate growth, to teach reading skills, and to develop
pupil interests and attitudes. These functions are fulfilled
primarily by the teacher helping pupils in their selection of
printed materials, offering guidance during individual conferences, keeping records of pupil progress, and offering individual and group encouragement during silent reading periods.

Description of the Individualized Reading Approach

Criteria   Rationale

1. The teacher with the help   1. Children differ in native

of the children selects a wide variety of reading materials (books, magazines, pamphlets, etc.) from all possible sources. These materials, representing varying degrees of reading difficulty, interest, content, style, format, etc., become the media for reading instruction.

ability, interests, and emotional needs. As a result, their purposes for reading will vary from one child to another. In order to better accommodate these differences there is no limit to the amount and kind of reading material needed.

2. The teacher encourages the children to become familiar with the material available by providing opportunities for them to browse, to discuss the materials, to hear passages or stories, to use book lists, etc.

2. Familiarity with material promotes more intelligent use. When children discover reading materials in the areas of their particular interests, they are naturally motivated to read and to appreciate the rich variety of reading material available. New interests are thus continuously aroused.

3. To prepare children for initial selection of materials for reading, the teacher guides children in the development of effective techniques for appraising printed materials quickly. Examination of preface, introduction, table of contents, index, topic sentences, pictures, etc., is encouraged. Skimming and other surveying techniques are developed through explanation, demonstration, and try-out.

3. Because of the great amount of printed material available today, it becomes a primary task of the teacher to provide each pupil with the necessary techniques for selecting materials appropriate to his individual needs and purposes. The pupil needs more than knowledge of the techniques, he needs also to be able to apply them in meaningful situations.

4. During the initial stages of using varied printed material in the classroom, the children are encouraged to "try out" different materials in terms of their own interest, purpose, and ability to

4. Since interest and purposes are individually unique, the children themselves are more likely to choose materials which are appropriate to their individual needs. Children are also more highly

Description of Three Approaches

Criteria	Rationale

read. They are allowed
complete freedom within the
range of material available
in arriving at their choice
of material which they will
make more concentrated
use of during the time
scheduled for reading.

motivated when they are
able to pursue tasks of their
own choosing. A more val-
id assessment of their true
ability to read print is possible under such conditions.

5. Children are encouraged to
proceed in their selected
material at their own rate.
Vocabulary growth, skill development, interest, and
time available are the major factors regulating this
growth.

5. A child will advance more
rapidly if he is encouraged
to proceed at his own rate
of progress, which is not
limited by the rate of progress of a group.

6. Guidance in developing
reading skills, vocabulary
growth, interests, and attitude is provided by the
teacher through scheduled
individual conferences with
each pupil as the need arises.
These conferences help the
pupil develop an understanding of the skills necessary
to his reading growth. The
teacher points out the areas
of the child's success in
reading and helps him to
plan additional reading experiences in areas where he
needs further development.

6. Because no two students
have identical specific reading characteristics at any
given time, instruction can
best be performed on an individual basis. The close
working relationship between
teacher and pupil inherent in
individual conferences helps
the child see that someone is
concerned about his interest
and progress and is willing
to give him needed assistance. In pointing out the
child's successes in reading,
the teacher is encouraging
the pupil to achieve future
success.

7. Group situations may be
employed when:
   a. Two or more children
      have similar needs in
      skill development.

7. Children will at times exhibit
common specific needs which
can best be taught in group
situations. They occasionally have need to identify with
a group situation wherein

b. There is an expressed desire to share reading interests.

c. There is need to share ideas of different students gleaned from their individual or common reading.

Structure of groups changes as needs change.

they feel they have peers in reading skills, interests, and attitudes and where they can see that different people bring different meanings to a reading selection.

8. An individual reading record for each pupil is kept by the teacher. In diagnosing the child's progress, the teacher keeps frequent anecdotal notations of the child's growth based upon daily observation. In this observation the teacher looks for evidence of the pupil's interests, attitudes, reading level, rate of progress, and difficulties with reading skills. The number of conferences and amount of time spent with each child is also noted. Over-all reading growth is recorded periodically to survey the pupil's variety of reading experiences and physical characteristics in reading situations. Results of informal and formal testing are also included.

8. An individual reading record facilitates the teacher's diagnosis of each child's reading strengths and weaknesses. This enables the teacher to work in individual conferences so that each child gains an understanding of his own progress.

9. Children engage in many types of creative independent activities during the time when they are not involved in group or individual conferences.

These activities are related to many areas of the curriculum but reading is given top

9. As children acquire new skills, interests, and attitudes from their reading activities, many opportunities are needed for them to fortify these new learnings and apply them in different situations.

Because reading is the core

Description of Three Approaches

Criteria	Rationale

priority.

A balance is maintained in that children participate in individual silent reading, oral reading in small groups, art, communication, and construction type endeavors.

from which these activities are extracted, it should receive the most attention. However, children need to realize the inter-relatedness of all the curriculum areas.

The creative nature of these activities promotes self-direction, which is a major goal of all instruction.

10. Opportunity is provided for individuals or groups of children to share what they have read with others.

These sharing activities may be carried on in small groups, total class situations, or during pupil-teacher conferences.

A wide variety of means of sharing are possible, among them being dramatization, use of audio-visual aids, oral reading, pantomimes, etc.

10. It is important that children be enabled to evaluate their own growth through self-testing situations. Of lesser importance, and yet a factor, sharing allows for teacher evaluation of pupil growth in all areas of the language arts.

Even though each child at any given time is reading self-chosen materials, he must receive encouragement and opportunity to develop new interests and understanding of the range of reading materials available.

What is Independent Reading Like?

by

Alexander Frazier

(This material is excerpted from the author's article, "Individualized Reading: More Than New
Forms or Formulas," which appeared in Elementary English in December, 1962.)

The teacher who is acting to sponsor a more important place for independent reading may be thought of as:

1. Scheduling time for reading and study by children
in and from varied materials chosen by them within a framework of such agreements as seem to suit the situation.

Time is provided to read what seems to those concerned to be worth reading as selected from whatever is
available. In general, on any given day, most children will
use all this time for reading. Conferences with individuals
or teaching sessions with groups may take some, but probably not the same pupils, out each day for part of the time.
Children have some scheduled time every day to read on
their own; that is the point.

2. Helping children clarify and extend interests and
purposes and deal with feelings through continuous observations and interaction.

With regular opportunities to review, select, and read
from varied materials, children provide the teacher with an
increasing fund of information about interests and feelings.
Guesses can be verified at many points of interaction--
through informal questions or remarks, in more formal
counseling or conference periods, in group sessions, in responses during class planning, discussing, or reporting sessions. The clarification and extension of interests and purposes cannot be confined to private colloquy.

Presumably reading widely will mean reading for all kinds of interests and purposes determined in part by agreement among learners and teacher, the results of which will be expected to show up in contributions made during many phases of study. The feelings of readers similarly will be revealed in behavior at the book shelves or in side remarks or in proposals for sharing enthusiasms and disappointments with other children as well as in conferences between the teacher and a pupil.

3. Facilitating the search for and through richly varied materials.

When a broader base of materials is used in helping children learn to read more effectively, the search for and through these materials becomes in itself the great opportunity for developing the kinds of abilities we must value-- skimming and sampling, locating needed information and ideas from many sources, comparing varied treatments of the same topics, reading deeply and extensively in specific books by the same author, and gaining experience with many books of a similar type or form.

In all these pursuits, finding, handling, reviewing, rejecting, and selecting what is to be read is central to learning how to learn more effectively. Thus, the teacher seeks to involve the reader in the search for, as well as the search through, an abundance of varied materials. The relationship between supply and such use is obvious. Yet even with very young readers, the direction should be toward going where the needed books are in greatest numbers rather than resting content with those that can be collected by or spared for a given class.

4. Providing many opportunities for making full use of what is being learned or experienced.

As readers gain more experience in wide reading, they become not only better informed but can serve as greater resources in every aspect of their living together. Independent reading, while it may lead to some interests being pursued more deeply or farther afield than will be of concern to other readers, can enrich the common experience in many ways. One child's "expertness" may lie in books on space travel, another's in foreign lands, others' in pioneer days, circuses, birds, tales of fantasy, or books by a favorite author.

In any aspect of study in which shared purposes are formulated, this variety becomes more closely focused through organizing, sharing, testing, and extending the information and ideas gained from many sources. The teacher who values range and variety of learning will find many enriching and strengthening opportunities for using what is being learned to forward individual growth as well as common understandings.

5. Assessing growth in ability to learn from many kinds of materials in terms of many interests and purposes.

Using some kind of framework of skills or abilities, the teacher assesses the needs children have for learning better how to deal with words unfamiliar in pronunciation or meaning. Attention goes also, of course, to abilities of the more advanced kinds as they are developing. The assessment is made in personal conferences of the formal variety and also on countless occasions when needs are revealed more casually. Much assessment is made in the setting of the total group at work with materials. Does a given child find something rewarding to read? Is he continuing his search with intentness and excitement? Is he active in sharing and testing what he is learning?

Assessment of how well a child can understand what he is reading and do something with what he has learned is continuous in a program that bases all learning on the use of many materials. Assessment includes also the whole range of personal approaches to reading--how interests and needs are pursued and extended through reading and learning, why a child wants to learn something and what he sees to do with what he is learning, and the pattern of his personal reading as it relates to his total development. Again, these many assessments take place all day long in reading as in other learning, although some aspects are checked out in the periods provided for more intensive personal conferring and counseling.

6. Providing needed help in developing specific abilities.

The base needed in learning to learn from reading found in the kind of program that uses many materials in itself provides much greater opportunity for so-called skill development. As we have pointed out, many of the skills we most value demand a broader base of experience for their

development than has sometimes existed. Moreover, under
a program that maximizes independence in reading, children
have greater need, as well as opportunity, to extend these
and the earlier, more easily measurable word attack skills.
Because they encounter so many more words they have to
learn how to pronounce and so many more for which they may
have only vague and imprecise meanings, children are im-
pelled to identify their own needs for help in a new way.

With this base and from the teacher's assessment, the
provision of opportunities for specific help can be much more
sharply defined. Some of this help goes to children on the
run, so to speak, as they ask for it in terms of pressing
problems. Some is provided for in conferences as a part of
further assessment. Some may be provided to several children at a time when needs are found to exist in common.
Some may be provided for the class as a whole. The help
comes as it is needed, in many kinds of contexts and toward
many kinds of needs.

7. Working to relate learning through reading to the
all-day search for new meanings, satisfactions, and values.

In a sense, this particular behavior is basic to the
others. With more materials to read and learn from, the
teacher finds that the information and ideas being gained by
children during reading and study time are inseparable from
those being sought during other portions of the day devoted
to explorations in the social studies or science or the arts.
What the teacher finds and encourages is the relevance of the
broader base of materials to learning in every aspect of the
program.

The content of children's experience is thus richer
and more varied than it ever could be when multiple materials were related to the basal materials in the program as
supplementary rather than central. Children not only learn
to learn more successfully, but they have, if our teacher
really knows what she is doing, much more to think about
and to think within every phase of learning.

These, then, are some of the desired behaviors that
teachers need to develop in moving to greater independence
in reading.

Are Skills Neglected in an Individualized
Reading Program?

by

Lyman C. Hunt, Jr.

(This material is excerpted from the author's article, "Individualized Reading: Teaching Skills,"
which appeared in Education in May, 1961. Copyright (c) 1961.)

They say it couldn't be done. They say it isn't being
done. Yet teachers are doing it. Teachers are teaching
children in the reading program as individuals, and they are
teaching them needed skills. It is exciting to watch teachers
who are trying to work out their own particular approach to
teaching skills to individual children.

These venturesome teachers use every resource for
improving skills. The textbook manual is a reference, not
a heavily beaten path from which they cannot depart. While
it may be true that the constant use of the manual gives
greater security, it is not necessarily the best way to help
each individual child learn skills. The days when the teacher,
manual in her lap, herds her three ability groups through
various exercises in revolving-door fashion are waning.

Many teachers say, "I want to try individualized reading, but will my children learn skills?" It is a sobering idea
for the teacher to "go it alone." Undertaking an individualized program requires courage, vision and know-how.

Advocates of the basal-reader program say that
teachers neglect skills if they try to individualize their reading instruction. There may be some truth in this contention.
But what about controlled vocabulary? What about sacred
sequences? What about organized structure? Have they
been successful?

It is becoming increasingly clear to many teachers
that many children do not learn reading skills according to
the organized sequences and structures of the textbook manuals. The theory upon which the prescribed patterns are
based may be sound; unfortunately, though, many children just
don't grow according to the pattern.

Successful teachers are finding ways to identify skills
needed by each individual child. Successful teachers are
finding ways of developing those skills with individual children. Successful teachers are finding ways of organizing
children into temporary groups for the purpose of studying
skills needed by the groups and for the purpose of giving individual children help at the moment of need. Successful
teachers are finding ways of showing children how to help
themselves with skills. Successful teachers are accomplish-
ing this in programs where every child is reading a book of
his own choice at a pace consistent with his purpose.

Four Major Skill Areas

Important skills lie in four areas: (1) sight-recognition vocabulary; (2) word study; (3) oral-reading fluency; and
(4) silent-reading efficiency.

Careful study will reveal that success must be built
on the first step. Without an adequate sight-recognition vocabulary and without assurance of constant accumulation of
words into the sight-recognition vocabulary, the child will
stumble and falter. He will not gain the foundation needed
to uphold the other three skill areas.

Word study is an important skill area primarily because it enables the child to help himself. It is always subordinate to accumulating a sight-recognition vocabulary, however.

Oral-reading performance is closely linked to a sight-
recognition vocabulary. We often err by expecting fluent oral reading when the child has not truly accomplished the first
step; he simply does not have sufficient skill in sight recognition to read well orally.

Sight recognition is a bond between the relatively separate processes of oral and silent reading. We unrealistical-
ly expect a child to read silently when his sight-recognition

vocabulary is insufficient for the vocabulary included in a
particular selection.

It is evident that skill development is intricate and
complex.   Nevertheless, we are becoming increasingly aware
of the variety of individual patterns through which children
learn skills in each area.   It will help to keep our focus on
truly important skills and to avoid over-emphasis on lesser
skills.   It is easy to become lost in a maze of minor skills.

Are the Sequences Sacred?

The advocates of the basal-reader program claim that
only through a controlled-vocabulary approach can the child
successfully acquire sight-recognition skills.   The proponents
say that the scientifically worked-out sequences and structures for related skills development are so well defined that
every child can succeed.

Let's examine the theory.   The basal-reader program
has a dual approach to word recognition.   First, and rightly
so, it begins with building a sight-recognition vocabulary
which rests on predetermined sequences of words, arranged
story by story, book by book, grade by grade, for the total
program.

Once accumulation of a sight-recognition vocabulary is
off to a good start, and even though there is an increasing
number of words to be accumulated with each new story, a
second skill task is introduced.   This new element, word
study, confronts the child with structures and sequences related to phonic development, to variations in word forms,
and to syllable sensitivity.

There is a dual approach, too, to the silent- and oral-reading steps.   With each story, provision is made for
directed silent reading of the material to realize some
teacher-designated purpose.

Following silent reading comes each child's opportunity to read orally or, at least, to listen as one of his
group-mates reads orally.   In this sequence of silent-fol-
lowed-by-oral reading, each child is given roughly equal time
and consideration.   In the individualized reading program,
with each child reading a selection of his own choice, silent
reading far exceeds oral reading in time and emphasis.   Yet

neither is neglected.

What Is the Issue?

The critical issue lies within this complex of sequences. The system which prescribes that particular words
are to be learned for each particular book during each particular year by every child must be carefully considered by
the teacher. Is this a sequence of controlled vocabulary or
overcontrolled vocabulary? Prescribing the particular time
for learning particular words is too brittle and too rigid a
system for many children and for many teachers. This system lacks flexibility.

The result of over-attention to a prescribed order for
learning words can be disastrous for both the able and the
unable. If the child does not assimilate the designated words
into his recognition vocabulary at the particular time they are
introduced (with the number of allowed repetitions) then this
vast, but fragile, superstructure can fall all about him.
This condition of accumulating specified words at a specified
time in order to be successful can serve as a handicap and
hindrance to many children even though it may be beneficial
to others. The able child bursts out of the structure; the
slow child struggles unsuccessfully to maintain the pace.

When teachers have realized this fact and certain other basic facts about words, they do not necessarily need to
become entangled with their children in this vast system in
order to help children accumulate an adequate sight-recognition vocabulary.

Common Ways to Word Recogniation

Any teacher who is endeavoring to help youngsters
build an adequate sight-recognition vocabulary, any teacher
endeavoring to help children learn ways to help themselves
study words must have instant command of the seven common
ways of helping children gain acquaintance with word forms.

1. Word form with pronunciation. Ordinary consideration is given to the word form, its pronunciation, and, if
needed, its meaning.

2. Visual scrutiny. The child is asked to exercise

extreme effort to study word appearance visually and to construct mental images of word forms.

3. Contextual meaning. Words are recognized through their stress on meaning.

4. Word structure. Attention is paid to changes in word forms which result from adding beginnings and endings, or from combining words.

5. Configuration or outline. Notice is given to lengths, shapes, and outlines of word forms.

6. Relationship or letter-sound blend phonics.

7. Syllables. Studying syllables as subparts of word forms.

The secret of success, discovered by teachers teaching skills to individual children, can be revealed. Success comes from combining several of the seven ways of recognizing words according to the child's needs and according to his present mastery of skills. Teachers can learn to utilize proper combinations effectively.

Teachers should sense the balanced relationships within the four skill areas and the major subdivisions thereof. They should be able to detect individual patterns of accumulation of sight-recognition vocabulary, to manage the two phonic systems, and to command the seven ways of knowing words. Then skills can be taught individually.

How Do Teachers Do It?

How do teachers detect the needs of each child when they have thirty to thirty-five children? Each teacher has her own individual approach, but a common practice is to maintain some kind of check sheet on which the basic skill areas are listed as major headings. This list may take the form of a graph or a notebook page for each child; the teacher, through individual conferences or through work in skill groups, notes the child's accomplishment and records needed work.

Sometimes teachers have children keep their own records with respect to performance in sight-recognition vocabu-

lary, word study, oral reading, and silent reading.   Children can work out word lists for self study.

A variety of ways for independent word study exists.
While most skills teaching is accomplished with the individual during conferences, many teachers form groups to work
on skills, according to needs of children within the group.
Sometimes teachers will announce to the class which skill
element will be developed and the children themselves volunteer to participate in that group.   If a child is not sufficiently aware of his need for working with the group, the
teacher will counsel with him.   He can learn to recognize
his own need for attending the group which has been formed
to work on double-consonant beginnings, if that happens to be
a point of weakness for him.

Word examples taken from the reading of one child
might be used to teach a particular skill to the group.   Word
examples taken from another child's reading might be used
in teaching another skill.   Many times the teacher, sufficiently skilled, can determine whether the children in this
group need to work to perfect recognition of the difficult wh
words.   This can be done through a game-motivating approach.

Appraising progress again rests on the ingenuity of
the teacher.   While record-keeping is primarily the responsibility of the teacher, valuable assistance can come from the
children.   A teacher must be able to discern and record
when any particular child is making great strides in accumulating a sight vocabulary; when he is barely crawling up the
steep incline; when he is perhaps stalled or even gradually
slipping backwards.

She must be able to discern and record the approach
most frequently used by the child as he tries to study out
words for himself.   She must teach students to look within
the word, to cover up endings, to use meaning, and/or to
use the seven common ways to help themselves.

She must be able to discern and record whether oral
reading is becoming more fluent, more enjoyable, more pre-
sentable to herself and to the group.   She must be able to
discern whether silent reading is becoming truly effective.
She must help children to concentrate on meanings when they
read to themselves.   She must constantly try to transfer to
the child her know-how in all the skill areas so she can help

him to help himself.

What Direction Do We Take?

It is most important to realize that many teachers are ready, willing, and able to put the manual aside and venture forth on their own in teaching skills. There is an urgent need to stop giving teachers recipe books which prescribe steps. Rather, teachers need to have a clear command of major skill areas, and need to utilize this source.

A great deal of our present word-study program as developed in manuals of the basal-reader program is repeated and duplicated in the spelling program. We should do more reading of an individual type during so-called reading class and place more emphasis on the word-study program in connection with writing where spelling fits naturally.

We should have, above all, faith that we as teachers can learn to know important reading skills and transmit to the children the ways of mastering skills on an individual basis. The happy result will be that all children may be engaged in reading books of their own choosing at their own rate of speed during reading class.

Chapter 2

Individualized Reading in the Primary Grades

The procedures described in the primary grades and the procedures described in the three selections included in this chapter are not presented as ideal programs. It is the purpose rather to give some examples of how individualized reading was actually approached by classroom teachers.

At the risk of being repetitious, the point must once more be made that no other teacher would use these identical procedures; individualized reading has no "manual;" it is dependent on the ingenuity of each teacher using that approach.

The first selection, taken from Elizabeth Senderling's master's thesis, describes the individualized reading program she used in a first grade.

Sylvia W. Roston described her experiences with individualized reading in a classroom of first and second grade children in her master's thesis. The excerpt included here describes some of the procedures she employed.

The third and last selection is taken from Janie K. Bollinger's master's thesis. It does not deal with individualized reading as such but is a survey study of ways in which 189 third grade teachers in Tennessee attempted to meet individual differences in reading instructions. The data presented in this excerpt show how the individualized reading approach meets the individual needs of widely differing pupils. The data also make it obvious that individualized reading is not by any means universally accepted.

How Individualized Reading was Used
in One First Grade

by

Elizabeth Allen Senderling

(This material is excerpted from the author's
Northern Illinois University master's thesis, Indi-
vidualized Beginning Reading Instruction--A First
Grade Program.)

The Second Year: Individualized Reading Instruction

By the beginning of the second year of the study, the
teacher was ready to try a completely different organizational approach. Since the children coming to her class had had
only kindergarten school experience, any plan of organization
in first grade would be new to them. It was felt it would
be as easy for them to adjust to one organizational plan as
to another.

Getting Ready to Read

During the first few weeks the usual standard readiness procedures were employed. These included the label-
ling of objects in the room, using the children's names in as
many ways and places as possible (on their desks, above
their coat hooks, on the chalkboard), experience charts and
stories, and the Scott, Foresman pupils' books, Before We
Read. In addition the procedures used in San Diego County,
described by Dr. Allen[1] were put into practice in a slightly
modified form.

After the children had been asked to draw pictures
relating to some experience each child described his picture
to the class. As the teacher held the picture, she wrote one
or two sentences on the back of it using the child's vocabu-

41

lary.   At the end of the day each story was rewritten in
manuscript and stapled onto the picture.   The next day three
or four children at a time were invited to the "reading group"
to read their stories.   The groups were chosen according to
the similarity of vocabulary in the stories.

In the small groups the pictures (now with stories attached) were held up one at a time while each child again
told about his picture.   The teacher then read the story,
pointing to each word as she read.   The group as a whole
then read the story as the teacher again pointed to each word
and supplied words as needed.   The stories were so short
that, after they had been "read" once or twice, most children
knew all the words.   Then the child who had made the picture read his own story.   Thus each child in every group
had an opportunity to read the other children's stories as
well as his own.

As the children began to acquire small sight vocabularies the teacher began pointing out similarities in the beginnings and endings of words.   Attention was also called to
similar initial consonant sounds in the children's names and
in the words on the various labels and stories about the
room.

The readiness book, Before We Read, was used as a
whole class activity.   It was felt that each child could profit,
according to his ability, from the readiness skills developed
in it.   After all pages had been discussed the class went
through the book again and retold some of the picture stories.
The teacher and the class cooperatively decided upon one
sentence to tell about each picture.   The sentences were
written on the chalkboard and read back to the class.   They
were then dittoed and a copy given to each child.   The pictures were cut from the Before We Read books, mounted on
colored construction paper with the captions pasted below
each picture.   The mounted pictures with captions were fastened together with pronged fasteners as they were completed thus creating the children's first "reading book."   The
stories in these reading books were reread many times.

In selecting the sentences for each picture an attempt
was made by the teacher to guide the choice of words to coincide as much as possible with the vocabulary in the Scott,
Foresman pre-primers.   Picture dictionaries, hung in every
available space about the room, illustrated such simple sentences as "See Sally jump," "Dick and Jane run," "Dick and

Father play," etc. Each child had made a picture for each
sentence and the most appropriate illustrations were mounted
on the chart paper with the sentence written in large letters
beneath. By the end of October a few children had learned
all, or nearly all, of the words in the first Scott, Foresman
pre-primer. These children were then given the book to
read by themselves, being helped with unknown words whenever they indicated the need. The beginning-to-read activities continued for the remainder of the class.

Beginning Independent Reading

        All children progressed at their own rate through the
three pre-primers of the Scott, Foresman series as their
vocabularies grew through the making of the Before We Read
booklets and the continued use of their own stories written
on their pictures. The progression through the series was
not direct, however. Other "easy" pre-primers were inter-
spersed along the way, according to the needs and abilities
of each individual child and chosen by the teacher to best
meet their needs and abilities.

        In the process of selecting other pre-primers for
each child to read, the teacher became aware of the great
diversity of vocabulary among the various pre-primers. Nine
complete series were available, comprising thirty different
books. These pre-primers varied greatly, even at the same
levels, both in the number and in the variety of the words
used. It was felt that this would present a problem of sequential vocabulary development as the children shifted from
one series to another. Random choosing among these books
by a beginning reader could result in frustration and loss of
security because of the difference in vocabulary load among
them.

The Reading Period

        "What are we going to do now? - Read? - Oh, boy!
My favorite stuff!" "Yeah! Oh, boy! Read!"

        This was the sort of response which, two or three
times each day, accompanied the teacher's suggestion, "Let's
read for a little while." We did not always read at the same
time every day, nor did one particular activity always follow upon another specific activity, so that often the announce-

ment of a reading period came as a pleasant surprise. In
general, however, the children read immediately after the
opening exercises, after morning recess, and after lunch.
There were some days of the week when this arrangement
was never followed, and there were no days when it was always followed. The awareness on the part of the pupils that
a reading period was about to begin was always accompanied
by expressions of pleasure. On one afternoon, when several
admonitions by the teacher similar to "Let's all take our
seats now" had gone unheeded, she finally said, "All right.
Get out your reading books." Immediately there was a scurrying to desks, exclamations of "Boy, oh, boy!," and soon
each child was reading at his own desk from his own book.

Reading period was never a completely quiet time,
but it always was a time when each child was occupied with
his own particular task. Whatever conversations, quiet comings and goings occurred in the various parts of the room affected only those who participated in them. Most of the children were busily reading and for the most part quite heed-
less of the activities of anyone else.

During the latter part of October all children were
reading independently, each from a different pre-primer,
orally to themselves. To the children, busily occupied with
the task of reading, this was not at all disturbing. One
teacher has said, "Children are seldom disturbed by the hum
of work when they are happy in their own activities. It is
only teachers who are worried by such sounds."[2]

It was felt that, at the very beginning stages of learning to read, it was necessary and important that each child
say each word aloud to himself. Hearing himself say each
word would enable the child better to relate the word to all
the associations he had ever had with it, and would not only
make it more meaningful to him, but would help to reinforce
the memory of the word by linking the visual with the auditory impression. Support to this view is given by several
writers.

Gertrude Hildreth has stated:

> ... Pronouncing a word while looking at the printed
> form is the first step in learning to recognize the
> word later from visual clues alone. After a num-
> ber of repetitions of this association a glance at
> the word recalls its meaning without noticeable vo-

vocalizing.

... These first "look and say" experiences with
reading vocabulary should underscore the say part
of the phrase; they should be oral. [3]

Each child had a movable chair and movable flat desk.
These were grouped in rectangles of four or six desks with
the sides of the desks parallel to the chalkboard. Children
sat with whom they wished and desks were regrouped periodically when there was an expressed desire. The arrangement proved very satisfactory socially, and it also afforded
easy and close at hand help from other pupils.

Most children had completed extensive reading in pre-
primers and had started the Scott, Foresman primer, Fun
with Dick and Jane, by January. Three had started it prior
to this time, and five started in February. At about this
time the teacher felt the children had gained enough facility
to begin learning to read silently. She told them that she
thought they were now ready to read the way grown-ups did--
without saying every word to themselves aloud--that they were
good enough readers now to just think the words to themselves as they read. By the end of January they were all
reading silently and had only occasionally to be reminded,
"Are you thinking the words to yourself?"

Children would thumb through their books looking at
the pictures and anticipating the story before they started
reading what the words said. There was often a quiet discussion about the books they were reading. They made such
remarks as: "This is a good book;" and, "That's a nice
book. You're going to enjoy it." They showed pictures to
each other and told one another about interesting or funny
things in their stories. One child was reading The Cat in
the Hat Comes Back and all the children who sat around
him were gathered at his desk while he showed them one of
the pictures and told what the story was about. Shortly they
all voluntarily returned to their desks and quietly resumed
their own reading.

Such busy, meaningful murmurings were accepted by
everyone but there were recognized limits. The teacher
spoke to those children who seemed to be making idle conversation, reading aloud, or who were otherwise being disturbing; but discussions about the books they were reading were
never interrupted. At one time, when the teacher suggested
to a child, "If you did not talk so much you could read

more," another child spoke up and said, "You know that book
I was reading? Well, Sandy was talking to me and I didn't
even answer her. I just went on reading my book."

The Individual Conference

During reading period the teacher held individual conferences with children who had finished their books and voluntarily indicated a readiness to read to her. She was also
available for help of any kind to anyone who needed assistance.

To each conference the teacher took a pencil, notebook, and a clipboard. In the notebook, opposite the name
of each child, was recorded the date, the name of the book
he was reading, and the title of the book he was to read
next. On the clipboard comments were jotted down about the
child's specific difficulties, or any other notations the teacher
felt would be helpful for later individual or small group instruction. At the end of each day appropriate recordings
were made in the daily plan book from these notations for
subsequent teaching. Much of the assistance which the children needed at the beginning stages of reading was concerned
with enlarging their sight vocabularies.

If a child came unprepared to a conference he was
given his book to reread. No pupil allowed this to happen to
himself more than once. If, however, the book was too difficult for the child, he was given an easier one. Occasionally a child would come to the teacher and say, "I'm finished
with my book but I'm going to work on my words some
more." One child asked, "Shall I read the last unit again?"
The teacher responded, "How sure are you of your words?
Do you think you should practice them some more?" After
a moment's reflection, the child replied, "I think I'll read
the last unit again." Jeanette Veatch has stated, "When each
child... is reading at his own pace, he presents his story to
his teacher because he is sure he can read it. [4]

Responsibility for their own progress was put directly on the children not only to indicate when they were ready
to read, but also what selections from their books they would
read to the teacher. The accurate reading of selections toward the end of the book gave the best evidence of vocabulary mastery, and it was these which the children invariably
chose. Choices were indicated by such remarks as: "Here

is a story I like." "I like the 'Merry-go-around' one;" or,
"I like the last story. It is nice."

Comprehension was checked either by judicious questioning, or by having the child read the beginning of the
story and then tell the rest of it.

Exceptions to waiting until the book had been finished
before a conference was held were made for very slow readers, or for those who at first were timid about indicating
their readiness to read. The teacher called these children
from time to time to check on their progress. Association
between teacher and child was continually maintained throughout each child's reading of his book as he came to her needing assistance of various sorts.

On occasion, when two or perhaps three children were
finished with the same book at the same time, they all came
to conference together and took turns reading. This happened infrequently but the children enjoyed it. For that
brief span of time each of these children was of about the
same competency in reading.

Conferences were held at the rear of the room,
teacher and pupil sitting side by side on small sized chairs.
The teacher's position was such that she could be aware at
all times of what was happening in other parts of the room.

There were a few times when bottlenecks occurred
as several children were ready to read from different books
at the same time. On these occasions some of the better
readers were pressed into service as helpers. This did not
happen very often and no child ever read to a pupil-helper
twice in succession. As the year progressed, however, and
more and more children were reading longer books, this aid
became unnecessary.

There were other times when no one was ready for
a conference. At these times the teacher circulated among
the children giving help where raised hands indicated the
need; stopped momentarily to hear a child read a short passage; or gave reinforcing instruction in phonetic skills.
Sometimes the teacher would remain at her desk while the
children came to her for help. This latter procedure was
less tiring for the teacher and provided the children with
needed exercise and relief from reading quietly for relatively long periods of time.

On occasion a child would come to the teacher's desk
only to share with her his enjoyment of his book.   Steve
brought Ted and Sally and said, "I'm almost up to the make-
believe stuff.   I'm really going to like that part!"   Another
time, David, with Day In and Day Out, delightedly exclaimed,
"I'm the luckiest boy in this class because I get to read this
book!"

During reading period every child was reading, either
orally to the teacher or silently at his desk.   It was understood that any child could interrupt briefly during a reading conference for needed help so that he could continue to
read his book.   The child reading orally to the teacher paid
no attention to the string of children quietly waiting their
turns for brief assistance.   The teacher whispered the word
which they silently indicated, then they unobtrusively returned
to their desks.   The teacher could meanwhile become immediately aware of a hesitancy in the conferee's oral reading or
detect a word incorrectly pronounced.   At times one of the
children who was the object of this divided attention would be
asked to wait a moment as the teacher focused her undivided
attention on one of them.   Every child accepted this sharing
of the teacher's time and assistance politely and graciously.

When children came for help which was too extensive
for on-the-spot teaching, they were simply told the necessary words and the teacher made a note for a follow-up later.

Sequential and Developmental
Features of the Program

Some writers have insisted that self-selection is the
heart of an individualized reading program.   The present
writer does not believe that free choice is advisable in the
beginning stages of reading.   Nevertheless, the program
described here was individualized as well as sequential and
developmental in vocabulary building and in the acquisition of
word attack skills.

The Scott, Foresman readers were considered the
basal program but other readers were a part of the program
also.   These books were used developmentally and sequential-
ly on an individualized basis.   No two children in the class
followed exactly the same reading program.   There was a
sequential list which was a "must" for each child, but supplementary books varied with each child in the class.   In

addition to the Scott, Foresman readers this sequential list
included four other primers and two other first readers. No
child in the class read only these books but every child read
all of them.   It was understood that the "required" books
would be read from beginning to end.   This was considered
necessary for sequential learning.

To supplement these books there were in the classroom about thirty readers from primer to third grade level.
In addition there was a generous stock stored in a large
closet not connected with any classroom, to which all the primary teachers in the building had access.   Supplementary
books were selected for the children at the discretion of the
teacher as the pupils progressed through the "basic" program.
Only the teacher was aware of the reading level of the various books.   Each child progressed through these books at his
own rate and in accordance with his ability, motivation, and
interest.

The development of the important reading skills was
not left to chance.   In addition to the two or three reading
periods each day--each lasting approximately twenty to thirty
minutes--there were usually two other periods of whole class
related reading activities.   With the amount of time taken up
by the program of individualized reading instruction, the
teacher felt it necessary to save time by teaching to the whole
class some skills which in previous years had been taught in
the reading groups.   Whatever teaching did not "take" during
the initial presentation to the entire class was followed up
later either individually or in small group instruction.   From
these initial presentations to the whole class, the teacher did
not expect uniformity of learning for all children.   However,
for all those children for whom this instruction was effective,
it meant time saved.   For those who needed later reinforcement there were benefits derived from previous instruction.

Phonics Instruction

During one of these periods the class received instruction in phonics.   Dr. Anna B. Cordts' books, I Can Read,
Reading's Easy, and Hear Me Read (published by Benefic
Press), were used by the teacher, and the material for each
lesson was written on the chalkboard.   One writer has said:

> Skills should be taught only when they are needed
> and if they are needed.   Otherwise teaching is a

waste of time. ... Once a teacher <u>knows what is</u>
<u>needed</u>, he can proceed to teach it singly, to a
group, or to the whole class. [5]

The justification for teaching these skills to the entire
class at one time was that it was new learning for all of the
children. Additional reinforcement was given in individual
conferences or in small group sessions.

The children looked forward eagerly to these sessions,
which never lost their character of a game thoroughly enjoyed by all. The children made such remarks as:
"O-o-o-h, I like sounds!" "Sounds are fun."

Most of the children became very adept at using
phonetic skills in unlocking new words. Steve approached the
teacher one day looking very puzzled. "What is this word?"
he asked. The teacher answered, " 'From.' " Then he said,
still puzzled, "I thought that is what it ought to be, but it
doesn't have any 'u' in it!"

Other Reading Skills

Another whole class activity involved the use of the
Scott, Foresman <u>Think and Do</u> reading workbooks which accompany the first grade readers. It was felt that the knowl-
edges and skills which are developed through this medium
could profitably be taught to the entire class. Although all
the children in the class were reading at different levels,
they all enjoyed and seemed to benefit from the workbook
activities.

The reading vocabulary was a minor problem as the
instructions on each page were read orally by the class in
unison. For a few of the children some of the words were
new, but for most of them the reading material represented
reinforcement of previous learnings. The reading of the directions proceeded smoothly under the leadership of the better readers. These were sometimes reread if there was any
question of meaning or vocabulary involved.

It was the skills development which these pages afforded which was thought important and which was emphasized. As soon as all children understood the directions,
they completed the page independently. Checking followed
immediately and help was given if needed. Children busied

themselves by coloring the pictures on the page while waiting their turns to be checked.   Often children spontaneously
got out their reading books while they waited.

Many other reading skills seemed to need no teaching,
but developed naturally out of the children's interest in and
love of reading.   Motivations and purposes seemed to be in-
trinsic in the program.   The purposes for reading were the
children's own.   They were not set by the teacher and did
not have to coincide with any other child's purpose at any
time.   Once when many in the class had expressed delight
because a reading period was about to begin, Mary came to
the teacher and confided, "I don't really want to read now,
but I said 'Yea!' because I want to finish this book and then
I get to choose."

At another time, when the teacher was selecting a
book for Julie to read she asked, "Do you want a hard book
or an easy book this time?"   Without hesitation Julie emphatically replied, "A hard book!"   When Steven began reading Poke Along, he said, "It looks like a kind of silly book.
I think I'll read it.   I like silly books."

The abilities to use picture and context clues seemed
to be a natural consequence of the responsibility which was
placed on each child for his own learning.

Arthur Gates has stated:

> There is increasing evidence that instruction in
> the past has depended too much on the teacher's
> activity in teaching every stage of reading and too
> little on the pupils' learning how to help them-
> selves learn to read.   ... It has been found that
> they are challenged by and delighted with the whole
> procedure of taking upon themselves the responsi-
> bility for helping themselves and others in the de-
> velopment of the insights and skills which enable
> them to read better.   There is a vast difference
> between teaching a pupil how to be taught in a typi-
> cal classroom, on the one hand, and teaching him
> how to learn by himself on the other. [6]

Jimmy came to the teacher with his finger pointing to
a word in his book.   "'Herself'?" he asked.   When told he
was right, he said, "That's what I said to myself.   I thought
that's what it was."

Randy was delighted when assured that his "guess" had been correct. " 'Radio'?" he asked, and then continued, "I thought that was 'radio'!"

Sandy, too, made an intelligent guess. " 'Pear'?" she asked. And then, "I kept guessing and guessing and finally I thought of that. "

There were many instances, under a variety of circumstances, of the children's enjoyment of reading. In passing Mary remarked one day, "I can hardly wait until reading time. I love to read--don't you?"

One afternoon when the children were finishing a project, the teacher asked, "What will you do while you are waiting for the others to finish?" A child asked tentatively, "Read?" When the teacher gave her assent, there was a general exclamation of "Oh, boy!"

Another afternoon, under similar circumstances, a child asked, "Can we do anything we want to do when we are finished?" Upon receiving an affirmative reply, he exclaimed, "Oh, boy!" and got out his reading book. Others, following suit, continued reading until the time was up.

A very average reader remarked one day, "Gee, it's fun to read!"

Davis came to the teacher's desk pointing to a word and emphatically declared, " 'ladder'!" "That's right, " the teacher said. Davis beamed. "I did it again. I looked at the picture and I saw a ladder so I knew the word was 'ladder'. "

Another child, pointing to a word, asked, " 'Busy'?" The teacher asked, "How did you know that one?" The child answered, "I don't know. I just say what I think it should be. "

These discoveries delighted the children who made them. Smiles of pleasure swept over their faces and lit up their eyes. The children gave evidence of real effort and searching in their struggles to learn to read and genuine pleasure accompanied their accomplishments.

Gertrude Hildreth has stated:

> For building reading vocabulary the best advice is
> to go right ahead and read and read without spend-
> ing too much time on preliminary or accessory ac-
> tivity, but with the sympathetic aid of the teacher
> always at hand. The pupil should try to get the
> new word from the context if he can, then he's
> more apt to recall it next time... In all reading
> activities encourage the child's own effort 150 per
> cent. Never give help ahead of the time it is
> needed, nor give more help than needed. ... Why
> deprive him of a little fun and a valuable learning
> experience? ... If they find they can get some sense
> out of the activity because they see the meaning in
> it, they will keep right on learning, and no one can
> stop them. 7

It was not necessary to instruct the children in reading with expression. Vocal inflection and phrasing seemed
to be a natural outcome of their interest and enjoyment.
They read for their own purposes, at their own speeds, and
under no pressures but their own absorption in the stories.
The story seemed to become a part of them; it gathered
meaning; and when a child was ready to read orally, he read
as though he were living the activities about which he read.
Reading with expression was present from the very beginnings
of oral reading.

One afternoon Julie was reading to the class from
Donald Duck and His Friends. Suddenly she started chuck-
ling and said, "Now you wait till you hear what happened to
him!"

The direction from the teacher to "Put your books a-
way now" was usually greeted with disappointed "O-o-oh's;"
"Why can't we read all day?;" or, "Just one more page!"
This last request was usually granted with the allowance of
a little extra time.

One child brought Round About to the teacher, and,
pointing to a passage, exclaimed with breathless awe; "This
is like a poem!" (The passage was: "Around the turn flew
the sled. Around the turn and down again. Down, down,
down until it stopped.")

The children all evidenced a much greater respect for
books than the teacher had noticed before. Books were constantly brought to the teacher for erasures and the mending

of small tears.

The children in this program had more time to read, they did read and problems concerning seatwork activities and discipline were in large measure eliminated.   Since during reading period every child was reading, "busy work" did not have to be supplied.   There were no groups of children occupied with activities of doubtful educational value while the teacher read with another group.

No child was pushed faster than he wanted to go, nor frustrated because more was expected of him than he could deliver.   Reading continued to be a pleasure for each child in the room.   Each child was at all times aware that he was making progress in his own way without comparisons with anyone else, and each knew that his joy in his progress was shared by his teacher.

It naturally became obvious that some children were better readers than others, but this was accepted and every child took pleasure and pride in every other child's accomplishments.   Children would remark, "Gee, Julie's a good reader!"

Self-Selection

As soon as the "basic program" had been completed (which included other readers in addition to the Scott, Foresman books), the child was free to "choose."   It was felt that he had by this time (having read three first readers) achieved a reading level sufficient to enable him to cope, on a self-selection basis, with the trade books and other readers which were in the room.   At their disposal, in addition to the many readers already mentioned, were approximately one hundred fifty easy-to-read trade books.

"Choosing" was a privilege to which all of the children looked forward and each one was delighted when he had earned this privilege.   This comment was typical: "Randy's lucky!   He's reading!"   After the teacher said, "You are reading, too," the child replied, "I mean--he's picking!"   Another child remarked, "I can hardly wait to choose!"   A story written by one of the children stated: "I have two more books to read then I can pick and I will be happy.   Then I will pick another book and another book."

Not all of the free choice books were displayed at once. Books were placed on low shelves and on two library tables. Before adding a book to these groups the teacher would sometimes read the book to the class, or just tell something about the book and show the pictures. These books would be immediately chosen by the next ones to complete their present books. At the book shelves several children were often gathered making their selections, discussing the books with each other and aiding in one another's selections.

It was the teacher's belief that self-selection without guidance could be disastrous. Occasionally when a child checked out a book the teacher felt that perhaps that book might be a little difficult for that particular child at that particular time. She would make a remark similar to, "That book is kind of hard. If you have too much trouble with it you may change it for another." One time David, after many return trips to the teacher to ask unknown words, finally said, "You were right. This book is a little too hard. I'll have to read a couple more books before I read this one!"

At another time, Mary, who had been coming back to the teacher to ask many words she did not know, said, "This book is too hard. I'm going to get another one."

By early spring most of the children were choosing their own books. After children reached the "choosing" stage, only an occasional book was read to the teacher. Always, however, each book was checked in and out with the teacher, help was given as needed, and a record was kept of the child's progress in reading.

In totaling the number of books which each child in the class had read, no pre-primers were counted. The count was made at the time the class was given a standardized reading test, the middle of May. This count, therefore, does not indicate the number of books read during the entire year, since all children read at least several and a few children read many books, during the subsequent month.

During this year the maximum class size was twenty-one...

Notes

1. Allen, Roach Van, 567, 568.

2. Nulton, 394, p. 24-32.

3. Hildreth, Gertrude "Getting Acquainted with Words"
   The Reading Teacher 8:96-98, December 1954.

4. Veatch, 583, p. 27.

5. Ibid., p. 31.

6. Gates, Arthur I. "Unsolved Problems in Reading, A
   Symposium I," Elementary English 31:331-32, October 1954.

7. Hildreth, op. cit., p. 97-99.

Individualized Reading in a Combination First and Second
Grade Classroom

by

Sylvia Willner Roston

(This material is excerpted from the author's 1962
National College of Education master's thesis, An
Individualized Reading Program in a First and Sec-
ond Grade.)

Environment

The environment was also carefully planned. The
bulletin boards at the beginning of the year were keynoted to
reading. Publishers had been exceedingly generous and supplied many book jackets upon request. One bulletin board
had a book tree with labeled apples telling what can be
learned in books. The grass underneath was the colorful
book jackets. Another bulletin board had a poem on it with
suitable pictures surrounding it.

The books were divided between two areas. Two
book cases were near the rug and two at the other end of
the room. An attempt was made to keep the poetry and science books separate. It worked with the poetry books but
not with the science books. Interestingly enough, later in
the study it will be indicated that poetry was read less than
anything else. Perhaps this was an unintentional environ-
mental control.

No effort was made to group the books by levels or
subject matter. As was stated earlier, the books were always so disorganized by the end of a school day it would
have proven to be an impossible task.

There was a round reading table in one corner of the
room where the teacher worked individually with the children.

It was away from either of the book areas and was close to
the blackboard.   It was here that she also worked with small
groups.

        In addition to books, the room was well supplied with
games and creative materials such as clay, paint, craft paper and drawing paper.   The children were free to use these
after the assigned work had been completed.

Grouping

        There were three types of group activities.   These
are comparable to those reviewed in the literature.   The
first was total group activities.   The early morning activities which usually involved planning were whole group activities.   At this time the assigned work for the day was explained and questions were answered.   If there was reading
involved in the work it was read orally by a child.

        This planning sometimes required that each grade be
worked with individually.   This occurred more often at the
beginning of the year than toward the end of the year.   Work
involving the Weekly Reader was a group activity of this type.

        There were other total group experiences that were
shared enthusiastically.   The mornings when the books were
brought from the library were interesting sessions when the
entire first and second grade came to the rug while the
teacher showed them the new books and related a little of
their contents.   As the children became more familiar with
authors, publishers and pseudonyms, they, too, became involved in the discussion.

        A letter from an author brought excited group re-
sponses.   The entire class was anxious to hear a child's letter.   Equally exciting an experience were those occasions
when the children shared their books with each other.   A
prerequisite for this was having already shared the book with
the teacher.   This was an audience situation.   One child told
about a favorite book and read a part of that book.   If he
had drawn a picture, written a book report or done some
other dominating activity this was also shared.   The sharing
experience with the group was rather an interesting one.   At
the beginning of the year book sharing was limited to once a
week and was a teacher guided activity.   By the middle of
the year the sharing lists (the children signed up on the
board voluntarily) were becoming so long that many children

had to wait until the following week for their turns.   This
began to result in disappointments.   It was finally agreed
that "sharing" should be in the program twice a week.   This
worked for a short time but again there was a backlog on the
board.   Through a class discussion it was decided that the
children would have sharing every day or every other day depending upon the need.   The period would last ten to fifteen
minutes and it would be led by the child who happened to be
at the top of the list.   During this time the teacher could
have reading conferences.   This seemed an ideal solution,
and it was for a period of about six weeks.   The children enjoyed it and were most cooperative.   At the end of the six-
week period, one or two asked for permission to stay in their
seats and not attend the sharing sessions.   Cooperation and
listening among the children began to diminish.   Sharing finally resorted to the original once-a-week program with teacher guidance that there was at the beginning of the year.

Much thought has been given to why this happened.
Perhaps many of the children no longer needed the approval
and encouragement of their peers in this area of reading.
Perhaps the reading span of some had increased so much
that the interest variance was too great.   The program may
have become too permissive due to the lack of teacher participation.   One final thought is that "sharing" was no longer
a special occasion because it happened so often.   At best, it
proved to be a learning experience for the teacher and a part
of the program which will need re-evaluation when tried a-
gain.

Other total group experiences were experience charts,
poetry reading and units in science and social studies.

The second grade children had poetry books of their
own which had developed through sharing favorite poems then
copying those they liked best and enclosing them in a booklet.   Favorite times were poetry sessions when all the children would come to the rug to have choral readings.   These
days were not often but well enjoyed.   The first grade shared
the books with the second grade.   It was a situation comparable to music, an experience shared by all.

The experiences described above are total group experiences involving reading.   There are certainly many other
types of activities participated in by the total group.

The small group experiences sometimes involved

skills which will be included in that area.   The other small
group experiences were usually on a spontaneous level organized by the children.   They came together in groups of
two or three to read to each other, each from the book of
his choice.   They sometimes worked on a particular skill
voluntarily.   Often a group could be seen before the phonics
chart or an experience chart reading together.   Two children
might be playing a game.   These are all spontaneous, basically social activities, which involved no ability levels but
children feeling comfortable with each other in an activity of
their own choosing through which they both could learn.   Another small group activity was working out plays or puppet
shows.   These were encouraged by the teacher and help was
given when requested, but they were completely organized by
the children.

Conferences

        The availability of books, the guided flexibility and
the conferences were undoubtedly the core of the program.

        As was stated earlier, this particular program was
conducted in the most flexible combination of patterns that
had been suggested by the literature.   Therefore, conferences were self-selective on the part of the child.   A list
on the blackboard designated which child was coming that particular day.   When a child wanted a conference he put his
name on the board and was taken in turn.   The number of
names usually ranged from seven to twenty.   The children
signed up as they were ready.   Obviously the teacher could
not get to all the children every day.   The remaining list
was copied, usually by a child, and put on the board the following day.   Occasionally a child had his conference out of
turn if the teacher felt that he needed the help immediately
for some particular reason.   This did not occur often but
did occasionally.   One of the reasons for taking a child out
of turn was if he had not had a conference in a long time
and the previous child on the list had had one the day before.
The conferences were not limited as to time.   Each child
was given the length of time he needed that particular day.
The only limits that were placed on the conference were that
the child was supposed to have done some independent reading in the book of his choice, and he was only permitted to
read orally out of two books, regardless of how many he had
completed since the last conference.   This was because of
the time factor.   It was not unusual by the middle of the
year for some children to come with four or five books.

These limitations were accepted by the children willingly and cheerfully.

The conferences were one of the most interesting parts of the program. Many times they were conducted alone, but it was not unusual to have other children come to sit at the reading table, sometimes to listen, but equally as often to work or read. Quietly this small group at the table might ask the teacher for help, but probably the security of working or reading near the teacher was one of the major reasons for coming. The second reason was curiosity concerning the book that was being read or discussed. At times it was almost as though the table had a magnetic force. The teacher would start out with one child and perhaps a few visitors. If an interesting subject arose, one by one, children would drop what they were doing and come to the reading table to enter into the discussion. At times there were ten to twelve children standing around. This is another example of a spontaneous group situation.

On one such occasion a child was reading a book which discussed the eardrum. Another time one of the boys was reading about the beginning of Marshall Field and Company. A discussion concerning the League of Nations is a third example of this type of spontaneous activity.

Goals in the reading conferences were different for each child and also different for each child that particular day. Sometimes the conference placed its emphasis on skills and word definitions, sometimes on oral reading... Teaching the child to think creatively or interpretatively was often the goal. Comprehension was certainly included. An effort was made to let the conferences assume different tones so that the child would not get into a boring routine.

Selection of Books by the Children

The manner in which the children chose their books proved to be one of the most interesting learning situations for the teacher. Each child had a reason or goal of his own. Each child also had a pacing procedure peculiar to himself. The characteristics which appeared to upset the so-called developmental process the most were (1) that a number of the children chose books which would have been classified as too difficult for them, (2) a number chose books which would have been classified as too easy for them and (3) a number of children chose to read more than one book at a time.

Because it had been decided before the study began that the children would have free choice, they continued selecting books which the teacher would actually not have chosen. The concern for the second grade was not as great as that for the first grade. The teacher was confident that the second grade children could read. It required great strength and confidence to permit some of the first graders to "struggle along" or so it seemed to her. Three factors were instrumental in helping her to permit the children to work in this manner. The first was the children's comments: "It's not too hard, it's interesting." The second was the confidence of the people working with her in the study and the third was the literature.

Bolstered by the literature and the children, the program continued along smoothly. The problem with the words became less and less. The important point to remember here is that it was never a problem to the children, only to the teacher. She attempted not to show her concern and the bridge was soon crossed.

The pattern of children reading more than one book at a time may have started because there appeared to be certain tensions in the room when new books were brought in which resulted in the attitude, "If I don't take that book now, it won't be on the shelf when I want it." However, it was also pointed out that many adults read this way. Why shouldn't children? A third cause was that often children left the book they were reading at home and chose another one to read during the school day.

Habits of self-selection as practiced by the study group were certainly considerably different than the teacher would have planned it. It is important to remember that the children's seeking, self-selection, and pacing demanded a new type of planning, organization and orientation on the part of the teacher, but planning it did demand. There was no chaotic permissiveness as some of the literature suggests.

Skills

The major part of the development of various skills was done in small groups and reinforced during the individual conferences. If a child was having a particular problem which no one else in the class was having, it was discussed at the time of the conference and, if necessary, a paper which would help reinforce the concept was given. Individu-

al flash cards were made and given to many of the first
graders at the beginning of the year.   Each child had an en-
velope in which he could keep his own cards.   Once the cards
were learned, they were discarded.

Groups were formed for phonics skills.   They did not
meet every day and most of them were disbanded by March.
Three children continued on until May, but this group did not
meet every day.   Five children, who appeared to need little
phonics reinforcement, met once or twice a week, but did
not continue after February.   Although many of these children did not meet as a group continuously through the whole
year, it must be emphasized that the tools they had learned
were used again and again in their reading, in conferences
and in paper work.

The children did read once a week in basal readers.
Three or four stories were assigned and group written work
was assigned with it.   Everyone in the first grade read as
one group and the fourteen second graders read as a group.
It was particularly interesting that children whose reading
varied so greatly could read together once a week with no
great problems.   The teacher read with the first grade most
of the time and the second grade had a child leader.   Once
a month the procedure was changed and the second grade had
the teacher as a leader.

Although the written work covered the same material
for each group, it was geared to different levels of independent ability.   Some children did varying amounts of board
work and some were given ditto sheets.

The purpose behind using the basal reader once a
week was to help the children to answer questions and develop techniques in a written manner.   Although some children
did it often through self-selection, there were those who did
not and this grouping once a week gave them the experience.

It must be acknowledged that some of the children did
not keep the place in the book as the others read.   A few of
the children looked forward to the day on which the basal
reader was used, but most of them were apathetic concerning it.

The two reading groups were not ability grouped.
Grade lines could have been crossed, as they were many
times, but they were not because the goal was not involved

with reading levels.   The children did most of their reading
individually on any level they chose.   Many of them commented that the reading on Wednesdays was easy, but the
written work was hard.

There was one group of three children that came together for flash cards until about the end of April.   The
children needed the reinforcement and really enjoyed working
with them.   These were first grade children.   A fourth child
joined them occasionally.   He was in second grade and was
often at gym when flash cards were used.   He did, however,
work with the teacher alone from time to time.

Class Time Spent Reading

The time spent in actual reading activities such as
conferences and small group work varied from one and one-
half to two hours.   Reading conferences had a period of one
half hour in the morning and one half hour in the afternoon.
The remaining time was spent in small group activities described above.   As the year progressed and less time was
indicated for small group activities, the time allotted to reading conferences increased.   The complete block of time used
for reading was flexible.   If the reading conference list was
very long on a particular day, the small groups did not meet.
The teacher was under no pressure to cover so much material by a certain date.   This was one of the factors that contributed toward the flexibility and feeling of relaxation in the
group.

During the reading period the children were never told
that they must read out of their individual books.   There
were specific assignments in arithmetic, spelling, skill pages
or creative writing.   Once these assignments were completed,
the child was free to select any activity he chose.   The a-
mount of free time was at least an hour.   In many instances
it was longer, depending upon how rapidly the child worked.
Many children spent a good part of this time reading or in
reading activities such as browsing through books.   It was
during this period that books were chosen which would go
home that night and checked out with a particular child.
These cards were later rechecked by the teacher.

At one forty-five in the afternoon, when all reading
activities were supposed to come to an end, the teacher usually had to walk around the room to remind the children to
put their books away.

Beginning Organization

The first grade started out the year with experience charts, poetry (which was actually due to influence from the second grade program), large books which were teacher-made and riddles written by the children. Books were readily available. This period lasted from six to eight weeks. During the period many of the children began to read books and sign up for reading conferences. They, too, continued with the group activities at the same time. They also began simple creative writing. The stories were put in a book entitled "Our Book of September Stories." All the material the children wrote was always included into books of this type and available for reading during free time.

The second grade children started with the individualized reading program immediately. All fourteen of these children had worked with a basal group approach in grade one. The teacher gave them a careful explanation as to how the reading program would work. They were also told that it was being organized in this manner so that they would be given the opportunity to read whatever they chose. Seven of the children she had had the year before were in her group again. The children accepted this as a matter of course with the exception of one. B. G. , a boy who had been in her room the previous year and who was quite a good student, immediately told her that he couldn't choose his own books, he would much prefer that the teacher choose them. Apparently, here was a child who required a highly structured program. It was explained to him that selecting a book was part of learning too, that teacher guidance was available to him but that he would have to learn himself. This was no longer a problem to B. G. by the end of the year.

The second grade also worked with poetry at the beginning of the year. The children would each bring a favorite poem about a pre-chosen subject and read it to the group. The one which received a majority vote was manuscripted on chart paper and put on the bulletin board. The children then copied it. In previous years, when the teacher had worked with grade one alone, she had used the same technique, but dittoed the poems and gave them to the children to decorate. The dittoed method is far superior. Copying poetry is long and laborious and actually serves no purpose. In retrospect she felt it detracted from the appreciation of poetry in the total program. Appreciation of poetry had been the goal, but the busy work of copying it detracted from that goal.

Neither the first nor second grade began to read in
the basal readers once a week until about six weeks after
school started. The teacher began this for the reasons
stated above, and also due to some concern for the children,
as she knew they would return to a basal text pattern the
following year.

Books Going Home

This was one of the major parts of the program.
Most of the children loved to take the books home. It is difficult to be sure, but a generality may be drawn to the effect that most of the reading was probably done at home.
Both the parents and the children were thrilled with this part
of the program.   This is certainly one phase of individualized reading which could be incorporated into any type of
reading program.

How 189 Third Grade Teachers Provided for
Individual Differences

by

Janie Keith Bollinger

(This material is excerpted from the author's 1966
University of Tennessee master's thesis, Provi-
sions for Individual Differences in Reading in the
Third Grades of Selected East Tennessee School
Systems.)

Questionnaire Statements and Distribution
of Responses by Number and Percent

	Response			
	Always	Fre-quently	Seldom	Never
	----Number/Percent--------			
1. My group is somewhat alike as to achievement as they were grouped that way before they were assigned to me.	22/11	34/18	29/20	96/51
2. All of my students receive reading instruction from the same reading text.	56/30	52/27	29/15	52/28
3. Time is set aside each week for "free" reading (when each child reads from different library books).	106/56	71/38	8/4	4/2
4. I form temporary and flexible groups with children who have similar needs and disband the group after a few days when the needs are met.	41/22	94/50	35/18	19/10

Questionnaire Statements and Distribution
of Responses by Number and Percent (cont.)

Statement	Response			
	Always	Fre-quently	Seldom	Never
	----Number/Percent--------			
5. When introducing a word recognition skill, I teach it to the whole class.	53/28	56/30	47/25	33/17
6. I assign stories and poems to be written by the total class.	29/15	96/51	37/20	27/14
7. Flash cards and experience charts are used with students as they need them.	92/49	80/42	13/7	4/2
8. I plan a conference with each child at least every two weeks, during which time he reports his reading activities to me.	17/9	49/26	73/39	50/26
9. I teach reference skills such as dictionary usage to different reading groups as a need arises.	136/72	43/23	9/4	1/1
10. I have each child read orally to me every day.	45/24	70/37	44/23	30/16
11. I (or resource people) give a vision test to each child every year.	158/84	18/9	10/5	3/2
12. I seat students advantageously who appear to have hearing or seeing difficulties.	183/96	4/2	1/1	1/1
13. When working on a unit, I assign different sub-topics to ability groups.	81/43	82/43	19/10	7/4

14. I give the same standardized
reading tests to the entire
class.   129/69   38/20   12/6   10/5

15. My reading instruction is
based on book selections which
students make to suit their in-
terests and abilities.   23/12   53/28   56/30   57/30

16. I introduce a new word recognition skill separately to
each individual when he is
ready for it.   19/10   53/28   75/40   42/22

17. Pupils construct their own
dictionaries or dictionary notebooks using words in which
they are interested and which
they need.   19/10   73/39   53/28   44/23

18. I observe and record each
child's interests, study habits,
and work habits.   72/38   91/49   16/8   10/5

19. I give teacher-made reading
tests to the entire class.   36/19   78/41   45/24   30/16

20. When working on a unit, I
permit each student to select
his area of interest to work
in.   46/24   107/57   26/14   10/5

21. I instruct from basic readers, but I do not attempt to
keep all groups reading the
same material.   147/78   18/10   10/5   14/7

22. I introduce new word recognition skills to groups as
their introduction is needed.   144/76   40/21   4/2   1/1

23. I teach reference skills to
the entire class at one time.   35/18   74/39   45/24   35/19

24. I encourage children to do
creative writing when they
feel the need for it.   94/50   79/42   12/6   4/2

Questionnaire Statements and Distribution
of Responses by Number and Percent (cont.)

Statement	Response			
	Always	Fre-quently	Seldom	Never
	---- Number/Percent------			
25. Among the first things I do in reading is to have each individual read orally and privately to me.	86/46	44/23	17/9	42/22
26. I teach reference skills individually as a need arises.	57/30	90/48	33/17	9/5
27. I thoroughly study the cumulative folders of each child.	130/69	48/25	10/5	1/1
28. I give different tests to different groups.	61/32	79/42	33/18	16/8
29. Rather than stressing phonetic or structural analysis, context or picture clues, I encourage each child to develop the work recognition skills which fit his needs and interests best.	25/13	68/36	58/31	38/20
30. I (or resource people) give a hearing test to each child every year.	107/57	37/20	22/11	23/12
31. I include Science Research Associates (SRA) materials in my reading program.	47/25	26/14	28/15	88/46
32. I provide a time when children may do creative and other writing if they wish to do so.	74/39	89/47	23/12	3/2
33. I teach reading from the same basic reader to the whole class at one time.	6/3	17/9	17/9	149/79

34. If a student is reading above
or below grade level, I supply
him with a basic text on his
reading level.   116/61   54/29   13/7   5/3

35. I invite children who are
interested in a previously an-
nounced topic to work with me
in developing an experience
chart.   28/15   103/54   35/19   23/12

36. I form ability reading
groups in which most children
remain for the year.   46/24   79/42   42/22   22/12

Chapter 3

Individualized Reading in the Intermediate Grades

The five selections in this chapter (all excerpted from recent masters' theses) describe classroom teachers' experiences in the use of the individualized reading approach to reading instruction.

Carol H. Peters' selection describes a fourth grade program; Glenda A. Gray, Floy Utz, and Marguerite P. Caliver discuss the use of individualized reading in the fifth grade; and Hazel S. Webb describes a sixth grade experience.

The reader will note the common elements in each of these programs even though each one differs from all the others in many respects.

Individualized Reading Procedures in a Fourth Grade

by

Carol Huenink Peters

(This material is excerpted from the author's University of Kansas master's thesis, A Comparison of Growth in Reading Rate in an Individualized Approach and in a Basal Reader Approach to Reading Instruction in the Fourth Grade.)

The experimental group was instructed following the individualized reading approach. The following specific procedures were followed in this classroom. On Mondays and Thursdays, the days before library periods, the reading periods began with two oral book reports. Pupils signed up for these on a sign up sheet. Reports took many forms. Some children dramatized an exciting portion of their chosen book. Others, especially those sharing scientific books, put colored chalk diagrams on the board beforehand and explained them in their report. Others used the opaque projector to show illustrations in the book, and used these as visual aids for their report. Some made T. V. 's using a box, rollers and long strips of paper. A favorite selection was at times read aloud, or at other times a pupil told a portion of the story in his own words, leaving the class in suspense and urging them to read to find out what happened. Oral reports were always followed by a brief evaluation period by the class.

The teacher kept record of these reports and conferences. At the end of most reports children raised their hands to be put on a waiting list for reading the book. The list was posted on the bulletin board. After one child finished the book he was to see that the next one on the list got it.

On other days of the week, Tuesdays, Wednesdays and Fridays, the lesson often began with instruction for the

entire class on such fourth grade skills as use of guide
words, diacritical markings, or prefixes and suffixes. Any
children having difficulty were helped in smaller groups.
Periodically on these days diagnostic tests were administered
to help locate those children with particular needs. These
tests helped in the formation of groups.

On these days there was also vocabulary sharing for
about five minutes. New words pupils had discovered in their
independent reading were defined from memory after having
been looked up in a dictionary and were used in a sentence.
Then the words were added to vocabulary sheets.

In every lesson there were vocabulary riddles for a-
bout five minutes. A pupil read a sentence he had made up
using one of the words, but he left out that word in reading
it aloud. Whoever guessed the word could in turn read one
of his sentences. About three of the most current sheets
were kept displayed at any one time.

The remainder of the reading periods, on all days of
the week, was given to group instruction based on particular
individual needs, to individual conferences (pupils signed up
on a posted sheet) or occasionally to helping with the selection of a book. While these activities were conducted by the
teacher other pupils either read independently, kept their
reading records, or worked preparing to share a book, the
latter activity being limited to just one period a week.
Preparation to share could be done singly or in small groups,
and could involve art work or rehearsals or this could involve making a book cover to advertise the particular book.

At the close of each period children were asked to
write their diaries for the day. Kept consecutively in the
reading section of their loose leaf books, this record was
quite simple. Only independent or small group activities
were noted, not whole class activities. This enabled the
teacher to check daily on at least half of the class plus any
other child that she felt needed checking, to be sure the time
had been well used and to keep up on what each pupil was
doing.

Reading materials which pupils read independently consisted of books from either the public or school libraries
and sometimes of pupil's own books, so long as they were
approved by the teachers. Several children lent personal
copies to the classroom library to supplement the public li-

brary books kept there.   If any classroom library book was taken home, a record was made of this by placing its card with the date and the child's name in a file box.

A library committee of three or four assisted in selecting books from the public library every four weeks. Their names were drawn, and everyone in the class went at some time during the year.   The class was encouraged to make their wishes known to the committee by writing down their favorite author, series, particular title, or a general subject area.   Taking pupils in small groups after school promoted considerable enthusiasm, as well as providing an opportunity for a lesson on the use of the library.   An effort was also made to take out books which would supplement the social studies and science units being studied.

After a pupil completed reading a book he wrote an outline, following this guide: A. Title,   B. Author and illustrator,   C. Dates begun and completed,   D. Summary, E. Vocabulary.   The summary was to be just a few thoughtful sentences, enough to give someone else an idea of what sort of book it was.   These were sometimes shown to classmates who asked for good books to read.   In the evaluation the reader gave his personal reactions and sometimes made suggestions about who would particularly enjoy the book such as scouts, girls, those with mechanical interests, etc.   New words were listed along with the page numbers on which they were found in the book.

Each book was also recorded in the class record book in which each child had his own pages.   On a single line he noted the date the book was completed, the title, and the author.

A Fifth Grade Individualized Reading Program

by

Glenda Arlene Gray

(This material is excerpted from the author's 1965 Marshall University master's thesis, A Study of the Individualized Reading Program at Holz Elementary School, Charleston, West Virginia.)

On November 9, 1964, the fifth grade class at Holz Elementary School began their individualized reading program. During the following five months, twenty-seven students participated in the program with only twenty-two actually beginning the program in November, 1964, and following through until March, 1965. A total of five students transferred in and out of the class during the period. Students new to the classroom were able to adjust quickly to the individualized reading program and required only a minimum of guidance in preparing their record books.

The students' reading levels ranged from fourth grade to tenth grade with one student totally unable to read. Another student who had resisted reading for four years suddenly discovered the joy of reading and was the pride of the entire class as they urged him to try their favorites. He later moved to another school and was unable to complete the program and the testing.

Several minor problems arose as the class progressed. All were examined and discussed. Some, however, should be avoided if the program is to be successful another year.

A basic problem underlying many of the smaller problems was due primarily to a lack of experience with the individualized reading program on the part of the teacher and to a lack of a sense of responsibility on the part of a few of the students.

The average and above average students progressed smoothly and quickly throughout the entire program. For the others, the individualized reading program was difficult in that the fifty minutes allowed for the reading period was too long a period of time. Daily conferences were scheduled by the teacher for these students.

In the case of one student, lessons were planned and assigned by the teacher. During his daily conferences, the previous day's assignments were checked and evaluated. An interesting sidelight developed with this student. Previously a disciplinary problem, his behavior altered favorably as long as the daily conferences were continued.

Another problem that occurred in the program involved the categorization of the library books. The classroom was not equipped with enough library shelves so the books were placed on the top of the shelf that lined one side of the room. Theoretically the method worked, but the sheer bulk of the books made it impossible for any child to remove or replace a book without help. It soon became apparent that if students were to get books whenever they needed them, they would have to dispense with replacing the book in the proper category. The categories were abandoned.

The county-adopted, basal text reading program followed at Holz School had been taught through the use of ability-grouping, with from two to four reading groups in each classroom.

The fifth grade had been following such a reading plan. The three groups were eliminated when the class began individualized reading. It was felt that the children would be able to complete their basal text and accompanying work-book as part of the individualized program with skills being taught three times a week for twenty minutes. This was not the case. The above average readers abandoned the text as being too easy, the average preferred to read other books, and the poor readers were unable to read it by themselves. All of them disliked the workbook.

By January, 1965, the students and the teacher realized that if the basal text was to be completed, they would have to begin soon. After much discussion, the basic problem underlying the reluctance to read the text seemed to involve the workbooks. The students were discouraged by the poor work that they had been doing.

Temporarily, the entire individualized reading program was halted. Students were told to try to forget about grades. The workbooks were not to be graded and the students were to concentrate instead on learning the skills presented in the workbook. Daily periods with the workbook skills meant that those students having the most difficulty received more individual help from the teacher while the other students were able to go on with their own independent reading. At the end of each period, they checked their own work, stopping to correct any mistakes before going on to another skill.

By the end of January all students had successfully completed both the basal text and the workbook and it was felt that all concerned had greatly benefited from this procedure. Scores from the test booklets accompanying the basal text indicated that higher and more consistent scores resulted as compared to the scores of previous years.

The individualized reading program had barely gotten under way again when the reading laboratory was brought into the room. The reading laboratory contained materials on twelve levels and was designed to increase reading speed, comprehension, and listening skills.

The laboratory was introduced to the class and for two weeks the class centered their reading around the laboratory materials. After that, and continuing until the end of the school year, the teacher scheduled time for one series of rate builders and one listening skill builder for each week with each student responsible for two or more individual reading lessons.

Many of the students preferred to choose their own materials and disliked the laboratory work because of the writing skills that were involved. Use of the reading laboratory during another year might best be utilized at the beginning of the year when the teacher was becoming acquainted with each child and his reading ability.

Several students asked if they might read a supplementary text as a group since they felt it would be more interesting and ideas could be more easily shared. The interest of these particular students had been aroused the previous year when, as fourth grade students in a split level room, they had observed the reactions of the fifth grade students to the particular supplementary text.

Three such groups were formed, each having a week-ly conference. Individually the children continued their read-ing and scheduled conferences as before.

Grouping occurred frequently throughout the course of the program; a student having difficulty with a reading skill joined another having the same problem; a student needing an audience so that he might practice oral reading usually found a volunteer willing to listen for a few minutes each day; and two or more students often joined together after reading the same material and planned some type of sharing activity to present to the class.

Early in March, 1965, the principal of Holz Elemen-tary School requested that the other fifth grade teacher and one sixth grade teacher inquire about the individualized read-ing program. After reading the text of the study of litera-ture and hearing of the experiences of the class, both teach-ers asked and received administrative permission to under-take the program for the remainder of the school year. Their particular advantage might well have been that they had already completed the basal text program and could benefit from the experiences of the individualized reading program described above.

The Individualized Approach to the Teaching
of Reading in a Fifth Grade

by

Floy Utz

(This material is excerpted from the author's 1961
University of Kansas master's thesis, An Individualized Reading Program in a Fifth Grade Classroom and its Effect on Pupil Attitudes.)

Fifty minutes was allotted for the reading period. It
was necessary to keep the time scheduled for any phase of
the reading program quite flexible in order to meet the needs
of the pupils in a period no longer than this. Usually all of
the pupils read individually at least the first twenty minutes.
If the more able readers were using workbooks or were assigned a basal reader for work on a given skill, they read
individually after completing their assignments. Other work
on skills followed the silent reading period. Individual conferences were held during the silent reading period. With
the exception of the very slow learners, pupils did not have
more than one conference a week. When the workbook or a
basal reader was used, the more able learners frequently
had ten days or more between conferences. Usually every
pupil received help in a group situation at least twice a
week. If time permitted, the last ten minutes were used for
sharing books. Some English periods were used for this
purpose. Science books were sometimes shared during the
science period.

The reading materials used during the program were
obtained in several ways. Books were borrowed by the pupils and the teacher from the bookmobile and the main library of the Topeka Public Library. During the first half
of the year there were over three hundred trade books in the
classroom library. Trade books were borrowed from the
classroom libraries of the primary grades. A central li-

brary for the school was started at the middle of the year
and most of the trade books in the classroom libraries were
placed in the central library.   This increased the number
and variety of books at all grade levels available to the pupils.   Books from the central library could be checked out
daily by both the pupils and the teacher.   At least four different basal readers were available for each grade level.
During the seventh month of school fifty-eight books of high
interest and low vocabulary were purchased for the school to
be used with retarded readers in the intermediate grades.
Much use was made of these books by the retarded readers
in the room.   In addition to several sets of encyclopedias,
over two hundred reference books for science and social
studies were available.   Books from the Arrow Book Club
were purchased by many of the pupils.   A few magazines for
children were loaned or given to the classroom.   Workbooks
on various grade levels were used.   Two primary teachers
were very generous in supplying mimeographed material for
use with retarded readers.

Each pupil used some type of notebook for a diary.
A record was kept of all material read.   The pupil was required to list the author and title of each book or story read.
Many of the pupils recorded some of the following: (1) the
date the book was finished, (2) the number of pages in the
book, (3) a short summary of the book, (4) the pupil's reaction to the book, (5) new words learned, and (6) special assignments.

On the teacher's desk was an index file with a 5" x
8" card for each pupil.   When a pupil was ready for a conference he wrote the title of the book he would use during the
conference period on his card.   The card was placed on the
teacher's desk.   Since there were usually several cards on
the desk, the card at the bottom of the pile determined the
next pupil in line for a conference.   Some exceptions had to
be made as some pupils needed more conferences than others
and some pupils asked for more conferences than time permitted.   It was necessary for the teacher to check frequently
to see if all pupils were getting conferences when needed.

Needed assignments were written on the pupil's card
during the conference period.   This served two purposes.
The pupil knew what was expected of him.   At the next conference the notation on the card reminded both the teacher
and the pupil to check the assigned work if it was an individual assignment.

The teacher's records were kept in loose-leaf notebooks that were indexed.   Colored index tabs in which the
pupils' names were inserted were used.   Each pupil knew
the location of his records and was free to examine them at
any time.   The majority of the pupils frequently checked
their progress.   The records were used also for reference
during conferences with parents.

The records were of two kinds.   On the left-hand page
was listed the following information: (1) the date of the conference, (2) the title of the book, (3) comments regarding the
pupil's reading, and (4) assignments.   On the right-hand page
was a check list.   Items on the check list were listed under
the following headings: (1) oral reading, (2) reading habits,
(3) vocabulary, (4) comprehension, (5) locating information,
(6) selecting and evaluating information, and (7) using information.   Quantitative statements were usually made for oral
reading.   For other items a check mark (✓) was made if
the pupil encountered difficulty and OK was written if the
pupil's work was satisfactory for the item being checked.
The date was recorded when an item was checked.

Since the reading was integrated with the other language arts, samples of handwriting were included in the notebook so that the pupils could check their progress.   Words
that were misspelled by a pupil in other areas of the curriculum were listed.   Each pupil added these words to his
assigned list in spelling.   Pupils referred to these lists frequently to see if the spelling in their written work was improving.   The interest inventories and parent questionnaires
were included for reference.   Each pupil listed what he needed to do to improve his reading.   He added to his list as he
discovered new needs.   The lists were kept in the notebooks.

An extra desk with attached seat for the pupil and a
chair for the teacher were placed in a corner in the front of
the room for use during the conference period.   In the desk
were kept the loose-leaf notebooks containing the individual
records and a record of the books the pupils took home to
read.   The pupils used the desk when they examined their
records during the day.

The individual conference periods varied according to
the pupils' needs.   When individual assignments had been
made, these were checked first.   Books listed in the diary
since the last conference were noted.   As the year progressed, the pupils gradually started bringing lists of diffi-

cult words to the conference for discussion. The pupil usually read orally a selection that he had prepared. Many pupils required much help before they were able to select a complete unit of thought for oral reading. Comprehension and the pupil's reaction to the material read were always checked. Occasional checks were made to determine how the pupil made out new words. Other skills checked depended upon the needs of the pupils. Individual help was given as needed. Ways of sharing the material read were sometimes discussed. Guidance in the selection of new material was given when it seemed advisable. Sometimes the reading of related material was suggested.

When two or more pupils selected the same material for reading, the teacher usually met with the group rather than with pupils individually, unless a pupil requested an individual conference. Groups of this type were formed on the following bases: (1) friendship, (2) a common interest, and (3) similar reading abilities. Pupils in these groups frequently met to read orally to each other. If questions were available, they checked each other on comprehension. This resulted in pupils voluntarily leaving the group when they discovered that the material being read was beyond their understanding.

Sometimes a group reading together dramatized one of the stories they had read. Some groups were formed for the purpose of dramatization.

When two or more pupils needed help on a given skill, they were grouped for this purpose. Any pupil who felt that he needed the help that was being given was permitted to join the group. For the majority of the pupils, assignments in workbooks were group assignments. When a basal reader was used for teaching or checking a given skill, this was usually done in a group situation.

Sometimes pupils having a common interest met in small groups to share their books. The type of books discussed in small groups included: (1) biography, (2) science, (3) dog stories, (4) animal stories, (5) humorous stories, (6) mysteries, (7) general fiction, and (8) general non-fiction.

Usually books were shared with the entire class. The most popular method of sharing was to form a large circle around the classroom and discuss the books being read. The ways of sharing books were:

1. Plays, stories, and poems were dramatized.
2. Poems, short stories, and selections from books were read orally.
3. Incidents from books were related.
4. The reading of a selection from a book was preceded or followed by a summarization of other interesting incidents in the book.
5. A book was read and summarized alternately.
6. An incident from a book was illustrated.
7. A movie telling the story of a book was made.
8. A panel discussion by pupils who had read the same book of non-fiction was held.
9. A riddle was made about a book that had been read.

At the beginning of the year much time was spent in overcoming the negative attitudes of some of the pupils and in helping them to become better adjusted as individuals. At the end of three months it became possible to include all of the pupils in an evaluation of the reading program. Frequent evaluations were made during the remainder of the year. Some of these were individual and some were group evaluations. The final evaluation for the purpose of this study was made at the end of approximately seven months and was both subjective and objective.

The Use of Individualized Reading in Another
Fifth Grade Class

by

Marguerite Pittman Caliver

(This material is excerpted from the author's 1964
Ohio State University master's thesis, A Comparative Study of Two Methods of Teaching Reading at
the Fifth Grade Level.)

During the summer preceding the study the investigator read more than one hundred children's books.   The title,
the author, the facts of publication together with a resumé of
the story, and three or four questions on the plot and the
characters in the book were written on a 5x8 file card.   The
books selected dealt with humor, fantasy, animals, adventure,
nature, science, fairy and folk tales, biography, sports, historical fiction, myths and legends, and poetry.   The books
ranged from early second grade to seventh grade in level of
difficulty.

A file of biographical sketches, anecdotes, and pictures of authors and illustrators was compiled.   A felt board
story of Many Moons, a mobile of characters from Grimm's
Fairy Tales, and a diorama of Miss Hickory were created
to spark an interest in these and other stories and to illustrate ways of sharing stories.

In the middle of September a letter was sent to the
parents telling of the new approach to reading and requesting
their help in getting the children to procure and to use library cards.   The parents were invited to visit the school
or to telephone the teacher if they had questions concerning
the program.

Materials--Arrangements were made with the Public
School Library to borrow from two to three books per child

every six weeks. This was in addition to those in the unit
library. Forty books a month were drawn from the Columbus Public Library, and twenty more monthly from the Ohio
State Library. Thus, more than one hundred and fifty trade
books were constantly at hand. The basal and supplementary
readers, maps, reference books, and dictionaries used by
the control group were available. Life, Jack and Jill, Humpty Dumpty, and the weekly National Geographic School Bulletin were supplied. The school library was available on the
same basis as it was to the control group. The investigator
purchased some Arrow Books. Pupils also purchased them.

Workbooks from several reading series, Russell and
Karp's Reading Aid Through the Grades, and several Dolch
games aided in instructing individuals, small groups, and, at
times, the entire class.

The investigator kept a loose-leaf notebook with a section for each child. Each section included the "Pupil Interest Inventory" and a mimeographed sheet for recording the
pupil's test scores, his hobbies and interests, the date of
each conference, the book discussed, and the investigator's
comments on the pupil's oral reading ability, comprehension,
and word recognition skills. On the back of the sheet the
titles of books read in addition to those discussed were listed.
Additional sheets were added as needed. Barbe's "Reading
Skills Check Lists" for third, fourth, and fifth grades, the
levels on which most pupils read, were placed at the front
of the notebook for ready reference.

A brief diary kept the investigator apprised of the
special needs of pupils, and noted skills which could be
taught more efficiently on a small group or class-wide basis.

Each pupil had a composition book in which he listed
the author, title, illustrator, publisher, main idea, thing he
liked best, date begun, and date finished for each book read.
If he found he did not like a story, he was permitted to set
it aside. This too he listed in his notebook, giving the
number of pages read, and stating the reason for his dislike. Beginning on the last page of the book and moving forward he listed the words which were difficult for him. These
were reviewed periodically.

Method--At the time the explanatory letter was sent
to parents the pupils were informed that beginning October
fifteenth they would use a new method during the reading

period. Instead of reading single stories they would read
whole books which they would choose themselves from books
in the classroom or from the public library. The method of
choosing a satisfactory book, the procedure in the individual
conference, the system of record keeping, and some of the
ways of sharing the books read were explained to the pupils.
Through teacher-pupil planning, orderly procedures for check-
ing-out books, for getting help with difficult words, and for
creating materials for the sharing period were worked out.
These agreements were made into charts.

Since the Department of Instruction of the Columbus
Public School system required that the basic series be used,
pupils were encouraged to read them for enjoyment and to
enrich the social studies and science programs. The fanci-
ful stories of Just Imagine were suggested as a starting
point for pupils testing on the third grade level on the California Reading Test. The section "Famous Americans of
Other Times" in More Times and Places enriched the study
of American history with stories on George Washington,
Daniel Boone, Francis Scott Key, and Clara Barton. The
expansion of the country into the Louisiana Territory and the
Far West became more real as pupils linked the stories in
Days and Deeds of children like themselves in a buffalo hunt,
on a pony express route, and in a wagon train. Brief whole
class discussions of folk tales, fairy tales, and legends were
illustrated by materials from More Days and Deeds.

At the beginning of the study the investigator administered the tests and the interest inventory described earlier
to the experimental group. The range of ability, and the interests revealed, together with the findings of research spe-
cialists on children's interests in the nine-to-twelve age
group, helped greatly in selecting a wide range of books
throughout the year. As pupils' interests expanded notes in
the Teacher's Record enabled her to provide for them.

In arranging the classroom areas had to be set aside:
(1) for a library corner where pupils could sample and check
out books, (2) for a center of creative activities, and (3) for
a teacher-pupil conference area. In the library corner a
display, "Let's Re-Discover America," introduced the children to stories of the different sections of the United States.
By choosing a section of the United States map that was
mounted on the chalkboard and by following the red, white,
or blue ribbon leading from it to a book displayed on the
table below, the pupil could find a story about that region.

Some books contained stories of long ago. Some told of life today. The stories, while on a fifth grade interest level, varied in difficulty from third to seventh grade levels.

The teacher's desk, her chair, and a small chair beside it constituted the individual conference area. The names of pupils due for an individual conference were posted on the chalkboard the preceding day. Approximately six pupils were scheduled each day.

Teacher-pupil conference--The most popular part of the entire program was the individual conference. Many pupils wanted daily attention. This period when the teacher gave her total attention to them appeared to fill a void in their lives. After the investigator had conferred with the pupils scheduled for the day, she devoted any time remaining in the conference period to pupils requesting conferences.

During the reading conference the pupil read a prepared selection of his own choosing. Observations on the child's ability to read orally, on his understanding and feeling about the story, and on his skill in using the mechanics of reading were recorded in the teacher's notebook. Many of the questions on the content came from the card file prepared the summer before and constantly expanded. Some of the questions generally asked during a conference were:

1. What interested you in this book? Why?

2. What kind of a book was it? Was it fiction, fact, a science story, a funny story, or what?

3. Which character was your favorite? Why did you like him?

4. Give briefly the main idea of the story.

5. Could you figure out the ending before you came to it?

6. Was it hard, easy, or about right to read?

7. Which words or ideas were difficult for you?

8. Were you able to figure out some of the new words yourself? How?

9. Do you feel that you are reading better now than you did a month ago?

10. How do you plan to share this book with the class?

Naturally if the book concerned science, nature, or biography the questions would be of a different nature. The type of material determined the kind of questions asked.

The evaluation of the pupil's oral reading and his comprehension indicated which skills needed special work. Assigning appropriate practice materials or giving directions on how to improve his performance usually terminated the conference.

Only the books being read at the time of the conference were checked. To check all the books read by the class would have consumed a disproportionate period of the school day. Time in the reading period was allocated roughly as follows: about five minutes to plan special activities for the independent work period, about twenty-five minutes for individual conferences, from five to ten minutes on a special group or class skill problem, and from five to ten minutes for sharing.

In the individual conference the investigator was able to use her knowledge of the pupil's home environment, peer status, school attitude, self concept, and ambition, to guide the pupils to books which would aid them with their personal problems. The story of the Man with the Purple Eyes enabled a pupil, whose parent was ill with tuberculosis, to realize that his problem was not unique, that healing takes time, and that faith on the part of the family is necessary.

Skill instruction--Skill instruction was given during the individual conference, in small temporary groups, and to the whole class. Instruction in skills lacked by only one or two pupils was done individually during the conference period. To improve such abilities as skimming for specific information, drawing inferences, and summarizing, which were lacked by small groups of pupils, temporary groups were established. Whole class instruction was given in structural analysis, and in such phonetic problems as three-letter blends, the sounding of double vowels, and syllabication.

Since no school subject is taught in total isolation, studies in other subject areas fed back into the reading pro-

gram. In working with the dictionary in spelling, diacritical
marks, multiple meanings, the effect of context on meaning,
the derivation of many words from a common root (i. e.
"tele" meaning "far off" in telegram, television, telescope,
teletype, and telecast), the effect of prefixes such as "un,"
"sub," "mis," "post," and the suffixes "-ness," "-like," and
"-able" on the root word, helped the pupil to unlock the meaning of words in his reading. Such research skills as the
use of indexes, charts, maps, library card catalogs, and
tables of contents in social science aided his reading of books
on science, history, and geography in the individualized
reading program. Creative writing, poetry, and dramatization, which were studied in connection with language enriched the reading program. The organization of reports on
science experiments aided him in placing ideas in sequence.
Word games and puzzles used during indoor recess led children to compose rebus stories, riddles, and puns in their
sharing of books. After hearing of Thomas Jefferson's invention of the dumb waiter, one pupil asked this riddle:

> Question--"What is a dumb waiter?"
> Answer--"A retarded servant."

The radio program "Uncle Dan from Froggy Hollow
Farm," while intended as enrichment for the science program, served as a medium for instruction in note taking.
Some pupils learned to take notes in outline form. This a-
bility to pick out the main idea and subordinate ideas greatly aided comprehensions. While instructing pupils in these
subject areas, the investigator clearly pointed out their relationship to the reading program.

Sharing activities--The sharing of books read enabled
pupils to express their enthusiasm for and pleasure in the
books read and to interest others in them. From the sharing the teacher picked up clues about skills which needed improving, interests, and special abilities. Some sharing was
done individually, some by small groups. Typical individual
activities were: (1) making a scrapbook, (2) arranging a collection of the items discussed in the book, (3) performing an
experiment, (4) reading a favorite passage aloud or telling
about a favorite character, (5) preparing a flannel board
story, (6) building a model, (7) making up "Who Am I?"
quizzes, (8) preparing posters advertising books. Typical
group activities were: (1) choral reading of poetry, (2)
painting murals, (3) imagined interviews with authors, (4)
pantomimes of parts of stories, (5) puppet shows based on

an exciting scene, (6) building miniature science equipment,
(7) writing and giving a skit, (8) building a model of a scene
in a story, (9) preparing a bulletin board, (10) writing a different ending for a story.

"Reading aloud" to the children was a sharing technique which the investigator found especially effective.   A
daily fifteen minute period was used to introduce pupils to a
wide variety of books.   Among the books "read aloud" to the
class were: The Jungle Book, Mrs. Piggle Wiggle, Simba
of the White Mane, Peacock Pie, Homer Price, King of the
Wind, Many Moons, Abraham Lincoln, Friend of the People,
and Mr. Popper's Penguins.   Pupils clamored to reread
these books as soon as they were finished.   Requests for
them were posted on the bulletin board, and they were passed
from hand to hand.   Occasionally after "reading aloud" a
whole book, five or six books were briefly presented by telling just enough to tempt the readers.   Sometimes to entice
a reluctant reader a book was presented to the class which
the investigator stated was chosen for _____ because of the
interest in the subject.   Such attention usually guaranteed
that this pupil would read the book.

The sharing of a letter from an author spurred pupils
to read many of his books.   Marion Rennick's letter to a pupil caused "a run on the library" for her books.

Audio-visual aids provided continual motivation and
built new interests.   The investigator made use of film strips,
commercial television programs, films, and records.   Film
strips of the legendary American folk heroes, Paul Bunyan
and Pecos Bill, spurred reading in this area.   A mural,
which included three heroes, along with John Henry and Casey
Jones, resulted from the interest of several boys in this
area.   On commercial TV Peter Pan and Walt Disney's colorful productions of classics sent pupils scurrying in search
of these books.   The movie "Make Way for Ducklings" was
intended for younger children.   It was used to introduce the
class to Robert McCloskey and to such humorous stories as
Lentil, Canterbury Tales, and Homer Price.   A highly realistic phonograph record entitled "A Trip to the Moon" prompted several boys to explore the solar system through literature.   As the program moved along the sharing of several
phonograph records and books by the peer group moved the
focus of motivation from the teacher to the pupils.   Since
this age group is in the gang stage, the interests of other
youngsters are more stimulating than those of the teacher.

The Eastside Branch of the Columbus Public Library
was an important community resource for the program. Because a multiplicity of books is a necessity if an individualized reading program is to provide material to meet the
varied interests of pupils reading on many levels, the investigator decided to encourage every pupil to procure and to use
a library card. Before school began the investigator had obtained permission to bring the class to the library in the
morning when it was closed to the public. A week before the
library appointment a sound film was secured from the Audio-
visual Department of the Columbus Public Schools entitled
"How to Use the Library." After viewing the film and discussing it, the class made plans for their trip. The investigator, then, passed out applications for temporary library
cards. It was explained that if their parents signed these
cards the pupils could take two books home on the day we
visited the library.

During the week prior to our visit the use of the card
catalog was explained. Charts showing the three methods of
indexing books were posted. Pupils discussed the kinds of
books they liked, and authors who wrote interesting stories.

On the appointed day the class walked to the library
where they were greeted by the head librarian. After a
brief discussion of the rules of the library, the method of
checking out books and an actual introduction to the card catalog, pupils were permitted to browse. Four pupils had
cards at the beginning of the school year. Twelve pupils
brought cards properly signed and were permitted to withdraw books.

On our return to school several pupils asked to paint
a mural entitled "Our Trip to the Library." Plans for independent work centered on the trip. While some pupils
planned and began the execution of the mural, four other pupils wrote "thank you" notes to the librarian. Sketches of
the interior of the library showed the card catalog promi-
nently.

In order to reinforce the pupils' interest in and use
of the library a second trip was made three weeks later.
At this time five more pupils were able to withdraw books.
The librarian read "The Duchess Bakes a Cake" to the class.
Pupils were urged to come to the library on their own in-
itiative.

Evaluation--The evaluation of the program was made through the administration of the California Reading Test, through the results of teacher-made tests, and from the observations of the teacher during the individual conference. The attitude of the pupil toward reading, the expansion of his interests, the amount and level of the reading done, all contributed to the evaluation of his growth. Pupil comments on the program also were indicative of its effectiveness in building interest in reading and in building the habit of reading.

Special Acitivities--All elementary schools held Open House the last week in October. The new reading program had been initiated two weeks before. A parent representing nearly every child visited the classroom. After the parents viewed the collection of books, and the bulletin board and other displays, a brief description of the program was given. A few pupils "walked through" the activities of the daily reading period. Many parents expressed the hope that their children would become more interested in reading during their free time.

How Individualized Reading Worked in a Sixth Grade

by

Hazel Sparks Webb

(This material is excerpted from the author's
1963 Ohio State University master's thesis, A Comparative Study of Two Approaches to the Teaching
of Reading at the Sixth Grade Level.)

Explaining to parents--The children's parents were
told about the reading program at the annual "Get-Acquainted
Tea" which is held at Broadleigh School during the second
week in September. The purpose of the tea is to provide an
opportunity for the parents to come into the individual classrooms, meet briefly with the teachers, ask questions about
policies and programs of the school, and to look over the
materials with which their children will be working during
the school year. It was explained to the parents that the
children would do a large amount of reading through a guided
program of self-selection of reading materials and, although
there would be some grouping for working on common problems and specific skills in reading, that reading instruction
would be on an individual basis. Each child would read alone
with the teacher during an individual conference instead of in
a group with other children. The parents seemed pleased
with this decision about the reading program and one parent
remarked, 'I'm glad to know that you think reading that important because it has been my son's trouble in school. He
is a slow reader." Another one said, "My daughter is very
happy because she likes to read and this way she can go as
fast as she wants to." There were no questions about how
the individualized reading program would be conducted or
whether the basic readers would be "completed" during the
year. Some of them had already heard about the new way
of reading because the children had asked permission to
bring in books for classroom use.

94

Those parents who did not attend the "Get-Acquainted Tea" were told about the reading program during informal telephone conversations, or when holding conferences with them about the child's progress in his classwork, or at the open-house period which is held for one-half hour or so before every Parent Teachers Meeting in the school.

Getting started--Before the arrival of the children in September, the teacher had obtained a large supply of books from the Columbus Board of Education Elementary Library, and from a personal library of children's books. An attractive bulletin board was arranged with displays of book jackets and book titles in colorful lettering. National Geographic magazines, sports magazines, copies of The Children's Digest, and other reading materials were arranged on a round table near the center of the classroom with chairs placed around it to provide an invitation to go there to browse. Since the proponents of the individualized approach to reading have suggested that three to five books be made available for each child, the investigator had made these preliminary plans in order to have enough reading material for the children. There were more than the prescribed 150 books for the thirty children who came into the classroom in September.

Carrying the program forward--Inasmuch as the teachers in the Columbus Public Schools are committed to the use of a basal reader series of books, it seemed best to start with each child according to the reader which his last year's teacher had suggested and then move out as soon as possible into individualized reading through self-selection of the books and materials read. The teacher talked with the children about this and explained that reading would be different this year and that they would be permitted to read many books of their own choices. It was further explained that even though each child would start with a basic reader, he would not need to read the stories in sequence but could skip around as he pleased. They were asked, also, to bring along to the conference with the teacher one other book or story that was separate from the readers and that the reading and discussion during the conference could be from either of the books they had brought. This plan was received with elation on the part of the children and many of them read all of the stories sometime during the year.

The children's enthusiasm for this new plan of reading brought forth many helpful suggestions for places to hold conferences, ways to organize and display books for easy ac-

cessibility by all, and ways to share their stories with others
in the room. Each child was given a colorful reading folder
with pockets large enough to accommodate notepaper and other materials which would be needed for reading. Various
ways to keep records of materials read were discussed at
length and the decision was reached that each child would
keep a list of all books and other materials read, the authors, and the illustrators. It was also agreed that the titles
of stories inside books would be listed and their page numbers noted. One child asked, "Do we have to make book reports this year?" He was told that most people would probably want to tell or write about some of the books they read
but that long, detailed reports would not be required. The
teacher asked the children to write a brief comment about
any book or story read if they wanted to do so. This was
not a specific requirement but later in the year a small alphabet file box for 3" x 5" cards was set up and the children
wrote brief reviews of the books they enjoyed most. This
card file was placed near the book exhibits and was helpful
to all since many of the childred liked to see what others
recommended before making their own book selection.

One hour each day was allotted to reading and this
was done in the early afternoon session of school. This
proved to be a good time for reading, especially on snowy,
cold days, when the children returned to school early. They
enjoyed selecting a new book or one already started and
would go ahead and read while the others played games or
worked in the science corner. The usual procedure was for
the teacher or a child to start the session by reading aloud
a story or excerpt from an interesting book and then the
whole group planned together for about five minutes in order
to clarify any difficulties which might have arisen in regard
to the work period or reading. The children went in small
groups to choose books and soon, most children had a book
on the desk already started so that it was easy to move into
the reading period. During the next thirty or forty minutes
the teacher held individual reading conferences with the children. A few minutes were usually saved for working with
a small group of three or four children who needed help
with the skills of reading such as prefixes, suffixes, or pro-
nunciations. Later in the year small groups were utilized
more and more for planning together on bulletin boards,
murals, displays, or creative writing. Sometimes they were
used to talk with children who had read the same books and
had things to say about the characters or authors. Approximately fifteen or twenty minutes were reserved for some

sharing with the large group of books and materials read, or
to tell about a book, character, or an event that was especially interesting.   These sharing periods were a vital part
of the program and the children showed great ingenuity in the
ways they chose to tell about or recommend books to others.
Drawings, paintings, character impersonations, scrambled
titles, and other techniques were used to make this period
an interesting and worthwhile one.   The teacher and children
compiled a list of interesting ways to tell about books they
had read.

Individual conferences--No part of the school day was
more eagerly anticipated than that period when the teacher
and children could talk individually about materials read, why
certain books were selected, and decide together about ways
to improve reading skills and enlarge reading interests.
This brief period of five to ten minutes was an excellent time
for giving guidance and direction to the children in making
wise selections of reading materials and increasing their interest in reading for pure enjoyment.

The teacher's questions about the children's reading
were varied to suit the child and the material read, but some
of these listed were generally used: (1) What kind of story
is this?   (2) Tell me about what happened to the most important people in the story.   (3) How do you feel about what
happened at the end?   (4) What do you think you would have
done if this had happened to you?   (5) Why did you choose
this book?   (6) What is different about the way these story
characters lived and the way we live?   (7) Would you like to
live in that country, and if so, why?   (8) Was this book
hard for you, easy for you, or just about right to enjoy reading it?   (9) Are you reading better than you did a few weeks
ago, if so, how can you tell?   (10) What will you plan to do
as a follow-up to tell or show others an interesting event or
character in this book?

At first, during the oral reading, many of the children had a tendency to start at the beginning of the story
even though they had often already read all of it.   The teacher would then ask for a part that was "exceptionally interesting," "a descriptive paragraph or two," or "read the part
where there was lots of action."   This tendency decreased
as the children grew more adept at finding key parts to books
and stories.

Individual conferences were held with each child at

least once a week and with many of them more often.   At
first, the children wrote their names on a chart to let the
teacher know when they were ready but this was not satisfactory since the children who read the most books were
scheduling conferences so often that slower, more shy children were not receiving enough attention.   The listing was
continued with the understanding that the teacher would write
other names between them when it was believed best to do
so.   This plan worked exceptionally well with the only draw-
back being the fact that the children demanded more conferences than they were able to get.   Many of them were held
at recess or noontime or at odd moments during the day.
This was easy to do because the teacher kept an alphabetical
notebook ready with the dates of the conferences, the books
and stories read, words to work on, comments made by the
children, and pertinent information about each child which
was helpful in understanding their needs.   As the teacher lis-
tened to the child read orally, notes were made of reading
skills which needed to be strengthened.   These were discussed with the child along with those things which he had
done well and on which he deserved to be commended.

        It was found that the children were neglectful in keep-
ing track of difficult words when they were reading alone.
This was discussed with the class and a plan worked out
whereby children and the teacher would list words that they
felt everyone would need to know.   When this list became as
large as fifty or more, they were made into fun games by
the children or the teacher and enjoyed together.   A copy of
these words was duplicated by the teacher and added to the
children's reading folders for further study if needed, while
a new chart was begun for more words.

        Perhaps the most gratifying part of the conference
for the teacher came when the children made comments on
the way they enjoyed the individualized method of reading.

Chapter 4

Individualizing Reading Practices

In this chapter as in the two preceding ones, information is given about the actual procedures used by classroom teachers when the individualized reading approach is employed.

One of the most interesting and outstanding research studies done on the subject of individualized reading is the longitudinal study reported by Frances V. Cyrog. Incidentally, the results of this study are strongly indicative of the effectiveness of this approach. The first selection in this chapter is Mrs. Cyrog's description of classroom procedures.

The selection taken from Beverly M. Dernbach's master's thesis presents the results of a survey of practices employed by 55 teachers in seven Illinois school districts who used the individualized reading approach.

Donna Delph reported in her master's thesis a study in which she interviewed in depth 17 teachers who employed individualized reading in their classrooms. A summary of what these teachers felt to be their principal problems is presented in this chapter's third selection.

The teachers of Baltimore County schools in Maryland engaged in an extensive study of individualized reading. Portions of the report of this study are given in the selection included next in this chapter.

In her thesis, Anna M. Rix queried 78 individualized reading teachers concerning their classroom practices. The results are reported in an excerpt from this thesis.

In the next selection, excerpted from an article by Professor Patrick J. Groff of San Diego State College, a number of teachers were queried concerning the difficulties they encountered in using individualized reading. The out-

come of these interviews seems to indicate that those difficulties most frequently associated with the use of individualized reading in theoretical discussions were not the ones
that primarily concerned these teachers.

It is often said that the ideal reading program would
be one combining the "best" features of both individualized
reading and basal reading. While there are serious short-
comings inherent in the implementation of this suggestion,
attempts have been made to carry it out. Beverly L. Mc-
Kay reports in her thesis on a survey of 250 teachers using
such a combination of approaches. Some of her findings are
presented in this chapter's final selection.

A Longitudinal Study of Individualized Reading

by

Frances Vanderhoof Cyrog

(This material is excerpted from the author's 1964 Claremont Graduate School master's thesis, <u>A Longitudinal Study of an Individualized Program in Reading.</u>)

Procedures used in primary grades. Although the basic premises of individualized reading were in use at all grade levels in the four schools in this study, procedures varied somewhat from grade to grade and class to class.

In general, first grade pupils began in the fall using a fairly typical program which included experience charts followed by pre-primers. During this period of several months the students were taught to read through the conventional basal text approach. They were placed in one of three or four groups according to reading ability and met with the teacher daily for a twenty to twenty-five minute period for group instruction. When a group had completed ten or twelve pre-primers of various basal series, or had attained a reading vocabulary of approximately one hundred and fifty words, the teacher introduced a new book to the group and discussed with them changing over to individualized reading.

In preparation for this discussion and change, the teacher procured from the district library a wide selection of pre-primers, primers, and simple trade books (an average of three to four per student) and displayed these attractively around the classroom--in a book corner, on open display racks, or on counter tops about the room.

Calling attention to the many new books in the room, the teacher explained to the students that they were about to begin a new way of reading. Each student at the reading table would from this time on read his book to himself, proceeding as fast or as slowly as was comfortable for him. The teacher would be there to assist with words or give other help, but she would also meet with one student at a time for a conference each day. Each student in the group would have this daily conference with the teacher and during the conference the teacher and student would discuss his book, the student would read a portion of it to the teacher, and the teacher would keep a record of the student's needs and progress. Other members of the group would remain around the reading table during these conferences, continuing to read their own books to themselves. As the teacher completed a conference with a student at her right, he [the student] would change places with another student at the table; and the teacher would confer with the student on her left. In the course of the twenty-five minute reading period it was possible for most teachers to confer with eight to ten students--the usual number in a group.

At the same time as she conducted her conferences, it was possible for the teacher to be aware of the reading habits of the other students reading at the table, their concentration, difficulty with words or meanings and their interest or disinterest in the books they had chosen. She could, if necessary, encourage a student as he finished reading, to choose another book from those displayed in the room and return to the table. The period of time which the teacher spent with the group previous to beginning individualized reading did not change--only the focus and pattern of the reading instruction.

As soon as most of the children were making independent reading choices the teacher re-established groups on a heterogeneous, non-ability, friendship basis.

At other times during the day, the teachers on occasion drew small groups together for brief periods to work on mutual problems in skills or comprehension. These groups were flexible and disbanded when their purposes were accomplished.

Independent activities for those students who were not reading with the teacher included simple reading and phonic games, puzzles, many art materials, and if they wished, books to continue reading.

In second and third grades, the procedures begun dur-

ing the individualized reading part of first grade were maintained.   A wide assortment of books, both trade and textbooks, of reading levels several grades above to several
grades below the reading range of the student group, were
chosen for each classroom by the teacher.   Books were not
exclusively in the fiction category; science, health, history,
biography, mathematics and other fields were represented on
the shelves of primary grade students.   Teachers were able
to procure these books from several sources--the district library, the city library, and school collections of old and new
state texts from many curriculum areas.

Third grade students continued to read in eight to ten
member reading groups around a reading table with the
teacher.   They read the books of their choices silently during the twenty-five minute period except for the conference
time with the teacher.   The teacher maintained a daily conference with each student on a much more flexible pattern.
Conferences at this stage were of increasing depth and a student might have a brief period with the teacher one day and
a much longer one the next.

Group discussions of books also arose within the
classroom and within the groups, about favorite books, characters, plots, or other topics.   Students read to each other,
completed independent activities which centered upon a specific skill or comprehension problem, prepared book reports
in a variety of creative ways, wrote stories and poetry,
played phonic and other skill games, and took part in many
other reading related activities during independent periods.

Procedures used in upper grades.   Although the self-
selection of materials from a broad assortment of pre-se-
lected books and the conferences with the teacher remained
the basic reading pattern for students in all classrooms at
all levels in which individualized reading was used, in the
upper grades the time students spent in reading independently became longer.   Early in the fourth grade the length of
the reading period might be approximately forty minutes for
the majority of the students, but by the middle of the year
and from then on it expanded to a fifty-five to sixty minute
period.   Teachers conferred less frequently with each student, but conferences were longer and emphases were on
greater depth of understandings, underlying meanings, inferences, seeing increasingly complex relationships.

The structure and routines which teachers used were

flexible. A teacher might set up a quiet corner in the room
for conferences or move from student to student, placing her
chair next to the pupil for this friendly but carefully planned
discussion of his book. She usually met with ten or twelve
students a day for detailed conferences, spent briefer times
with others who might need momentary help, and led a book
discussion or book chat with another group for a ten to fifteen minute period during the reading hour.

    A wide assortment of books, which were changed regu-
larly, was provided by the teacher. This assortment was
composed in part of books which reflected students' interests
and in part of books which challenged and channelled new interests and reading pursuits. As in primary grades, the
reading range of the class was considered and books from
several grades below to several above were represented in
the collection.

    The conference period with each student was consid-
ered a most vital part of the program. During this meeting
between teacher and student the teacher helped to develop
understandings, depth of comprehension, word attack and
meaning skills. The student usually related important aspects of his book to the teacher, discussed the book, and
read a portion of it to the teacher. Both student and teacher
kept records of the student's needs and decided together what
to do to meet them.

A Survey of Individualized Reading Practices

by

Beverly M. Dernbach

(This material is excerpted from the author's 1965 DePaul University master's thesis, Approaches Toward the Individualized Reading Program in Selected School Districts in Cook and Du Page Counties, Illinois.)

Grade Levels Included

First	Second	Third	Fourth	Fifth	Sixth
10	9	13	5	9	9
19		18		18	

Sources of the Individualized Reading Programs

How was the Individualized Reading Program brought to your attention?

Superintendent	9	An educational conference	12
Principal	16	Parents	1
Other Teachers	24	Your own idea	9
Educational magazines	15	The children	4
		Didn't answer	3

Why was the Individualized Reading Program tried?

Lack of interest in the basal reader	9
Difference in reading abilities in the classroom	31
Need for more personalized approach to reading	27
Lack of motivation when using the group-ability plan	8
Variety of interests among the children	17
Variety of backgrounds of the children	9
Desire to try a new approach in reading	30
Suggestion of a supervisor	6

Whom did you notify when you began the Individualized Reading Program?

The district superintendent	3	The school librarian	2
Your supervisor	4	The public librarian	0
Your principal	40	Other teachers in your	
The parents	9	school	9
None of these	8	The children	17
		Didn't answer	2

How was the program initiated in your room?

Started with the top group	16
Started with the middle group	3
Started with the bottom group	1
Started with the whole class	38
Didn't answer	1

The Administration of Individualized Reading Programs

How long is your reading period (per day)?

1-20 minutes	2	121-140 minutes	0
21-40 minutes	8	141-160 minutes	1
41-60 minutes (1 hr.)	23	161-180 minutes (3 hrs.)	1
61-80 minutes	1	Varies with child	2
81-100 minutes	7	Didn't answer	1
101-120 minutes (2 hrs.)	9		

What activities are usually included in a daily reading period?

Selecting books	37	Group meetings	27
Individual conferences	48	Sharing time	25
Individual activities	37	Activity for class as a	
Silent reading	53	whole	27

What levels of ability are present in your class?

Average ability	52	Above average ability	50
Below average ability	42		

Have you ever excluded any child from this program?

Yes   12   No   43

What was the reason for excluding the child?

Immaturity	5	Inability to work inde-	
Lack of native ability	2	pendently	8
Rebellion to plan	0	Troublesome nature of	
Failure to cooperate	1	child	0
		Lack of interest in plan	0
		Hadn't planned to use with	
		entire class	2

Records Kept in Individualized Reading Programs

Do you keep an individual record on each child?

yes   46 no   9

a) Is this a running record noting problems and achieve-
   ments over the course of the year?
yes   38 no   8

b) Do you make a notation during or following the individual conference with a child?
yes   33   no   1   sometimes   12

c) how often is something written about each child?

Daily	3	Twice a month	1
Twice a week	4	Once a month	5
		Following the conferences	23

d) Do you make notations as a result of group work,
   sharing activities or work done in other areas over
   the course of the day?

yes   17 no   29

Does each child keep some type of record of his reading?

yes   38   no   17

a) What type of record is used?

A standard form adopted by the class   26
Individual child selects his own form   2
A variety of recording methods used by each child   10

b) Do you make a periodical check on the child's individual record to see that it is in order?
yes   33   no   5

c) Do the children keep a list of new words that they
   have encountered?
yes   19   no   19

Are there any visible charts, graphs or tallies in the room
which show the number of books read by each child?
yes   11   no   44

Are there any charts or graphs showing the variety of material read by the individuals?
yes   7   no   48

Are there any charts or graphs showing the reading level
of the books read by each child?
yes   3   no   52

Materials Used in the Individualized Reading Programs

Do you use a basal reader?

Not at all   4
Finish it before starting Individualized Reading   12
As a supplementary book   12
Children may select these books if they want to read
   them   17
Alternate it with Individualized Reading on different
   days   8

Alternate it with Individualized Reading on the same
    day   8

Finish part   5

Didn't answer   1

How are the reading materials selected?

Textbooks	33	School Library	47
Supplementary books	37	Public Library	27
Trade books	33	Book sales	8
Newspapers	9	Auctions	0
Magazines	17	Children bring books from	
Reference books	21	home	36

Self-Selection of Reading Material in the Individualized Reading Programs

What is the reading level of the children in the room?

Two years	2	Six years	11
Three years	10	Seven years	4
Four years	9	Eight years	3
Five years	14	Nine years	1
		Ten years	1

How are the books arranged for selection?

No arrangement	21	Size of book	1
Subject matter	11	Fiction - nonfiction	9
Level of difficulty	11	Author's name	6
		School Library	2

How does a child select his book?

The teacher aids in finding something suitable	44
The child finds it entirely on his own	45
Other children help by means of book reports, skits, etc.	39

What usually motivates a child to choose a particular book?

The teacher	24	Size of book	8
The child	29	Difficulty of book	27
Other children	43	Type of book	36
Other books by this author	36	Pictures in the book	18

Must the children finish a book once they have selected it?

Yes	1	Usually	16
No	24	Except in certain cases where the decision was unwise	21

What if a child keeps selecting the same type of book?

Insist on a change	0	Leave him alone	12
Encourage a change	41	This has never happened	2

How do you stop a child from constantly reading books beneath his reading level?

Insist on a change	2	Leave him alone	8
Encourage a change	43	This has never happened	2

Workbooks in the Individualized Reading Programs

How do you normally develop reading skills?

The entire class	23
Certain permanently established groups	14
Temporary groups who need the same skill	37
The individual when he needs a skill	38

How is seatwork distributed?

To some children	29
To the whole class	22
The individual creates his own	13
None	11

Do you use reading workbooks?

For the whole room	22	For the faster children	3
For certain groups	11	For the average children	3
For particular individuals	14	For those needing vocabu-	
For the slower children	8	lary help	4
		For those needing help with a certain skill	20
		Do not use	10

How do you use the workbooks?

Follow the order in the book	18
Use certain pages when the need arises	24
Do not use	10
Varies	3

Development of Reading Skills in the Individualized Reading Programs

		1st & 2d Grades	3rd & 4th Grades	5th & 6th Grades
Do you follow a sequential development as in the Basal Readers?	Yes	11	10	3
	No	4	4	10
	with some children	4	4	5
	D. A.	0	0	0
Do you check on certain skills with each child during the course of the year?	Yes	17	15	16
	No	2	3	1
	D. A.	0	0	1
Do you teach only those skills that you notice the child is lacking?	Yes	2	8	6
	No	17	10	12
	D. A.	0	0	0
Total no. of teachers		19	18	18

Oral Reading in the Individualized
Reading Programs

How do you take care of remedial reading?

In the individual confer-ence	23	Don't even consider this concept since the child is working at his own pace	11
In small groups	24		
Remedial reading teacher	9	Didn't answer	3

Is there oral reading in your room?

Yes	53	No	2

Who is the audience?

One or two other children	17	You in the individual conference	45
A group of children	30	The whole class	39

Who helps with unknown words?

The teacher	51	Dictionaries	29
Another child	42	Content and context clues	46
Make a word list	20	Skip over	3

The Number of Individual Conferences
Averaged in a Day

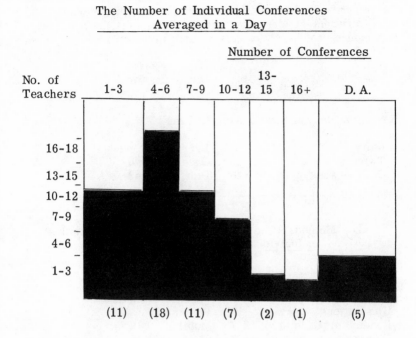

Number of Conferences

No. of Teachers	1-3	4-6	7-9	10-12	13-15	16+	D. A.
	(11)	(18)	(11)	(7)	(2)	(1)	(5)

Grouping in the
Individualized Reading Programs

Do you have grouping of any kind?

Yes	42	No	11
		Didn't answer	2

a) Is the grouping temporary?

Yes	38	No	4

b) What is the specific purpose for the group?

A particular skill	24	Enjoyment of a particular	
Remedy of a difficulty	26	story	19
Similar reading material	18	Work on a group project	20

Do you have a sharing time during your reading period
when different children are allowed to present their reading
experiences to the class in a variety of ways?

Yes	50	No	4
		Didn't answer	1

How often do you have a sharing time?

Daily	5	Every other week	8
Twice a week	8	Once a month	5
Once a week	20	Didn't answer	9

The Methods Used Most Often to Report on Reading in Individualized Reading Programs

Oral reports	27	Guess my book	1
Written reports	18	Murals	1
Skits or plays	15	Character sketches	1
Illustrations	10	Poems	1
Reading portions to class	7	Mobiles	1
Dioramas	7	Clay	1
Puppets	6	Charts	1
Home-made movies	5	Show and tell	1
Sales talks	4	Tape record selections	1
Individual conferences	4	Bulletin boards	1
Book jackets	4	Letters of appreciation	
Oral discussion of se-		to the author	1
lected stories	3	Check on vocabulary	1
		Didn't answer	12

Reactions of Parents, Other Teachers and Principals to the Individualized Reading Programs

What is the reaction of the parents?

Much in favor	27	Not particularly in favor	0
Moderately in favor	6	Definitely against	0
Slightly in favor	0	Not particularly interested	6
Don't know 8 Mixed	2	Didn't answer	6

What is the reaction of the other teachers in your school?

Much in favor	20	Not particularly in favor	1
Moderately in favor	13	Definitely against	0
Slightly in favor	1	Not particularly interested	6
Don't know 4 Mixed	6	Didn't answer	4

What is the reaction of your principal?

Much in favor	35	Not particularly in favor	1
Moderately in favor	7	Definitely against	0
Slightly in favor	2	Not particularly interested	1
Don't know	5	Didn't answer	4

Effects on the Progress of Students in Individualized Reading Programs

How does Individualized Reading affect the child?

	yes	no
Progresses at own rate	51	1
Slow reader not stigmatized	44	4
Shows much enthusiasm	46	3
Sustained interest in reading	48	2
Competes with himself	38	6
Reads more books	48	1
Reads a variety of books	49	1
Increase in reading ability	49	1

Grade Level and Effectiveness of the Individualized Reading Programs

What teachers should use this method?

All teachers	1	Only experienced teachers	13
Those interested in trying it	44	Didn't answer	4

Do you think this method can be used effectively in any elementary grade?

Yes	39	No	13
		Didn't answer	3

Is there any grade where you think this system would be particularly effective?

All grades	14	Fourth grade and up	3
Upper grades	2	Past first grade	2
Intermediate grades	10	First grade	2
Primary grades	5	Didn't answer	17

In what size class would you consider this plan to be most effective?

Below twenty	10	Size shouldn't matter	6
From 20 to 25	18	Didn't answer	5
Under thirty	16		

Student Participation in the Individualized Reading Programs

How does the discipline compare with discipline under the Basal Reading Plan?

Easer than with Basal Reading	21
About the same	26
Harder to maintain	4
Didn't answer	4

What is your opinion of the record keeping?

Tedious	4	Time consuming	18
Essential	32	Rewarding	10
Non-essential	10	Didn't answer	4

Does this system call for more preparation on your part?

Yes	29	No	23
		Didn't answer	3

Do you find it more rewarding to teach?

Yes	44	No	5
		Didn't answer	6

Does this system seem to increase the children's reading outside of school?

Yes	47	No	5
		Didn't answer	3

Do you believe that the children develop into better readers through the use of this plan?

Yes	38	No	7
About the same	4	Didn't answer	6

Progress Ratings in the
Individualized Reading Programs

"In relation to these reading skills how would you say your children have progressed? (Consider the children's abilities.)"

	Excellent	Good	Fair	Unsatisfactory	Didn't answer
The children are able to see and hear words clearly and recognize their meanings.	12	31	2	0	10
The children are able to understand sentences, paragraphs, pages and stories	13	27	6	0	9
The children are creative readers.	15	20	7	0	13
The children are able to find the information they need and seek.	15	21	9	0	10
The children are able to read aloud effectively.	9	28	8	0	10

Teachers' Problems in Using Individualized Reading

by

Donna Delph

(This material is excerpted from the author's 1963 Ball State Teacher's College master's thesis, An Investigation of Problems in Individualized Reading Felt by Selected Elementary Teachers in the Public Schools of Hammond, Indiana.)

A Description of the Selected Group

The seventeen elementary teachers who agreed to cooperate with the investigator were teaching in eight different public school buildings in Hammond, Indiana, during the interview period. Seven of these teachers were teaching primary grade classes; the remaining ten teachers were working with fourth, fifth, or sixth grade students. Three men and fourteen women were interviewed. All teachers included in this group held bachelor degrees and ten of the teachers interviewed had earned the master's degree. Twelve teachers in the selected group had more than five years' teaching experience as elementary classroom teachers; five teachers had fewer than five years' teaching experience in the elementary grades.

Reasons Teachers Chose to Initiate Program

The elementary teachers who in 1957 initiated programs of individualized reading did so as members of an "action research" committee. Although most of them had expressed previous interest in this approach, five of the six teachers interviewed in this group felt the request by their supervisor had been the impetus which caused them to take part in this experimental program. All of the teachers said they had felt free to refuse the request to work with individualized reading.

The teachers who implemented this approach to reading in their classrooms the following two years said they were influenced by discussions with teachers involved in the program and by attendance at a series of meetings about individualized reading sponsored by the local organization of the Association for Childhood Education International. The teachers in this group expressed general dissatisfaction with areas of the basal reading program and attended the meetings because they were interested in an approach to reading instruction which might better meet the individual needs of students.

The five teachers interviewed who began working with individualized reading during the 1960-1961 or 1961-1962 school years stated various reasons for entering the program. Two of these teachers were prompted by requests from students in their classes who had enjoyed working with the program previously, two others felt experience with individualized reading as student teachers had aroused their interest, and another teacher became interested in an individualized approach to reading instruction through attendance at the above mentioned meetings.

II.   How Teachers Prepared to Initiate Program

The literature contains numerous suggestions for teachers who wish to implement programs of individualized reading in their classrooms.   ... Educators feel that in addition to a strong commitment to the idea of individualized instruction, teachers must also possess necessary insights regarding the reading process.   Teachers should be sure they feel secure in beginning the program, have a real desire to work with it, and understand that there is no single method each teacher must follow.   A variety of suggestions to aid teachers in book selection, classroom procedure, record keeping, and evaluation can also be found in the literature. The necessity of keeping each classroom approach flexible and individualistic is often mentioned with these suggestions. The interviewed teachers employed several of the above mentioned techniques as they prepared to initiate individualized reading programs.

The six teachers in the "action research" group met with the supervisors for a discussion of the program.   At this first meeting many of them were skeptical about the feasibility of an individualized approach.   Most of the teachers read the articles and books about this subject that were available in 1957. None had an opportunity to discuss this program with anyone who had worked with it, or to visit classrooms where this type of program was in progress.

Four of these teachers decided to initiate the program gradually. They thought beginning with one ability group, a few children, or working with an individualized approach certain days of the week might help them feel more secure. Their apprehensions were described by one teacher who said, "What if the program fails? What about the children?"

However, two teachers in the "action research" group felt the best way to experiment with the program was by a complete commitment to its philosophy. After a discussion with their students and detailed planning, they decided this instruction would be the reading program for the entire class.

The eleven teachers who prepared to initiate individualized reading programs after 1957 had members of the "action research" group available as resource persons. The in-service meetings were mentioned by many of the teachers as being extremely helpful to them.

Every teacher who initiated this program from 1958 to 1960 read articles about an individualized approach and felt ideas contained in these articles were helpful as they prepared to enter the program. There were many articles appearing in the educational periodicals at this particular time. Several books containing background materials and other suggestions were available. Teachers in this group mentioned help received from reading one or more of these books.

Everyone in the 1958-1960 group discussed the programs with at least one teacher who was working with individualized reading. Four members of this group visited at least one classroom before they initiated the program. Although they found these observations interesting, they felt even more impressed with the flexibility of this new approach. Most of these teachers remarked how it was impossible to get anything more than a "feeling" of individualized reading from these visits.

As was mentioned earlier, two teachers in the 1960-1962 group became familiar with individualized reading as student teachers. They both felt the experience they gained working with the program as student teachers was extremely helpful to them as they prepared to implement it in their own classrooms. One of them remarked, "I would have been a-fraid to try had I not worked with individualized reading as a student teacher."

One teacher in the 1960-1962 group attended the meet-ings held by the Association for Childhood Education. All five teachers interviewed in this group mentioned discussing the program with the teachers experienced in this approach, four said they reviewed the literature on individualized read-ing, and three visited classrooms as they prepared to initi-ate this new approach to reading instruction.

Of the seventeen teachers interviewed, fifteen men-tioned reviewing the literature on individualized reading. Most of them felt it had been of great value to them. Some said they gained a better understanding of the philosophy of the program as a result of reading an article or book about this subject. Others found suggestions in the literature for book selection, classroom organization, record keeping, and evaluation were helpful to them as they planned their indi-vidualized programs.

Teachers who had an opportunity to attend meetings and group discussions on an in-service basis said they learned much about the new approach from them. The teachers a-greed that these experiences gave them an opportunity to ask questions and discuss areas of the program they did not fully understand.

Classroom observation was a possibility to members of the 1958-1960 and the 1960-1962 groups. Approximately one-half of these teachers visited one or more classrooms prior to implementation. Many felt they gained a general picture of classroom organization, but realized they could not duplicate what they saw. The teachers who did not have an opportunity to visit other classrooms said they thought it might have been of value to them. But as one teacher ex-plained it, "I think observing might be helpful, but I feel I grew faster because I was on my own."

Although all of the above mentioned experiences were thought helpful to some degree, there was general agreement among the interviewed teachers that anyone interested in in-itiating an individualized reading program should read as much as possible about it and think through his individual situation carefully before implementing this new program in his classroom.

III. Problems Felt by Teachers When They Initiated Programs of Individualized Reading

The data compiled from the interviews revealed that the seventeen teachers faced numerous problems when they implemented individualized reading programs in their classrooms. Each of these problems was placed in one of seven categories.

The remainder of this chapter is devoted to an interpretation of specific problems mentioned by the teachers during the interviews. These results are analyzed in the seven established categories.

Problems Related to the Changing Role of the Teacher

Ten teachers commented on a problem that related in some way to the special or different demands the new reading program made on them. Many of the ten felt keenly the change in responsibilities in moving from a basal reading series into a broadened reading program.

This new approach was recognized as "individualized" for the teacher as well as the child. Flexibility of the entire curriculum was viewed by most of these teachers as a must for success with this new program. One teacher remarked, "In this program, teachers must be willing to expect and accept change."

Another felt the basal reading program was one period in the day that did not "fit" because it was, "... too formal and restraining." He believed real teacher-pupil planning could take place in an individualized approach and recognized this new program as a problem-solving approach to reading instruction.

A majority of the teachers found individualized reading a more time consuming method. They discovered it took a great deal more planning, especially during the implementation period. Some found that it became less difficult with experience, but one teacher remarked, "It does not get 'easier' because each group is different and as a result, the program is always changing."

Several teachers, especially those in the "action research" group, faced problems created in "fitting" the new program into a basal reading framework. Most felt this happened because they felt secure with the routines of the established reading program. When convinced that individualized reading would work and when more accustomed to the role of helper and advisor, felt problems created by attempting to be a leader and a director gradually disappeared.

A comparison of problems felt by teachers who initiated the program in 1957 with those initiating it since that time. The teachers who were the first to work with individualized reading in Hammond expressed much more concern over their changing role than did the teachers who entered the program later. This lack of anxiety on the part of the latter group was probably due to the opportunity these teachers had to discuss the program with those who had experience with it. Many of the teachers who entered the program after 1957 were convinced it could be done. They had shared the experiences and problems of the teachers in the "action research" group and believed their problems could also be solved.

A comparison of problems felt by primary grade teachers with problems felt by intermediate grade teachers. How responsible are young children in making their own reading choices? How much freedom can they handle? These are questions that many primary teachers asked themselves as they initiated individualized reading programs.

A first grade teacher felt hesitant about giving the beginning readers freedom of selection. This problem bothered her a great deal, but as she observed how wisely these children chose their materials, she felt she should allow her students more freedom of choice.

One third grade teacher said, "The children loved it, but I didn't know if I would live through the first month. I felt so swamped with decisions!"

This teacher gradually shifted more responsibility for reading progress onto the children and felt much more at ease with the program.

Several primary teachers were troubled as they initi-

ated the program by the seeking, self-selection, and pacing
philosophy of the individualized reading program.   They
wondered if very young children could make satisfactory
reading progress without a planned developmental program.

Developing flexibility within the school day seemed to
be the main concern of the intermediate grade teachers.
Most of them, who considered this a problem, felt individualized reading was more demanding and time consuming.
These teachers found that when the reading program became
the "hub" around which many of the other subject areas re-
volved, the whole school day began to run more smoothly.

A comparison of problems felt by teachers with fewer
than five years' teaching experience with problems felt by
those with five or more years' experience.   Teachers with
less than five years' teaching experience mentioned propor-
tionately fewer problems concerned with their changing role.
This was perhaps due to the fact that these teachers had not
become so established in the routines of a basal reading program.

One teacher, who introduced individualized reading during her second year of teaching, told how satisfied she was
with the program, but remarked, "I don't consider myself a
real 'progressive' teacher.   This just seems to me to be the
most sensible way to teach reading."

The teacher, who said she would have been afraid to
try individualized reading had she not worked with it as a
student teacher, offered this opinion, "I think when you are
an experienced teacher, you tend to try more new things,
don't you?"

Problems Related to Selecting and Obtaining Materials

The availability of appropriate materials is often one
of the concerns expressed by teachers contemplating an individualized reading program.   However, the interviewed
teachers did not find this a serious problem.

Many of the teachers did praise the excellent cooperation they received from the children's department of the Hammond Public Library that supplied each of their classrooms
with a large rotating book collection.

The school system also provides each elementary classroom a sum of money annually for the purchase of trade books. Every intermediate grade has classroom reference materials.

The six teachers who mentioned problems that were included in this category most often referred to problems associated with quality rather than quantity of books. Others felt that organization of available materials, although not a continuing problem, was a difficult project during the period of implementation.

Four teachers mentioned problems of organization in connection with their skill-building programs. Although they had a wealth of materials, they faced the time-consuming task of locating and organizing them into usable form. Many, who depended upon workbooks for the development of certain reading skills, found it difficult to locate this material in a form that could be used independently of the basic textbook. Others searched for materials which were more or less self-explanatory so the children could work individually or in small groups with a minimum of instruction.

One teacher felt she needed a wider variety of subject areas and grade levels in her book collection when she initiated individualized reading.

Another teacher, who was working in a new classroom with a very small book collection, was provided with a sum of money to increase the size of her library.

Many of the interviewed teachers felt that over a period of years, the money saved on reading textbooks and workbooks could be used to build an adequate book collection for any classroom.

Familiarity with the ever-growing numbers of children's books was thought the real problem of material selection by many teachers. They mentioned sources they had found helpful; among the most helpful was the annual book fair held in the city. Reading reviews of children's literature in current magazines, newspapers, and publisher's brochures was another way these teachers learned of recently published trade books for boys and girls.

Teachers working with beginning readers were pleased with the growing numbers of beginning-to-read books. They related how much the children enjoyed the content of these books and how "perfect" they were for an individualized approach.

Many teachers felt they possessed inadequate knowledge of children's books as they initiated individualized reading. Most of them said they became much more "aware" of the literature as a result of working with the program.

A comparison of problems felt by teachers who initiated the program in 1957 with those initiating it since that time. The first teachers who worked with individualized reading made the initial requests for book collections from the children's department of the library. Those who initiated programs after that time seemed to profit from this experience.

Many teachers who initiated individualized reading after 1957 mentioned help received from the members of the "action research" group who had located and organized various skill building materials.

A comparison of problems felt by primary grade teachers with problems felt by intermediate grade teachers. Both primary and intermediate grade teachers found the selection and organization of materials the most difficult problem in this category. The primary teachers had more difficulty finding and using skill-building materials. They made more use of basal reading materials than did the intermediate grade teachers. Many intermediate grade teachers felt their classroom libraries lacked the wide range of reading materials necessary when they initiated the program. They were able, with the help of the library, to correct this problem quickly.

Intermediate grade teachers seemed more concerned with knowing the content of books and stories their pupils read than did the primary grade teachers.

Problems Related to Familiarity With Children's Interests, Attitudes, and Capabilities

"Knowing" their students when they began an individualized approach to reading instruction was a concern of a majority of the interviewed teachers. A few named it a major problem. All felt it was an important consideration in "getting the program off to a good start."

A member of the "action research" group, referring to her first experience with individualized reading, remembered thinking:

> Was I so learned as to know when I met with these children, what their problems were and did I know the reading program so well that I could provide for them all the things they should have, step-by-step, from first grade through eighth? I definitely felt inadequate.

The teachers in the experimental group began their programs by administering reading achievement tests of various kinds to their pupils. Other teachers who have initiated this program since that time have also felt reading test scores would be helpful in determining the abilities of their students. Some found the remarks and recommendations of other teachers helpful as they attempted to learn each of their student's interests and abilities. Intelligence test scores were available for most pupils. Many teachers found these scores useful as they formed a "picture" of each child's reading abilities and capacities.

Although most teachers felt test scores and teacher recommendations aided them in recognizing children's capabilities, they found individual conferences held with students the best single method of determining needs and interests.

Intermediate grade teachers found that many children who experienced difficulty with reading as primary grade students had developed antagonistic attitudes toward the whole reading process. One teacher said her biggest problem was with "... the children who would not read, the ones who just hate books!"

Although this attitude toward reading created many problems during the initial period, the remarkable effect individualized reading had upon the negative attitudes of many of these students was regarded by a number of teachers as the strongest aspect of this program. "In all my years of teaching," remarked one teacher, "I have never seen children so enthused about reading."

The teacher who felt inadequate about her ability to cope with the individual needs of her children said,

In spite of all my misgivings, I felt satisfied at
the end of that first year.   From completely subjective opinion, I felt sure the children who had
not been interested in reading were reading and
pursuing reading.

Problems Related to Classroom Organization
and Procedure

Individualized reading is a new approach to reading
instruction and requires many changes in the established
teacher-directed, three-ability-group plan of most basal reading programs.   The fact that twelve of the seventeen interviewed teachers mentioned problems relating to classroom organization and procedure indicates that many problems met
in the initial stages of this program are probably due to the
many changes and adjustments necessary in the daily reading
period.

The literature contains many articles which warn that
class size should be considered in any program which involves individualized instruction.   A few of the interviewed
teachers agreed that the size of the class makes "a big difference;" most of them did not.

The average size of the classes of the interviewed
teachers, when they initiated individualized reading programs,
was thirty-one.   The largest class had thirty-seven pupils,
the smallest twenty-five.   A majority of these teachers felt
that the actual size of the class made little difference. Many
agreed that most instructional programs are more successful when the teacher has more time to spend with individual
students.

Several teachers mentioned problems they experienced
because they lacked time.   One replied, "I could not be at
as many places as I wanted to be.   It seemed in the beginning that so many needed help."

"I felt I needed to work with every child right in the
beginning, which of course, I could not do," related another.
"The first few weeks are the most difficult.   The initial interview is the most important thing in getting the children
started."

A primary teacher stated her concern this way, "Sec-

ond graders like to read aloud.   I couldn't hear them all
read every day."

"My biggest problem in the beginning was not getting
to them often enough, at least I didn't feel I was.   I feel I
had solved this by the end of the year as I eliminated many
things I found unnecessary," remarked an intermediate grade
teacher.

Another teacher had a problem getting children to
continue independently when she was conducting individual
conferences.   She felt this problem occurred because she
was not meeting each child often enough in the beginning.

Several other teachers felt problems during the initial
stages of the program similar to these.   Many of these
teachers found that they had much more time to meet with
individuals and groups when they became better acquainted
with the needs of the children and more proficient at conducting individual conferences.

One second grade teacher actually found she had more
time to work with children than she had had when she worked
with a three ability group plan.

The elementary classrooms in the Hammond Public
Schools are heterogeneously grouped.   Fourteen of the interviewed teachers felt the groups of children with whom they
first initiated individualized reading programs were of "average" ability with the expected number of fast and slow learners.   Two said most of their students were definitely above
average readers and one felt that a majority of her pupils
were below average in ability.

Although some teachers began the program with the
idea that it would be better for the exceptional learners,
most agreed that individualized reading seemed to work well
with all types of groups and with children of varying abilities.

Classroom organization was varied.   Although there
was almost a complete rejection of ability grouping, many
teachers told how they worked with small groups of children
in "needs" and "interest" groups.   Some started their entire
class at one time.   Others introduced the new approach
gradually.   One third grade teacher said, "I do not feel I
could ever start my whole class at once."

But a first grade teacher worked with her children in
"interest" groups to build sight vocabularies and then moved
the children into individualized reading.

There were other problems mentioned which related
to classroom organization and procedure. An intermediate
grade teacher felt the biggest problem she faced was the continual changing and revising of the program.

Another said, "My biggest problem was getting the
children to select and stay with books. Perhaps it was the
sudden freedom of choice, because later they showed a great
deal of improvement."

Most of these problems were typical of the difficulties
encountered by teachers experimenting with any new instructional method. Nearly all of the teachers and students had
worked with a basal reading program. It was obvious that
many problems they faced were ones of adjustment to a new
approach. As was mentioned earlier in this chapter, many
teachers found they could not "fit" individualized reading into
the old or traditional reading framework. They told of problems, which at first seemed insurmountable, that seemed to
solve themselves when the teachers and students planned,
changed, and revised their reading program.

A comparison of problems felt by primary grade
teachers with problems felt by intermediate grade teachers.
A large number of both primary and intermediate grade
teachers experienced problems that were related to classroom organization and procedure. The primary teachers,
especially those working with beginning readers, felt it essential that they work with each child daily. This created
a problem for some, but they were all able eventually to organize their time so they felt more satisfied with the amount
of help each child received. For some teachers this meant
working with every child daily. Other primary teachers felt
it unnecessary to work with each student individually every
day although most found some type of daily group work was
desirable.

The intermediate grade teachers found it possible to
work with reading for longer periods of time than could the
primary grade teachers. Many were pleased with the growing independence and feeling of responsibility for their own
progress that individualized reading fostered in their pupils.
They found that the children became interested in planning

what they hoped to accomplish in reading each day.   A lack of independence and interest among their pupils had troubled some of these teachers when they first introduced this program.

Problems Related to Organizing Systems of Record Keeping and Evaluation

Devising systems of record keeping created problems for many of the teachers as they implemented programs of individualized reading.   Some were also troubled when they found it necessary to change and revise methods of evaluation.

Record Keeping.   As the teachers planned for the introduction of this new approach, most of them created experimental record keeping systems.   Many attempted, as had been suggested in the literature, to formulate a dual record keeping system.   They planned to keep records of each child's reading interests, needs, and growth that would then be supplemented by the child's own records of his reading progress.

During the initial stages of the program many found it necessary to revise and modify their plans.   An intermediate grade teacher had this to say, "Record keeping was somewhat of a problem at first, until I discovered what things were important to keep.   At first, I was attempting too much, too many details.   Later, as you come to know the children better, many of these can be eliminated."

One teacher felt, and this problem was implied by others, that she had been so concerned in the beginning with keeping records of reading skills that she neglected recording the growth of each child's reading interests, methods of book selection, and attitude toward reading.   As she began to feel more sure of herself in her new role, she found more time to record these other aspects of each child's progress that she had come to consider equally or more important.

Other teachers experienced difficulties working out record keeping methods that were acceptable to the children and helpful to them as they worked with individual pupils. They found some children became so involved in keeping records they had little time to read and other students be-

came disturbed if record keeping did not allow them enough
time to read. As a result, the record keeping methods that
evolved were very different from classroom to classroom,
and often varied from child to child within a group.

Another problem was created by children who thought
they should read as many books as possible and as a result
did not read with understanding. "My biggest problem with
third graders," remarked one teacher, "was to encourage
them not just to see how many books they could read. It
was a 'headache' for the first six weeks. After that they
began to get the idea that quantity is not the important thing."

Evaluation. "There are times," said a teacher,
"when I would like to know how well the children are doing."

"How can I be sure they are increasing their vocabularies?" asked another.

These and other problems related to evaluation
troubled the teachers as they introduced individualized reading.

Most teachers felt satisfied with what they knew about
the reading ability of their students because they had administered reading achievement tests when they introduced
the program, but some worried about their ability to measure
the day-to-day growth that was taking place.

This problem, like so many others, seemed less important as the program progressed. Some teachers, especially the more experienced ones, said they knew the children were "growing." Many used reading tests and other a-
vailable materials for measuring reading capabilities, to
check on this belief, and found it confirmed.

Several teachers mentioned a change in their attitude
toward children's growth in reading. They felt that previously, they had been interested only in achievement in areas
such as reading comprehension and vocabulary development.
This new approach made them more aware of "intangibles,"
such as growth in interests and attitudes toward reading.

Problems Related to Skill Development

How can reading skills be taught unless a develop-

mental reading program is employed? The interviewed
teachers reported that they were asked this question more
than any other during discussions of the new program with
interested teachers, administrators, and parents. The literature on individualized reading reveals scores of articles that
ask this question, or attempt to answer it.

Eight teachers described problems that related to
skill development, but the group, as a whole, did not find
this general area the most perplexing, nor the problems associated with it the most difficult to solve.

There was a difference of opinion among the interviewed teachers concerning the development of the reading
process. Some felt all children progressed through the various skill levels in similar ways, but at varying rates. Others believed that no two children learn to read in the same
way, therefore the development of skills must be individualized.

The teachers who expressed the first opinion tended
to use a developmental skill building program, making use
of materials from various basal reading series. One of these
teachers continued to use workbooks for her skills program
because she felt the reading "experts" had a richer background in this area than she did.

Another teacher said, "I was afraid in the beginning I
might miss some skills, so I held on to the workbooks and
checked faithfully. "

Whatever approach was used, identifying each child's
needs was the most difficult problem related to skill development faced by these teachers when they initiated the program. Most teachers made use of individual conferences to
discover their student's needs in this area. This information was also helpful when they planned their skill programs,
established "needs" groups, or provided individuals with necessary help.

After these needs had been recognized, selecting and
organizing suitable materials became the next task. A first
grade teacher found it necessary to plan and construct many
of the materials she used in her skill program. Most teachers made use of basal reading workbooks and specially constructed skill-building series. Many teachers mentioned using other subject areas to introduce or reinforce skills. They

found reading skills instruction could be incorporated in spelling and language arts lessons. Several intermediate grade teachers introduced various reference skills and other related reading skills as part of social studies and science units.

One teacher, who was admittedly apprehensive about his ability to develop reading skills on an individual basis, related, "In the skills area I found I was doing more good in a fifteen minute conference than I had been doing in group work in a week's time."

Problems Related to Interpersonal Relations

Because individualized reading is a new approach to reading instruction, the teachers who decided to work with it anticipated a certain amount of interest in, and some criticism of the program. Most of them found the problems they faced with parents, other teachers, and administrators far less serious than they had expected.

Four of the six teachers who described problems that related to this category had experienced them with parents of their students. Although a majority of them held individual conferences or group meetings to explain individualized reading, most felt that many parents did not understand the new program.

After one such meeting, four parents requested that their children be excluded from the new program. The teacher agreed to keep these students in a basal reading series. After a short time, these parents asked that their children be allowed to work in an individualized program. This teacher has had no other problems with parents.

Another found the best way to acquaint parents with the new program was to have them visit the classroom and observe during the reading period.

The parents who objected to the program usually did so during the implementation period. Later most of them became interested and often enthusiastic about this new approach. The interviewed teachers said they had received many compliments from parents about the favorable effect this reading program had on the children's reading habits and attitudes.

"The parents liked the idea so well," reported one teacher who had initiated individualized reading with part of her students, "I decided to put my whole class in the program."

Although many expressed interest in the program, no problems were created by teachers who worked closely with those interviewed. One teacher, however, did remark, "No one said anything to me, but I felt some of the other teachers were quite skeptical about what I was doing at first."

A primary grade teacher felt substitute teachers presented a problem. She explained, "I feel as if I can't be ill. The substitute can get by for a day or two, but after that she's lost."

Other teachers implied that this could become a problem and felt it would be desirable for teachers doing substitute work to become more familiar with this approach.

The teachers found their supervisors, and in most cases their administrators, interested in the new program and anxious to help in any way they could.

Many of the interviewed teachers had worked with student teachers. Although they did not feel this was a problem directly related to initiating individualized reading, several were concerned about their responsibility to the student. Some thought they should give the prospective teacher some experience with a basal reading program. Others thought it unnecessary. Although opinions varied, none felt working with the individualized approach has been a detriment to the student teacher.

Survey of Teaching Practices in Individualized Reading
on a County-Wide Basis

by

Baltimore County Board of Education

(This material is excerpted from A Pilot Study of
Individualized Reading in Baltimore County Elementary Schools, published in 1959.)

A pilot program of Individualized Reading was carried
on in twenty-five elementary schools in Baltimore County,
Maryland, during the school year 1957-58. After the year
was over, in fact about six months later, a five-page questionnaire was prepared and sent to 59 teachers in the twenty-
five schools, for the purpose of evaluating the pilot program.
The fact that the data presented in this analysis were collected some time after the year was completed, should be
kept in mind by anyone wishing to generalize on the basis of
the pilot program or its analysis.

It should not be inferred that there is not now an on-
going program in Individualized Reading in the Baltimore
County Elementary Schools. As a result of the pilot program, there is more work being done, and some attempts
are being made to compare some of the methods of teaching
reading.

In their comments on the program, most teachers
seemed to feel that the program increased interest and a-
chievement among the pupils participating. Implied or directly expressed in many of the comments made by the
teachers, is the opinion that the program also tended to increase rapport between teacher and pupil.

136

PARTICIPATION

Table I

Distribution of Classes by Grade Level

Grade Level	Number of Classes
1	4
2	12
3	8
4	8
5	13
6	9
Total	54

Not all pupils in every one of the 54 classes participated in the Individualized Reading Program. Teachers reported as small a percentage of participation as 20%, and the range extended to 100%. To test the hypothesis that the percentage of participation varied with the grade level, an analysis of variance of the following table was made.

Table II

Per Cent of Pupils Enrolled by Grade and Class

Class	Grade					
	1	2	3	4	5	6
1	30	25	41	100	36	23
2	100	37	33	56	44	41
3	40	26	54	40	54	58
4	100	50	33	44	39	19
5		23	100	30	83	39
6		30	34	100	54	50
7		20	50	37	48	26
8		39			38	41
9		35			100	
10		52			35	
11		36			65	
12		50				
Total	270	423	345	407	596	297
Av. % enrolled.	67. 5	35. 25	49. 28	58. 14	54. 18	37. 12
	Overall average enrolled = 47. 71%					

Reading Level of Participants

Table III refers to reading level of pupils before beginning Individualized Reading. In general, where less than the whole class was enrolled in Individualized Reading, the more advanced students were enrolled. Therefore, where teachers reported "Average" or "Below Average" reading level, this is likely due to class grouping on the basis of reading level.

Table III

Reading Level of Participants

Reading Level of Participants	Number of Teachers Reporting
Above average	47
Average	4
Below average	3

WHAT WAS DONE IN INDIVIDUALIZING READING?

Use of basal reader

Fifty-five of the teachers reported that they used the basal reader in the Individualized Reading Program.

Table IV

Frequency of Use of Basal Reader

Frequency	Number of Teachers Reporting
Daily	12
Periodically	29
Other	14

Method of keeping records

Table V

Records Kept on Individualized Reading

Method	Number of Teachers Reporting	
	Teacher records	Child's Records
Card system	24	15
Notebook	35	44
Other method	5	12

Some of the methods of keeping records reported under "Other" were: Diaries, charts, "reading train" with a different card for each type of book read, individual folders, individual reports, and "projects."

Facts recorded in records

Table VI

Distribution of Teachers by Kinds of Facts Recorded

Kind of Fact	Number of Teachers Reporting
Skills	45
Choice of stories	47
Projects completed	47
Conferences	46
Other	20

Under "Other," teachers reported that they recorded such things as attitudes, emotional adjustment of child, problem areas discovered, and number of pages read per day.

Time spent in preparation and keeping records

There was a large variation in the amounts of time reported to have been spent in preparation. A detailed an-

alysis indicates that there is a significant difference in the
amount of time spent per week in preparation, between those
teachers who enrolled 1/3 or less of her pupils in the program and those teachers who enrolled more than 1/3 of her
pupils.   The increased amount of time for preparation for
the larger enrollment is so small, however, that it would
be fair to say that not much more time is required when the
whole class is enrolled, as far as preparation time is concerned.

Table VII

Distribution of Time Requirements

Number of hrs. per week	Number of Teachers Reporting		
	For preparation	For records	Total time
1	4	17	0
2	12	20	8
3	6	4	7
4	5	0	8
5	6	3	8
6	4	0	4
7	2	0	4
8	0	1	5
9	0	0	0
10	2	0	4

Perhaps it should be emphasized that these data do
not represent actual time records, but only the estimations
of the various teachers concerned.   A reasonable generalization might be that most of the teachers thought they spent a-
bout 2 hours a week in preparation, and about the same a-
mount of time in keeping records.   There is much more a-
greement about the amount of time for record keeping than
there is on the amount of time needed for preparation.

Selection of Reading Material

Table XIII
Freedom of Selection

Degree of freedom	No. of Teachers reporting
Children had complete self-selection of material	11
Children were allowed to choose from material which had been previously selected for them	37
Other	20

Teachers reporting under "Other," indicated several interesting approaches to control of selection, usually by some application of principles of democracy, so that choice was controlled in terms of pupil understanding of appropriate goals. Notice that some teachers used more than one degree of control.

Table XVI
Extent of Control by Teacher's Opinion of Pupil Ability

Degree of control	No. of Teachers reporting
Always	10
Frequently	20
Sometimes	19
Seldom	4
Never	1

The question of whether a teacher should control or limit the pupil selection of reading material using a criterion of pupil ability is an interesting one and might well be debated. According to scientific opinion, bumble-bees have insufficient wing-spread, and are therefore unable to fly!

It appears that the average length of time that the several teachers conducted the Individualized Reading Pro-

gram was 15 weeks, and that there was no significant difference between grades as to the length of time that the program was in operation.

TIME REQUIREMENTS OF INDIVIDUALIZED
READING IN CLASSROOM

Average amount of time spent per day
on Individualized Reading

Table XIX

Distribution of Teachers by Amount of Time Spent Per Day

Minutes	30	45	60	75	90
Teachers Reporting	17	19	12	2	3

Median time spent per day = 45 minutes

Times per week teacher works with each pupil

Table XX

Distribution of Teachers by Number
of Individual Contacts Per Week

Number of contacts	1	2	3	4	5
Teachers reporting	19	17	8	6	4

Median contacts per week per child = 3

Average amount of time spent per week with
each pupil, individual basis

Table XXI

Distribution of Teachers by Minutes
Spent Per Week Per Pupil

Minutes	5	10	15	20	25	30 or more
Teachers Reporting	11	10	9	5	1	7

Median time per week per pupil = 15 minutes

Generalizations on time requirements

The average enrollment per teacher was approximately 19 pupils. If teachers average 15 minutes per week with each pupil, this means approximately 285 minutes per week per class, or 57 minutes per day per class spent on individual pupil help. This figure does not quite check out with Table XIX, wherein we see that 45 minutes per day per class was spent on the whole program. However, it would be more than unusual if the figures checked exactly. A reasonable generalization might be that teachers spend a little less time on individual help than they think they do. The amount of time that can be spent on individual help is one of the limitations of the program, as well as one of the strengths of it. Averages and distributions will not tell us on which pupils the teacher ought to spend the most time.

GROUPING PRACTICES IN INDIVIDUAL READING

All but four of the teachers followed the practice of bringing the pupils together in a group for the purpose of group evaluation. The frequency with which teachers did this ranged from daily, to less than once per week. Thirty teachers used group evaluation less than once a week.

Table XXIII

Miscellaneous Considerations

Survey question (abridged)	Teachers answering	
	Yes	No
Could you more easily identify the reading problems of participating children than those not participating?	33	5
Were you able to provide for a variety of reading interests for each child?	53	1
Do you feel individualized reading encourages critical thinking and creative thinking?	54	0
Do you feel that children enjoy this method of reading?	54	0
Do you feel that children in the program read books as opposed to simply handling them?	54	0

Table **XXIII**   (cont.)
Miscellaneous Considerations

Survey question (abridged)	Teachers answering	
	Yes	No
Would you wish to continue an Individualized Reading Program in your classroom?	51	1
Has a situation been set up in your school to accurately determine whether individualized reading is superior to some other method of reading?	8	46

Table **XXIV**

Effect of Individualized Reading Programs
on Library Services

Effect	Number of librarians reporting
The circulation of books was increased through individualized reading.	14
There was an increase in reading among the children in the program.	12
The program created additional problems for the library staff.	6
The library was not affected.	2
It was difficult to serve the needs of other children because of the demands made on the library by classes in individualized reading.	1
The program caused children to become too dependent upon classroom materials.	1

Table **XXIV** is based upon a questionnaire sent to 18 librarians and completed by all eighteen.

Most of the librarians felt that the demands of the program on the library would be directly proportional to the number of classes in the school having the program, and that the library could handle the demands, given sufficient warning, so that sufficient books could be placed on the shelves.

SUMMARY AND RECOMMENDATIONS

Among the fifty-four teachers who took part in the pilot program, there is very apparent agreement that the Individualized Reading Program is a success, as far as they are concerned. There is less agreement on the question of what Individualized Reading is, or just how one individualizes reading; but the main conclusion is favorable.

Can we then say that every teacher in elementary schools should "individualize" the teaching and practice of reading? It would be very risky to stake very much on the truth of such a statement. For every method of teaching anything, there exists a range of abilities of individual teachers to use that method. We can say that certain methods are very efficient in the hands of some teachers, and we may even say truthfully that some methods are best for almost all teachers, but we ought never say that there is <u>one best method</u> of teaching, which all teachers should use.

Perhaps we should conclude that all elementary teachers ought to give serious thought and study to this question: "Is each and every one of my pupils acquiring skill of reading to the best of his individual ability, and if not, is it because he is being held back by the "lock-step" of group methods?"

It is one thing to be "sold on" something, but quite another to be able to make use of it. Before teachers embark on a program of Individualized Reading, they ought to do some reading about the techniques of individualizing the learning process; they ought to plan very carefully just how it will be done; and they should give some consideration to the problem of evaluating the effectiveness of the new plan.

How 78 Teachers Employed Individualized Reading
in Their Classrooms

by

Anna Marie Rix

(This material is excerpted from the author's 1962
Kutztown State College master's thesis, A Survey
of Individualized Reading as Practiced by Teachers
in Several Elementary Schools in Pennsylvania.)

Number of Children in Classes

Grade Level	Teachers	Number of Children	Average
First Grade	6	25 to 36	29
Second Grade	6	21 to 35	36
Third Grade	5	23 to 38	28
Fourth Grade	10	24 to 33	26
Fifth Grade	4	15 to 32	26
Sixth Grade	10	9 to 35	27
Team Teaching Group	31	28 to 45	40
Combination Grade	2	27 to 29	28
Special Grades	3	12 to 17	14
Consultant	1	30	30
Total	78		30

Range of Ability and Reading Achievement of Children

Grade Level	Range	Number of Teachers	No Response
First	-	6	0
Second	1. 4-5. 0	6	1
Third	1. 2-6. 1	4	1
Fourth	2. 1-7. 9	10	1
Fifth	2. 0-9. 0	4	1
Sixth	4. 0-10. 0	10	0
Team Teaching Group	2. 1-11. 2	31	0
Combination-Grade	3. 2-8. 5	2	0
Special Classes	PP - 4. 5	3	0
Reading Consultant	-	1	1
Total		77	5

Time Given to Reading in Class Groups
(In Minutes Per Day)

Grade Level	No. Teachers	30-44	45-59	60-74	75-89	90-104	105-120	No response
First	6	2	1				3*	
Second	6			1		4	1	
Third	5			1		2	1	1
Fourth	10			3	2	2	1	2
Fifth	4		1	2				1
Sixth	10		3	4	2	1		
Team Teaching Group	31		7	24				
Combination Grade	2	2						
Special	3			1			2	
Consultant	1			1				
Total	78	4	12	37	4	9	8	4

* Varies - These teachers noted "depends upon type of difficulty" or "as needed" but did not give number of minutes.

Number of Individual Conferences

Grade	No. of Teachers	No Response	Number of Conferences per Day									
			*Var.	1	2	3	4	5	6	8	10	15
1	6	1				1	2		1		1	
2	6	1						1	2		1	1
3	5	2			1		1					1
4	10	3	2	1	1						1	2
5	4	2	2									
6	10	1	2		1		1	2	1	1	1	
Team Teaching	31	24	1		1	1		2				2
Combination Gr.	2								1		1	
Special	3		1				2					
Consultant	1						1					
Total	78	34	8	1	4	2	7	5	5	1	5	6

* Varies - These teachers noted "depends upon type of difficulty," or "as needed" but did not give number of minutes.

Reading Levels and Number of Books
Used to Initiate the Program

Grade Level	No. of Teachers	Grade Range in Books	Range of Books to Initiate Program
1	6	PP-3. 2	10 - 83
2	6	PP-5	60 - 300
3	5	1-8	50 - 280
4	10	2-8	40 - 120
5	4	2-10	25 - 250
6	10	1. 5-11	50 - 600
Team Teaching	31	1-12	40 - 200
Combination	2	2-7	25 - 50
Special	3	PP-4	40 - 80
Consultant	1	2-7	250

Types of Individualized Reading Practices

Grade Level	No. of Teachers	Complete Self-Selection	Per Cent	Comb. Basal & Self-Selection	Per Cent
1	6	1	1. 3	5	6. 4
2	6			6	7. 7
3	5			5	6. 4
4	10			10	12. 8
5	4			4	5. 1
6	10	2	2. 6	8	10. 2
Team Teaching	31	7	9. 0	24	30. 8
Combination	2			2	2. 6
Special	3			3	3. 8
Consultant	1			1	1. 3
Total	78	10	12. 9	68	87. 1

Difficulties Faced by Individualized Reading Teachers

by

Patrick J. Groff

(This material is excerpted from the author's article, "A Check on Individualized Reading," which appeared in Education in March, 1964. Copyright (c) 1964.)

Nineteen primary grade teachers and fifteen intermediate grade teachers who had successfully used individualized reading were asked to react to certain key criticisms that have been made of the individualized reading approach.

Difficulties Experienced

To begin, these teachers were asked what difficulties they had faced in using individualized reading.

Forty-seven indications of difficulties noticed in using this approach were given. About 75 per cent of these were (a) that the teachers did not have enough books in their programs, (b) that they were not familiar enough with the books they did have, and (c) that pupils could not work independently under individualized reading. Only about 15 per cent of the difficulties they indicated had to do with the actual problems of teaching word recognition.

Word Analysis

Next, the teachers were asked, "Some say pupils should first be taught word analysis using basal reading or workbooks, etc., before individualized reading is begun. Do you agree?"

150

Eighteen of the thirty-four teachers said "Yes" to this question. Another five gave a conditioned "Yes." These twenty-three teachers felt pupils would need to have developed word analysis skills before they were expected to begin individualized reading. Otherwise, they felt the limited amount of time the individualized reading teacher has for each child in this approach would preclude teaching the word analysis skills thoroughly.

The eleven teachers who did without basal readers believed more meaning could be given to word analysis through individualized reading, since the words used to develop word analysis here are taken from the individual pupil's peculiar reading needs as these come up in his individualized reading. Both groups of teachers insisted on the need for a strong word analysis program, in any case.

Then the teachers were asked, "It has been said a systematic program of word analysis cannot be carried on using individualized reading. What is your opinion of this statement?"

Only four of the thirty-four teachers queried believed this to be so. As seen above, many believed the word analysis program should be first taught through the use of basal reader materials, however. While the teachers, by and large, were optimistic that a systematic word analysis program was possible using individualized reading, they were impressed with the difficulty of the task. The importance of keeping accurate, complete records, and the need for teachers to have a thorough knowledge of both word analysis and the readability of pupils' self-selected reading materials were stressed. The word analysis practices reported most often were pulling pupils with common needs together for instruction, and conducting word analysis elsewhere in the curriculum outside the reading program, e. g. , in spelling.

To complete this line of inquiry, the teachers were asked to describe what they taught in word analysis as they used individualized reading and how and when, and how well it was taught.

Only four of the teachers reported that the content of the word analysis program they used was different from that ordinarily found in basal reading materials. Two of these teachers used a modified linguistic approach, that is, a controlled sound system. The other two used the SRA Reading

Laboratory.

Practically all the teachers grouped their pupils for instruction in word analysis. Furthermore, most of them said they taught word analysis every day. Only two teachers reported that they taught word analysis on a totally individualized basis. About one-fourth of the group of teachers indicated that they taught it through the spelling program.

The main departure from basal reading practices came when these teachers decided how instructional groups should be formed, and what word analysis instruction in particular was appropriate for any given group. Here they relied heavily for guidance upon the results of the individual conferences they held with pupils, and upon the records that were kept in these conferences. They claimed this allowed their groupings to be flexibly adjustable to the needs the individual pupil exhibited during the teacher-pupil conference. The individual conference also was used to determine the extent to which pupils could correctly use the word analysis skills which they previously had been taught.

Readiness for Reading

The teachers next were reminded that much has been said by critics of individualized reading of an apparent lack of attention in the approach to the development of readiness for reading, especially for recognition of "new" words. Seven of the thirty-four teachers indicated they thought this a valid criticism and consequently believed that under individualized reading pupils guess too much about words and practice faulty word analysis.

Four out of five teachers disagreed with this, however. They contended that the teacher-pupil conferences, help from other pupils, grouping for word analysis, word analysis activities in the spelling program, pupils' listing of "hard" words for later study, use of the dictionary, use of context clues, emphasis upon comprehension, the wise choice of materials on the pupil's reading level, and other procedures satisfactorily solved the problem of readiness.

One teacher, moreover, believed that not all children needed readiness activities. Another was aware of no objective evidence about her class that confirmed the critics' suspicions. Two said the enthusiasm and interest of their pupils for individualized reading was a factor in overcoming this. Another two reacted that the criticism was just as valid for ability-grouping, which to them also failed to provide adequate readiness.

Four teachers, on the other hand, believed the problem could be avoided only if pupils were first taken through several basic readers before individualized reading was started, or if individualized reading were delayed until pupils were in the intermediate grades.

Group Relationships

Because individualized reading has been criticized as isolating the child from the stimulation to learning possible in a group situation, the teachers were asked if the lack of social interaction under individualized reading had any adverse effects on their pupils' interests and efforts in reading.

The teachers' answers to this were almost unanimous in certain respects. First, they agreed that a total lack of social interaction in the individualized reading program would be a mistake. Second, many were convinced, however, that sharing through groups was necessary only for certain children. More teachers emphasized the need for poor readers to share than for good readers to do so. Finally, because of these reasons, almost all the teachers stated that they brought their pupils together, generally in small groups, to share what they had read. A great many different activities for this were mentioned. Several teachers indicated that such grouping was a frequent routine.

Individual teachers disagreed about the value of grouping. One did no grouping. Another teacher, who did not group for sharing, had never felt that it had any effect on interests. Sharing in other curriculum areas took care of the problem, a third teacher thought.

Study Skills and Interests

Critics of individualized reading also have questioned whether this approach develops study skills and wide reading interests. The teachers, in conclusion, were asked to comment on these two allegations.

In response to the first part of this criticism only
five of the teachers indicated they believed that individualized
reading does not develop study skills adequately.   Also, one
of these five thought that it did so in the intermediate but not
in the primary grades.   These teachers either felt that there
was not time enough in the individualized reading program to
make this possible or that pupils, to be successful under this
approach, must already have developed strong study skills.

The remaining twenty-nine teachers believed study
skills were properly learned under individualized reading.
Two of these felt the criticism wholly unjustified.   To them
the gain in study skills possible was the greatest advantage
the approach offered.   Many others remarked that the wide
reading and high pupil interest integral to the approach made
study skills easier to learn and teach.   Four teachers maintained that for individualized reading to build the study skills
there must be a "good foundation" laid in the study skills at
the beginning of the program and/or that the study skills
must be reviewed regularly.

All of the thirty-four teachers rejected the contention
of some critics that individualized reading is likely to develop
narrow reading interests.   "Just the opposite," many teachers
reported, "interests are broader."   Eight teachers stressed
the crucial nature of the teacher's role in this matter, however.   The teacher was reminded he must be on guard a-
gainst inattention to this matter, and be sure to provide a
variety of good books.

Also, narrow interests under individualized reading,
as under other programs, cannot always be condemned, insisted two teachers.   One described how a poor reader
started off in individualized reading with narrow interests but
after being allowed to read his fill of books in two categories,
branched off into other topics.   With poor readers, the other
teacher observed, it may be better to have good, narrow interests than none at all.

Survey of 250 Classroom Teachers Combining
Individualized Reading With Basal Reading

by

Beverly Lee McKay

(This material is excerpted from the author's 1964
Drake University master's thesis, Individualized
Reading as Part of an Eclectic Reading Program.)

Method of Incorporating Individualized Reading
Into the Reading Program

Method	Number
To fill out a year or semester for only the superior group	11
To fill out a year or semester for any group which finishes basal readers	24
As a special approach for retarded readers	30
As a supplement to the basal reader, used regularly even though the basal reader has not been completed	88
Other	19

Basis of Students' Book Selection in Reading Programs

Basis	Number
Interest	77
With teacher guidance	25
From group teacher has selected as being at his level and suitable	25
Relation to reading and other subject units being studied	20
From books and stories suggested in basal reader	8
Individual ability	8
Guidance of librarian	6
Recommendations of friends	4
Appearance, physical characteristics	2
Availability	1

Sources of Books Available to Children

Source	Number
School central library	82
Public library	73
Classroom library	67
County library	24
Home	22
Book clubs	7
Teacher	6
S. R. A. Reading Laboratory	4
I. S. E. A. Library Service	1

Types of Materials Used in Reading Programs

Type	Number
Fiction trade books	102
Non-fiction trade books	99
Various basal readers	83
Periodicals	73
Content texts	67
S. R. A. Laboratory	5
Newspapers	1
School newspapers	1
Comic-type	1

Methods of Keeping Records of Children's Reading

Method	Number
Filing cards	33
Student notebooks	29
Charts	28
Written reports	22
No records	14
S. R. A. procedure	4
Graphs	3
Check sheets	3
Cumulative folders	2
Questionnaires	1

Activities Which Take Place During
Teacher-Pupil Conferences

Activity	Number
Child telling story in own words	68
Oral reading	56
Question-answer session	45
Check for comprehension, vocabulary, etc., and help in correcting difficulties	13
Discussion of story, characters, incidents, etc.	12
Dramatization	6
Taping of oral reading or reporting	3
Activities varied to meet needs of children	3
Pupil evaluation of own achievement	2
Discussion of written report	1
Discussion of book to be read next	1

Occasions for Group Instruction Specifically
Related to the Individualized Reading
Part of Programs

Occasion	Number
Group needs help with a particular skill	19
Sharing individual ideas or discoveries with class	18
Oral book reviews	9
Preparation of class to select and evaluate books	9
Number of students choose same or related materials	8
Planning by whole class for a particular activity	6
Introduction of new concepts	5
Stressing reading skills in teaching the content areas	5
Follow-up activities	3
Wide interest shown in some phase of work	2
Oral reading to class	2
Panel discussions	1
Word building and analysis	1
None	27

Goals of Individualized Reading

Goal	Number
Love of reading	37
Broadened interests	36
Increased comprehension	22
Increased knowledge	20
Enriched vocabulary	19
Greater independence in work	14
Mastery of skills	13
Adoption of reading as a leisure activity	11
Development of literary appreciation and taste	10
Improved fluency	10
Increased speed	10
Increased amount of reading	8
Reading of wider variety of materials	8
Improved self-expression	8
Improved research skills	7
Independent application of work attack skills in context	7
Broadened background	5
Development of ability to select materials wisely	4

Chapter 5

Orientation to Individualized Reading

A major problem in the implementation of individualized reading programs is the proper orientation of all concerned prior to its initiation. Three selections in this chapter have to do with aspects of orientation.

Patrick J. Groff, Professor of Education at San Diego State College, has written extensively on the subject of individualized reading. In the first selection in this chapter, Professor Groff suggests ways in which a teacher who plans to institute individualized reading in his classroom may prepare himself.

In the next selection Glenda A. Gray describes the procedures used in orienting her fifth grade class to an individualized reading program.

In her doctoral dissertation Dr. Phylliss S. Adams, Associate Professor of Education at the University of Denver, carried on a carefully planned and well executed experiment comparing individualized reading and basal reading in the first grade. As part of her experiment she prepared detailed guides for the teachers of each of these approaches. The final selection of this chapter presents the guide for individualized reading in full.

How Does a Teacher Prepare Himself to Use
Individualized Reading

by

Patrick J. Groff

(This material is excerpted from the author's article, "Helping Teachers Begin Individualized Reading," which appeared in the National Elementary
Principal in February, 1964.)

There are many questions about individualized reading
that must be considered if the teacher would insure both his
success and satisfaction in using this approach.   Through individual or group conferences, the principal should make sure
that his teachers are aware of the problems in successfully
using individualized reading.   He should take the initiative in
seeing that teachers are prepared to explain the program to
parents and should be sure that the school patrons understand the purpose of individualized reading.

The following twelve questions and comments indicate
the kind of information and procedures which will help both
teachers and principals in planning and initiating a program
of individualized reading.

Teachers should be led to ask themselves:

1. Do I understand the purpose and techniques of individualized reading?   For example, what are the five essential parts of the program? [(Planning; individual silent reading and oral reading with partners; pupil-teacher conferences;
sharing what has been read; and cooperative evaluation of
these procedures.)]

2. Will it be possible for me to see individualized
reading in action?   Will at least two teachers in our school
be using it so we can exchange visits and ideas?

The principal can be instrumental in encouraging teachers to work in teams on individualized programs. The support and encouragement teachers can give each other will help a great deal in making the program successful. If no other arrangements can be made, the principal might take over a teacher's class so he can observe in another class-room. If possible, provisions should be made for teachers to see individualized reading in action in other schools.

3. Do my principal and supervisors understand individualized reading?

The principal of any school in which an individualized reading program is contemplated should be familiar with the theories and practices of individualized reading. Knowledgable supervision of a constructively critical nature is crucial to this approach.

4. Does my school have available the professional literature from which I can learn the details of individualized reading?

5. Do I know enough about children's books to use individualized reading? Does my school have sources from which I can learn about children's literature?

The school's professional library should include at least the following books on children's literature. Of course, nothing can supplant a good college course in children's literature.

Arbuthnot, May Hill   Children and Books   Chicago, Scott, Foresman & Co. , 1957.

Huck, Charlotte S. , and Young, Doris A.   Children's Literature in the Elementary School   New York, Holt, Rinehart & Winston, 1961.

Larrick, Nancy   A Teacher's Guide to Children's Books   Columbus, Ohio, Charles E. Merrill Books, 1960.

Tooze, Ruth A. , and Krone, B. P.   Literature and Music as Resources for Social Studies   Englewood Cliffs, New Jersey, Prentice-Hall, 1955.

6. Do I know where to find the right book for the right child at the right time? Does my school have refer-

ences which will assist in this search?

The teacher using individualized reading must be especially concerned with seeing that the books brought into the classroom meet both the children's interests and their reading abilities. Analyses of the pupils' interests and abilities should be made frequently.

7. Do I know enough about the techniques of teaching reading to use individualized reading? Can I teach reading without guidance from a teacher's manual?

With individualized reading, the teacher does not depend on the teacher's manual for direct guidance as he does when using a textbook for reading instruction. Consequently, he must know in detail at least the following aspects of reading methodology: word analysis and recognition; comprehension and study skills; flexibility of speed; oral reading; and appropriate independent review. Teachers need to self-evaluate frankly whether or not they will be able to develop these skills in an individualized reading program.

*   *   *

9. Can I find the time necessary to make an individualized reading program a success in a class of normal size?

There are many time-consuming aspects to individualized reading: for example, holding conferences, record keeping, directing sharing sessions, and teaching needed skills in groups. A well-organized time schedule should be developed. Further, in almost all cases it is better to begin by individualizing the reading of a small subgroup composed of dependable, industrious children. The amount of time needed for conducting individualized reading can be determined at this point.

10. Am I psychologically suited for this type of teaching? Is my personality such that I would feel a great loss of security if I could not depend on the teacher's manual for day-by-day directions?

Each individual teacher must judge for himself in the light of his experience, education, and personal characteristics whether or not he is suited to use individualized reading. The principal should, of course, be able to provide certain professional insights into this intricate and subtle problem.

11. Will I be able to explain the individualized reading program to parents?

Teachers, as well as principals, should be able to explain the advantages of an individualized reading program over ability grouping in terms of: pupil achievement; provisions for individual differences; pupils' attitudes toward reading; pupils' self-direction and control; and long-range effects. Teachers and principals should also be prepared to explain how the program differs from simple "free" reading.

12. Can I answer the objections that have been made to individualized reading?

The faculty of any school using individualized reading should be prepared to answer the various charges that have been made against this approach. Among the objections which are made are these:

* Individualized reading procedures are too disorganized, irregular, and time-consuming for the average teacher.

* Individualized reading is too unsystematic to allow for sequential learning.

* Individualized reading does not develop children's reading tastes and interests.

* Parents do not want their children to use individualized reading.

* Reading achievement is low. Reading skills are neglected and faulty word recognition habits and weak study skills result.

* There is no possibility for group learning with individualized reading.

* Most teachers do not have the personality or the knowledge of books, children, and reading procedures to use individualized reading.

* Most authorities are opposed to individualized reading; therefore, it must be wrong.

* "Flexible grouping" will adequately take care of individual differences.

* There is not enough control or repetition of vocabulary. The reading level of tradebooks (non-textbooks) is unknown. There is no provision for reading readiness.

* Discipline problems develop with individualized reading. Most children do not have the self-direction or control to work under this approach. They are inattentive and develop slovenly work habits.

* Most classes are too large for individualized reading to be used effectively.

* There are not enough books in most schools to make individualized reading work.

* Individualized reading will not work with slow learners.

* Individualized reading will not work in the primary grades, especially the first grade.

How a Fifth Grade Class was Introduced to
Individualized Reading

by

Glenda Arlene Gray

(This material is excerpted from the author's 1965
Marshall University master's thesis, A Study of
the Individualized Reading Program at Holz Elementary School, Charleston, West Virginia.)

I. Orientation Program

Administrative permission was granted to undertake
the individualized reading program and to integrate it with
the county-adopted basal text reading program during the
school year 1964-1965.

During September, 1964, two conferences were held
with the principal of the school in order that both teacher and
principal become fully aware of the principles involved in initiation of the new program. It was during these conferences
that the principal read the text of the review of literature
and offered suggestions as to its use.

During the school months of September and October,
1964, repeated references to the individualized reading program were made by the teacher to the students in her classroom. As the months elapsed, the children become quite enthusiastic and eager to begin the individualized program.

On Tuesday, October 20, 1964, a meeting was held
for the purpose of explaining the individualized reading program and to enlist the support of the parents. It was felt
that without this support and understanding, the teacher might
be accused of not teaching reading since the approach was
quite different from the reading program currently in use.
After an explanation of the program, a question-and-answer

167

period indicated that the parents were interested and would offer their support by lending their children's libraries for use in the program.

Beginning on November 2, 1964, and continuing throughout the week, the children took part in an orientation period. During this time they and their teacher discussed the new reading program, its purposes, and its responsibilities.

The class chose a corner in the back of the room for their conference corner. The particular area was thought to be out of the way and would afford privacy for those having conferences.

A committee was chosen from volunteers to "dress-up" the conference corner. Committee members brought in two chairs and thus created but not wholly closed off the corner. This was necessary since the teacher needed to be aware of the activities of the entire room; yet it provided for a sense of privacy.

Upon completion of the conference corner, mock conferences were held. Through this procedure the students learned of the importance of the conference and how it was to be conducted. They learned that they were to bring with them to the conference the book they wished to discuss or read aloud from, their reading record book, and any other materials they felt were necessary at the time.

Further discussions during the orientation period included the independent aspect of the program. The children learned that they could begin their reading whenever they were ready and without waiting for other students or for the teacher. They were to go quietly to the library and choose a new book whenever they needed one. In order to insure that they did not get a book that was too difficult, they learned to count the number of unknown words on any page of the book. If there were more than three unfamiliar words, then the book was probably too difficult and they were free to choose another one. Once chosen, however, they were expected to complete the book.

They also learned that grouping would be used only for definite, temporary needs and would be kept extremely flexible.

The Effectiveness of an
Individualized Reading Program

by

Phylliss Stevens Adams

(This material is excerpted from the author's 1962 University of Denver doctoral dissertation, <u>An Investigation of an Individualized Reading Program and a Modified Basal Reading Program in First Grade.</u>)

Conditions Essential for Success in an Individualized Reading Program

The success of an individualized reading program is dependent upon the existence of certain conditions relating to personnel, to materials, and to organizational procedures and classroom management.

Essential conditions relating to personnel include the following:

1. The teacher
   - (a) has a favorable and enthusiastic attitude toward an individualized reading program.
   - (b) possesses a thorough knowledge of the reading process and is well-informed about the skills and abilities involved in reading.
   - (c) knows content and level of difficulty of books used in the program.

2. The members of the school administration
   - (a) encourage flexibility in use of time.
   - (b) encourage teacher participation in classroom experimentation.
   - (c) assist in informing the community about the reading program.

Essential conditions relating to materials include the following:

1. Large numbers of books and other reading materials on many different subjects and at many different difficulty levels are available.

2. A wide variety of practice materials is provided.

Essential conditions relating to organizational procedures and classroom management include the following:

1. Time is provided for both group and individual reading.

2. Individual pupil-teacher conferences are held frequently and regularly.

3. Arrangements are made for pupil-teacher planning and for pupil-teacher evaluation.

4. Pupils are given adequate guidance in selection of reading matter.

5. A time for giving instruction in skills is arranged.

6. Suitable independent work is available for each child.

7. Individual reading experiences are shared.

8. A systematic method of keeping records is employed.

9. Certain necessary routines are established in order that the reading period may proceed smoothly.

10. The classroom environment encourages and stimulates interest in reading.

11. Appropriate evaluation procedures are utilized.

Materials of Instruction

Reading Materials

One of the requirements for success in an individualized reading program is a rich and varied supply of reading materials.   This collection of materials includes teacher-pupil prepared materials, teacher-prepared materials, basal readers, supplementary readers, trade books, magazines, newspapers, pamphlets, brochures, and filmstrips.

Teacher-pupil prepared materials.   One kind of reading material which is of great importance in first grade is the experience story dictated by the children to the teacher. These stories, written on the chalkboard by the teacher and later transferred to charts, may center around any number of experiences shared by the group.   Experience charts include:

> Accounts of trips taken by the class.
> Accounts of activities in the classroom.
> Records of experiments.
> Accounts of "Things We Want to Find Out" in relation
>   to units of work.
> Records of plans.
> Diaries of things happening each day at school.
> News reports.

In addition, experience charts may be developed following discussion of such topics as how to be a good worker in the classroom, playground rules to observe, directions for fire drills, and so on.

Experience charts are valuable during both the pre-reading period and the beginning reading period.   Among the purposes served by experience charts are:

1. They help children to acquire the idea that reading is "talk written down."

2. They foster the habit of reading for meaning.

3. They develop in children a feeling of sentence sense.

4. They provide experience in left-to-right progression.

5. They serve as a basis for developing sight vocabulary. [1]

A second type of experience record of use in an indi-

vidualized reading program is the story dictated to the teacher
by the individual pupil.   This type of reading material is often produced in connection with a picture drawn by the child.
Booklets can be made from the individual stories and placed
on a book table where all children in the room can select
them for reading.

Teacher-prepared materials.   There are times when
the teacher prepares a chart story without benefit of class
dictation.   Such stories are often developed for the purposes
of introducing specific sight words or for providing additional
repetition of previously introduced sight words.   A few examples of such teacher-prepared materials are:

Announcements of coming events in the classroom.

Stories designed to pique the child's curiosity (i. e. ,
    "We will have a surprise today. . . ")

Daily news stories.

Poetry charts.

Stories developed around large colorful pictures of
    people or pets.

Books.   Basal readers, supplementary readers, trade
books--all kinds of books are used in an individualized reading program.   Although these types of books are utilized in
other kinds of reading programs, the major difference lies
in the manner in which they are used.   In an individualized
program all types of books are used as the basis for reading instruction; in other programs the reading instruction is
usually centered upon basal readers and supplementary readers, with trade books being used chiefly for recreational or
free reading periods.

When using basal readers and supplementary readers
in an individualized reading program, it is more desirable
to have a few copies of many different series than many
copies of one or two series.   When a trade book is likely to
be in great demand, it is a good plan to have two or three
copies on hand.   In some instances, one copy of each book
is sufficient.

Many books are provided during the year.   Estimates
made by teachers carrying out individualized reading pro-

grams indicate that a minimum of three titles per child is needed; therefore, in a class of thirty pupils, at least ninety books are required.

Since a wide range of reading ability is present in any one grade, books are available on many difficulty levels. At the first grade level books ranging in difficulty from the easiest picture books on a pre-reading level to books of at least third grade difficulty are provided. Continually throughout the year the range of reading ability within the class is assessed and the difficulty levels of materials adjusted accordingly.

Subject matter of the books is varied in order that there be material of interest to each class member. Animal stories, realistic stories dealing with commonplace happenings, science stories, social studies stories, and fairy tales are included in the collection of books.

Several procedures are useful in increasing an individual classroom supply of books. These include: (1) making arrangements with other teachers in the school to exchange books; (2) checking out books from the supply at the control administration building; (3) asking pupils to bring books from home to share with the class; and (4) obtaining books on a loan basis from the public library.

Other kinds of reading material. Some magazines such as Humpty Dumpty's Magazine and Highlights for Children contain stories written on a first grade reading level. If these magazines are not available at school, children may be asked to contribute copies from home.

Newspapers such as My Weekly Reader comprise another type of reading material; in some cases pamphlets and brochures such as those distributed by the National Dairy Council and the National Safety Council provide suitable reading materials.

Filmstrips designed especially for use in reading programs make a valuable contribution. These include such materials as the Textfilms which accompany The Alice and Jerry Basic Readers, filmstrips of well-known stories, and filmstrips intended for use in teaching phonetic and word-analysis skills.

Practice Materials

Numerous practice materials are needed in an individualized reading program. These practice materials are either teacher-prepared or commercially-prepared.

All practice materials are used to overcome a particular weakness or to reinforce a specific reading skill. If several children exhibit the same need, they are given the same exercise. In other cases, practice exercises are assigned on an individual basis.

All types of commercially-prepared reading workbooks are used. Since they are not used on a class-wide basis, it is better to have a few copies of many different workbooks than many copies of one or two workbooks.

If there are two copies of the same workbook available, the following procedure might be advisable: (1) tear the two workbooks apart; (2) mount on stiff paper the even pages from one of the workbooks and the odd pages from the second workbook; (3) cover each page with clear plastic; (4) file the pages according to the reading skill involved. When it is noted that a child needs practice on a specific skill, he can be given an appropriate exercise to complete (using either a marking pencil or a grease pencil). After the exercise has been completed and checked, the writing can be rubbed off and the page placed in the file ready for use by another pupil. Teacher-made exercises can also be prepared in the same manner and filed with the workbook exercises; thus, at all times, a wide variety of practice materials is ready for use.

Reading games and devices are valuable to provide needed practice on reading skills. Some of these are purchased commercially while others are teacher-prepared. Many suggestions on types of worthwhile teacher-prepared materials are offered in the following publications: Reading Aids Through The Grades, [2] Independent Activities for First Grade, [3] Purposeful Activities for Primary Grades, [4] Independent Activities for Creative Learning, [5] and Let's Play A Game. [6] Teachers' manuals accompanying textbook series and textbooks devoted to reading instruction also provide additional help to the teacher interested in preparing her own practice materials.

Grouping

Both total class group work and small group work are an important part of an individualized reading program.

Total class group work may be profitably employed when: (1) plans are being made for the reading period; (2) there is a desire to share reading experiences; (3) the reading period is being evaluated; and (4) the class is preparing a cooperative story based on a common interest or experience.

Small groups are formed for instructional purposes when: (1) two or more children share a common need in skill development; (2) two or more children have read the same book and wish to discuss the story; (3) there is a need for planning or sharing of ideas gained from individual reading. These small groups are flexible, short-term in nature, and brought together for a specific purpose. The membership of such groups changes as the needs change.

Skill Development

Skills cannot be neglected in an individualized reading program. However, there is no predetermined program for teaching skills to all pupils at specific times throughout the year; nor is there any limit to the number of skills which are introduced at the first grade level. The particular skills introduced and the rate of introduction depend upon the individual child; that is, skills are taught when they are needed and if they are needed.

In order to carry out an individualized reading program effectively, the teacher must be well-informed about reading skills. These skills are taught singly to an individual, to a small group, or, on rare occasions, to the total class.

Reading authorities use different classifications for the skills involved in reading. Regardless of the categories into which skills are divided, there is overlap, with some skills falling in more than one category. The following composite listing represents the skills mentioned for development at the primary level in literature which pertained to the teaching of reading:

I. Word Recognition Skills

   A. Recognizing whole words by sight
   B. Using configuration clues (studying the length, height, and peculiar characteristics of a word)
   C. Using context clues (examining the known words around the unfamiliar word in order to get a hint concerning the unknown word)
   D. Using picture clues (scrutinizing the picture for clues to the unknown word)
   E. Using phonetic analysis (associating appropriate sounds with printed words)
     1. Auditory discrimination
     2. Sounds of initial consonants
     3. Mental substitution of initial consonants
     4. Sounds of final consonants
     5. Mental substitution of final consonants
     6. Initial consonant digraphs (th, ch, sh, wh)
     7. Initial consonant blends
     8. Vowel sounds
   F. Using structural analysis (examining the structure of a word to gain a clue to its recognition)
     1. Inflectional endings: s, es, ed, ing
     2. Compound words
     3. Contractions
   G. Using the dictionary
     1. Picture dictionaries
     2. Beginning knowledge of alphabetical order

II. Comprehension Skills

   A. According to the reader's purpose
     1. Reading to find the main idea (i. e. , selecting the best title for a page or for a class-composed story)
     2. Reading to select important details (i. e. , answering such a question as "How old was Bobby?")
     3. Reading to answer questions (i. e. , reading a story to find out who went to the circus)
     4. Reading to establish sequence (i. e. , telling what happened first, next, and last in a story)
     5. Reading to follow directions (i. e. , drawing a picture from written directions)

      6. Reading to predict outcomes (i. e. , telling what is likely to happen next in a story)

      7. Reading to gain visual images (i. e. , describing what is visualized after reading a specific passage from a story)

B. According to the length and nature of the selection

      1. Phrase meaning (i. e. , matching phrases with words of similar meaning)

      2. Sentence meaning (i. e. , drawing a line under the one sentence which is illustrated by a picture)

      3. Paragraph meaning (i. e. , telling in one sentence what a paragraph is about)

      4. Meaning of longer selections (i. e. , telling in several sentences what a total story is about)

III. Study Skills

A. Selecting and evaluating information (i. e. , finding the part of the story that is exciting or humorous)

B. Organizing what is read (i. e. , telling what items belong in specific categories: animals, food, toys, colors, and so on)

C. Following directions (i. e. , following directions that are written on the chalkboard)

D. Locating information (i. e. , using the table of contents to locate a story)

IV. Critical Reading Skills

A. Comparing and contrasting
B. Drawing conclusions
C. Evaluating conclusions
D. Making inferences
E. Predicting outcomes
F. Arriving at generalizations
G. Distinguishing fact from fancy
H. Making judgments
I. Determining relevancy of statements

Critical reading involves all the skills of word meaning and comprehension; it also demands that the reader interpret the ideas which he has encountered. The abilities involved in critical reading are closely related to the abili-

ties involved in critical thinking.   (The listing above does not
represent all of the abilities involved in critical reading.)

The same methods are used in teaching reading skills
in an individualized program as in any other type of reading
program.   Teachers' manuals which accompany the different
basal reading series outline effective methods for teaching
reading skills and are consulted by any teacher needing help
in this area.   On Their Own In Reading[7] is an excellent
source to consult concerning the teaching of word recognition
skills.

Record Keeping

Teacher's Records

Systematic record keeping on the reading status of
each child is of utmost importance in an individualized reading program.   In order to facilitate the keeping and use of
the reading records, each teacher has a large loose-leaf notebook to serve as a record book.   For each class member,
several types of records are kept in this notebook.   These
records are: the Reading Readiness Check List, the Running
Log Record (anecdotal record), the Individual Reading Conference Record, the Cumulative Book List record, and the Reading Inventory.

In addition to the records kept in the loose-leaf notebook, a folder is established for each child in which samples
of his reading work are filed throughout the year.

Reading Readiness Check List.   Teacher observation
is one very important way to assess a child's readiness for
reading.   During the first few weeks of school, the Reading
Readiness Check List is completed for each child.   (See
sample on pages 179-182.)   After appraising each child's
readiness, definite provision is made in the instructional
program for work in the areas in which weakness is noted.

Reading Readiness Check List

Directions: Check (✓) in the appropriate column.

Name: _____

Date: _____

Physical Factors	Yes	No
Visual Development		
Is the child free from symptoms of visual difficulty, i. e., watery eyes, blinking, red eyes?		
Can he see printed material on the chalkboard when seated at his desk?		
Can he see likenesses and differences in work forms?		
Auditory Development		
Does he show through his responses to questions that he is able to hear?		
Is he able to discriminate sound elements in words (house, horse)?		
Speech Development		
Does he exhibit accurate enunciation and pronunciation?		
Does he use mature speech rather than baby talk?		
Is he free from gross speech defects, such as stuttering or lisping?		
Motor Development		
Does he have well-coordinated bodily movement in such activities as running and jumping?		
Does he have well-developed eye-hand coordination, e. g., can he trace a line with a crayon?		
Can he use scissors without difficulty?		

Reading Readiness Check List (Cont.)

	Yes	No
General Health		
Can he engage in normal school activities without undue fatigue?		
Is he free from evident physical handicaps?		
Does he appear to be getting an adequate amount of sleep?		

Social-Emotional Factors

	Yes	No
Social Development		
Does he like to work with a group?		
Does he accept authority?		
Does he share his belongings with others?		
Is he willing to share the teacher's attention with other pupils?		
Does he offer to help other children when they need help?		
Emotional Development		
Is he free from shyness and timidity?		
Is he willing to let other children be the center of attention?		
Is he generally happy and cheerful?		
Does he appear to be at ease in school?		
Does he accept criticism or opposition without crying, withdrawing, or displaying outbursts of temper?		

Prereading Interests and Skills

	Yes	No
Does he enjoy stories and poems?		
Does he show curiosity about signs, labels, and words?		
Does he voluntarily go to picture books and look at them?		
Can he interpret a picture?		

Reading Readiness Check List (Cont.)

	Yes	No
Does he have the reading skill of left-to-right progression?		
Mental Maturity		
Does he appear to be mentally alert?		
Does he pay careful attention for a short period of time?		
Does he follow simply stated directions?		
Can he remember the sequence of events in a story?		
Can he predict outcomes of a story?		
Does he seem resourceful in solving a problem?		
Is he able to memorize easily?		
Language Development		
Does he speak in sentences?		
Does he enjoy taking part in class discussions?		
Does he use correct English?		
Does he grasp the relationship between printed symbols and words?		
Does his listening and speaking vocabulary appear to be adequate for beginning reading?		
Ways of Working		
Does he stick to a task?		
Does he take care of books and other classroom materials?		
Does he enter into group activities with interest?		
Does he take pride in doing neat systematic independent work?		
Can he work independently for a short period of time?		

Reading Readiness Check List (Cont.)

Experiential Background	Yes	No
Is he acquainted with nursery rhymes, story books, and fairy tales?		
Is he familiar with common things in the environment (animals, food, transportation)?		
Does his family usually speak English at home?		
Is he acquainted with the community through trips?		
Does he have toys, books, tools, and other play materials?		

Running Log Record. In addition to the Reading Readiness Check List, during the prereading period it is desirable to record pertinent comments made by the child, behavior exhibited in reading situations, and reading interests expressed. This information is recorded on the Running Log Record (or anecdotal record). Each child has a page in the record book with his name at the top; then when the child says or does something which the teacher feels to be significant in relation to his performance, the information is recorded. (See sample below.) Comments about every child are not recorded daily or on any scheduled basis.

Running Log Record

Jane Bell

9/25 After the chart story was written, Jane was asked if she could read it. Knew all the words.

9/29 After school Jane said she wanted to show me something. She went back to the book table and got the book I Like Red. She pointed out three words she knew--I, red, the.

10/4 Jane said: "I read a book at home last night. I just love to read!"

Individual Reading Conference Record.   When children begin to read in books, a record of the progress of each individual as noted during the pupil-teacher conference is needed.   These records, one for each child, are inserted into the loose-leaf notebook, and additional records added as needed.   The record for the individual reading conference covers a double page spread--right and left sides of the notebook.   (See sample on pages 184-185)

Cumulative Book List.   Since some of the books a child reads may not be listed on the Individual Reading Conference Record, a page for each pupil entitled Cumulative Book List is included in the loose-leaf notebook.   (See sample below.)   This list, which is a recording of the titles of books read, can be placed immediately following the child's Individual Reading Conference Record.

Cumulative Book List

Mary Jones

1.   The Big Show

2.   Splash

3.   At Home and Away

4.   Come to the Farm

5.   Come with Us

6.

7.

Individual Reading Conference Record

Name: _____   *Reading Readiness Score: _____

Age: _____   *Mental Maturity Score: _____

**Read-ing Turn	Date	Book, Level, Pages	Skills		Oral Reading	
			Strengths	Weaknesses	Strengths	Weaknesses

* These items may be deleted if the teacher wishes to show parents the record form.
** The number of individual conferences each child has had throughout the year is recorded in the "reading turn" column.

Individual Reading Conference Record (cont.)

Interests	Special Work Needed	Group or Individual Assignment	Sharing	General Comments

Reading Inventory. In order to be sure all aspects of oral and silent reading are being evaluated, the Reading Inventory Record is completed at least once each month. (See sample on pages 186-189.) This record gives at a glance an indication of the pupil's present weaknesses as well as showing his progress throughout the year.

Folder of pupil's work. A folder is set up for each child in which samples of his reading papers are filed. It is not necessary to include every reading exercise completed by each child; only enough papers are included to show evidence of the child's progress.

Pupils' Records

For the first part of the year first graders are usually too limited in their writing ability to keep their own individual reading records. However, by the latter part of the year, some pupils who have the ability may desire to keep a simple listing of books read. One way that this may be handled is to give each child a sheet of lined writing paper on which he merely records the titles of the books read... [Samples follow.]

Reading Inventory Record

Directions: Check (✓) if the item applies

Name:_____	Book: Level: Date:	Book: Level: Date:	Book: Level: Date:	Book: Level: Date:
Oral Reading				
1. Poor comprehension				
2. Rate reads rapidly				
reads haltingly				
3. Voice control reads too loudly				
reads too softly				
high pitch				

Reading Inventory Record (cont.)

Directions: Check (✓) if the item applies

	Book: Level: Date:	Book: Level: Date:	Book: Level: Date:	Book: Level: Date:
sounds tense				
reads without expression				
4. Faulty enunciation				
5. Rhythm				
reads word by word				
phrases inappropriately				
reads through punctuation				
6. Word recognition poor sight vocabulary				
inadequate use of phonetic-analysis skills				
inadequate use of context clues				
inadequate use of picture clues				
inadequate use of structural-analysis skills				
add words				
skip words				
repeat words				
substitute words				
reverse words (was, saw)				

Reading Inventory Record (cont.)

	Book: Level: Date:	Book: Level: Date:	Book: Level: Date:	Book: Level: Date:
Silent Reading				
1. Habits				
finger pointing				
head movement				
tension movements (moves hands, legs, feet, body)				
vocalization silent lip movement				
posture holds book too close				
holds book too far away				
visual factors squints				
rubs eyes				
blinks				
frowns				
2. Rate				
reads haltingly				
reads rapidly				
3. Comprehension				
inability to state main ideas				
inability to answer questions				
inability to predict outcomes				
inability to recall details				

3. Comprehension (cont.)				
inability to recall sequence of events				
inability to locate information				

Established Routines

Some routine procedures are established with children in order that the reading period proceed smoothly. The routines which every first grade teacher plans (what a pupil should do if he cannot locate his pencil, what he should do when he completes an assignment, what he should do if he has difficulty in completing an independent assignment) are also carefully arranged for in an individualized program.

In addition to the usual routines encountered in every type of reading program, two routines given special consideration by teachers using an individualized reading program are: (1) developing a procedure for pupils to follow when selecting and returning books; and (2) planning for ways to help pupils with unknown words which they encounter in their independent reading.

Selecting and Returning Books

After the first few weeks in first grade, some pupils are ready to engage in individual reading. At that time, they will require much teacher help and guidance in choosing reading material which is of interest to them and which is at the proper difficulty level. These are ways in which this assistance is given:

1. A special time is set aside each day when the teacher will be at the book table to aid individual pupils in selecting a book.

2. Several appropriate books are suggested at the time of the individual pupil-teacher conference.

3. Suggestions are offered to individual pupils during the sharing period. For example, a comment such as this might be given: "John, I'm sure you would enjoy the book that Mary just finished reading.

Maybe you can read it next."

4. A spot of colored tape (one color for hard books, one color for easy books, and still another for books "in between") is placed on the inside of the book to indicate the difficulty level. Children are informed of the meaning of the various colors of tape, and use this key to gain an indication of the difficulty of the book. For example, if a child read a book which he thought was too easy for him, one distinguished with a spot of red tape, when selecting the next book he might look for a book with green tape--an indication that this book was more difficult.

This listing does not exhaust the possibilities for aiding pupils in their selection of books; numerous other ways can be developed by teachers.

Children keep the books they are currently reading in their desks; however, a procedure for returning the books after they have been read must be worked out with pupils. The procedure followed depends to some extent upon the procedure developed for selecting books. One or more of the following ways can be used:

1. Pupils return all books to the teacher at the time of the individual reading conference.

2. A few minutes are taken at the end of each reading period to return books to the proper place.

3. Pupils return books to the tables or shelves any time during the reading period.

4. One shelf in the room is labeled "Returned Books;" monitors are then selected to place the books on the appropriate shelf or table.

Helping Children With Unknown Words

Especially at first grade level, children are likely to encounter several unknown words when reading silently; therefore, some procedures for giving assistance are developed.

Assistance is provided by:

1. Keeping experience charts in evidence around the
   room; when the child comes upon an unknown word,
   he can read through the charts and possibly locate
   the word in familiar context. Then he will be able
   to recognize the word in the new context.

2. Having picture dictionaries--either commercial or
   class-made--available.

3. Encouraging children to help each other in recognizing an unfamiliar word.

4. Planning the seating arrangement of pupils in such
   a way that a more-able child is seated by a less-
   able child.

5. Enlisting the aid of upper grade children to serve
   as assistants during the reading period. (Perhaps
   a different pupil could come to the room each day
   until all have served as assistants; then the schedule could be repeated. In this way, the problem
   of several pupils missing a great amount of their
   own instruction would be eliminated.)

6. Having a small group gather at the reading table
   for silent reading and individual conferences. With
   this arrangement, pupils are near the teacher, and
   she can quickly help each child having difficulty,
   even during the time an individual conference is being held.

Getting the Room Ready

All types of materials reflecting the importance and
joy of reading are utilized in the classroom. Bulletin boards,
displays of books, labels, signs, experience charts--all these,
as well as countless other ideas, are employed to encourage
and stimulate interest in reading.

In each classroom there are several activity centers
such as a cut and paste center, a paint center, a dramatic
play center or doll corner, a puzzle center, a reading activity center, and an arithmetic center. Careful teacher-
group planning is needed concerning rules and procedures pupils are to follow while working at the centers. In this way,
children are guided toward self-direction and self-control

while working independently, and many problems concerning pupil behavior are avoided.

These activity centers are introduced one at a time, with a new one being set up only after the ones already in use are being used profitably by the children.   Early in the school year the teacher moves around the room and is available to supervise while pupils are working at the centers. Gradually, as children develop self-direction, the teacher withdraws this supervision; thus she is free to carry out individual pupil conferences or small group instruction.

The supply of books is located conveniently on either low shelves or a large table.   A check is made to make sure that children can move to and from the book supply with relative ease.

A quiet spot in the room is selected as the place to hold the individual reading conferences.   Here pupils come one at a time for conferences or a small group of pupils come to the conference corner at the same time.

Furniture of the room is arranged in such a manner that space is available for small group work.

In making a final check to determine if the room is ready for individualized reading, these points, then, are considered:

1. Does the room offer pupils a constant invitation to read?

2. Are several activity centers ready for use?

3. Are the books and other reading materials conveniently located?

4. Is there a place where the individual reading conferences can be held?

5. Is there a place for small groups to meet?

If the teacher can answer these five questions in the affirmative, then the room is ready.

Initiation of the Program

Getting Children Ready for Individualized Reading

The teacher working toward an individualized reading program works in the same way as the teacher getting children ready to read in any other type of reading program. The same published readiness materials are utilized; however, they do not constitute the total readiness program, as more emphasis is given to developing readiness through a variety of classroom experiences.

Results of the Reading Readiness Check List and the standardized readiness test administered during the first few weeks of school help the teacher in appraising the level of development of each child.   For those pupils needing additional readiness activities, suitable experiences are provided. Valuable suggestions concerning types of worthwhile experiences are offered in such sources as Growing Into Reading,[8] Readiness for School Beginners,[9] and Reading Readiness.[10]

During the readiness period a start is made on developing initial sight vocabulary.   Sight vocabulary is developed through total class group work, small group work, and individual work.

The following procedures are used:

1. Reading many cooperative teacher-pupil composed chart stories.

2. Reading many individually composed stories-- stories which have been dictated by an individual pupil to the teacher.

3. Reading teacher-prepared news stories.   (Each day a story is developed by the teacher, one related to a current classroom event.)

4. Using the preprimers of one or more basal reading series with one or more small groups.

In using experience stories and teacher-prepared stories for building initial sight vocabulary, the teacher is faced with the problem of deciding which words to develop as sight words, since in an individualized program pupils

will be reading in many different books.   It is impossible to
know precisely which words the child will encounter; however,
analyses of vocabulary load in various books have been made
and lists compiled of the most frequently used words.   These
lists provide a core of words which children are likely to
meet repeatedly, regardless of the type of book read.   Any
words appearing on these lists would then be suitable to develop as sight words.

The following two lists serve as sources from which
to select words to develop for initial sight vocabulary:[11]

115 Words Introduced in Seven Basal Reading Preprimers

a	dish	in	pretty
airplane	do	is	puppy
an	dog	it	
and	down		ran
apple		jump	red
are	father		ride
at	fast	kitten	run
away	find		
	fine	like	said
baby	fish	little	see
ball	for	look	she
be	funny		show
bed		make	sleep
birthday	get	may	something
blue	girl	me	splash
boat	go	mitten	stop
bow-bow	good	mother	surprise
	good-by	morning	
cake	green	my	table
call			thank
can	has	near	that
cap	have	no	the
car	he	not	three
Christmas	help		to
come	her	oh	toy
cookies	here	on	two
cowboy	hide	one	
	home		up
daddy	house	party	
did		pie	want
dinner	I	play	we

what	will	work	your
where	with	yellow	

109 Words Common to Six or More of Seven
Basal Reading Series
(preprimers, primers, and first readers)

a	happy	out	went
all	have	over	what
am	help		when
and	her	play	where
at	here	put	white
away	him		who
	his	ran	will
back	home	red	with
be	house	ride	
big		run	you
blue	I		your
boat	in	said	
boy	is	sat	
but		saw	
	jump	see	
call	just	she	
came		so	
can	know	something	
come		stop	
could	laugh		
	like	thank	
did	little	that	
do	look	the	
dog		then	
	make	there	
eat	man	they	
	may	this	
farm	me	three	
fast	mother	time	
for	my	to	
from		too	
fun	night	toy	
funny	no	two	
	not		
get	now	up	
go			
good	of	want	
	on	was	
had	one	we	

Introducing Individualized Reading

Children are ready to start on individualized reading in first grade as soon as they have established a beginning sight vocabulary and can read independently in beginning books.

There are two major ways to introduce individualized reading: (1) one-group-at-a-time change-over, and (2) individualizing reading all at once with the entire class. [12]

One-group-at-a-time change-over works as follows: as soon as the teacher has appraised each child's stage of readiness, children with similar reading abilities are placed into groups. In most cases three groups are formed. Reading instruction is given in groups, although total class experiences are also provided through such an activity as developing experience charts. When a group has developed an initial sight vocabulary, has read one or more preprimers, and is well underway in learning to read, they are allowed to engage in individualized reading--selecting their own reading material, and meeting for individual conferences with the teacher. The rest of the class continues to meet in groups for reading instruction. Gradually, as children participating in individualized reading are settled and making progress, a second reading group is disbanded and these pupils start on their way in individualized reading. This procedure continues until all children in the class are reading on an individualized basis.

This description illustrates the one-group-at-a-time change-over plan:

> In the fall my first grade class was still in ability groups and many of the children were still not quite ready to read in books. The fast group had written many short stories, used readiness materials, the big book (state series), and had read several preprimers... Our library corner contained many other preprimers. I noticed a few of the children looking through these books. One day a boy who was reading very well brought up one of the books to me and said, "Mrs. Young, some of the books over there are easy to read! May we read them?" Before long others were doing the same and gradually the faster readers began to choose books to read. [13]

In this particular classroom the pupils themselves developed
the interest in reading self-selected books; in other cases the
teacher explains to the pupils in the group that they can now
select their own books and thus the children start in individualized reading.

Individualizing the reading programs all at once with
the entire class works in this way: The first few weeks are
spent in getting acquainted, and carrying out the readiness
program using published readiness materials as well as numerous class activities. At this time sight vocabulary is being developed through the reading of many group experience
stories, individually dictated stories, and teacher-prepared
news stories. When it is noted that several children (or
even one child) have developed a small sight vocabulary, they
are introduced to reading from a supply of varied pre-
primers--fifteen to twenty-five or more--with each child selecting the book he wants to read. These children then meet
individually with the teacher each day as well as engaging in
the on-going group activities. As other children develop
sight vocabularies, they, too, meet individually with the
teacher. This procedure continues until all children in the
room are engaging in individualized reading.

Modifications of both of the procedures mentioned for
initiating the program can be made. For example, in the
one-group-at-a-time change-over, each group can start by
being only partially individualized; that is, they continue to
meet as a group during the morning reading period but read
on an individualized basis during the afternoon reading period.

Each teacher initiates individualized reading in the
way which seems best suited to her own class; in addition,
the procedure selected is the one which she feels secure in
using.

The Reading Period

Schedule for A Reading Period

After all pupils are engaging in individualized reading,
these activities are included in the reading period:

Teacher-pupil planning.
Independent reading, related reading activities, and

work at the centers while pupil-teacher conferences
are being held.
Small group instruction on skills.
Total class group work--composing experience stories.
Sharing of books read individually.
Teacher-pupil evaluation of independent work.
Total class evaluation of the reading period.

All these activities are not included in every reading period;
neither would every reading period be carried out in exactly
the same way.

In first grade approximately two hours are scheduled
for reading, the time being divided into a morning and an
afternoon period. A suggested reading schedule for the day
includes the following:

Morning Period

Planning with pupils; giving directions for independent
work.
Small group instruction on skills--two or three
groups. (On some days individual pupil-teacher
conferences might be scheduled here.)
Teacher-pupil evaluation of independent work.
Total class group work--sharing of books or composing a chart story.

Afternoon Period

Planning with pupils; giving directions for independ-
ent work.
Individual pupil-teacher conferences.
Teacher-pupil evaluation of independent work.
Group evaluation of the reading period.

In planning the reading period for first graders, the
length of children's attention span and their need for varied
activities are considered. The period is planned in such a
way that children move from one type of instructional situation to another, rotating among total group instruction, individual instruction, and small group instruction.

Activities in the Reading Period

Teacher-pupil planning. The reading period will not

proceed smoothly unless children in the class have developed
the ability to work for short periods of time without close
teacher supervision.   Therefore, an important goal for each
teacher is that of helping children develop good independent
work habits.

Teacher-pupil planning is essential for developing pupil self-direction while engaging in independent work.   There
is a time for planning before each reading period begins.   At
the end of this planning session each child understands exactly what he is to do and is able to proceed without further assistance from the teacher.

A chart listing all of the possible activities is made by
the teacher; then, during the planning time, names of pupils
who are to engage in each activity are added to the chart.
(Name tags are inserted in slots on the chart in order that
the same chart can be used again and again.)   Some of the
activities are assigned by the teacher, such as assigning to
certain pupils the task of completing practice exercises; for
other activities, each child makes his own selection according to his interest and special reading needs.

Usually first graders cannot work on any one thing for
a long period of time.   Therefore, plans are made for each
pupil to engage in more than one activity during the independent work period.

During the planning session, the conference schedule
for the day is developed.   The names of those children who
wish a conference (or who are scheduled for a conference)
are recorded.   If small group instruction is planned for the
period, names of pupils who are to meet are also posted.
The same procedure is followed if a sharing time is scheduled for the period.   Time is saved if the teacher makes a
chart for recording the conference schedule, the sharing
schedule, and the small group work schedule.

Independent work.   If a grouping arrangement is used
during the reading period, children engage in silent reading
when meeting with the group; however, if a grouping arrangement is not employed, the first independent activity for each
child is reading his book (or part of his book) silently.

The same types of practice materials used in any other reading program are used in an individualized reading
program.

These exercises, either teacher-prepared or commercially-prepared, are assigned on the basis of need. If several children exhibit similar needs, they are given the same exercise. In many instances, exercises are assigned individually to one child.

There are many creative types of independent work which can be developed in relation to the child's individual reading. Some of the types which are suitable for first grade children include:

1. Art Activities (cut and paste, painting, and crayon)
   (a) Illustrating the main characters in a story
   (b) Illustrating the main events in sequence
   (c) Drawing a cartoon picture of a funny part of a story
   (d) Drawing a picture of the part of a story liked best
   (e) Making a book jacket for a story
   (f) Making a cumulative picture story book
   (g) Making simple puppets for the characters in a story
   (h) Illustrating a different ending for a story

2. Writing Activities
   (a) Keeping an individual record of the books read
   (b) Listing titles of stories liked best in a book containing several stories
   (c) Writing a riddle about a character in a story
   (d) Listing several words from a book (such as boy, apple, bear, car); then finding a picture to illustrate each one
   (e) Writing sentences to tell about three illustrations in a book
   (f) Making a list of all the words beginning with a certain letter (such as b) on two or three pages in a story

3. Activities Involving Both Art and Writing
   (a) Making picture scrapbooks organized around such topics as animals, food, people, transportation, clothes, plants
   (b) Making an alphabet scrapbook, writing the letters on each page and finding pictures to illustrate them
   (c) Making a consonant scrapbook
   (d) Organizing a scrapbook showing rhyming words

(e) Organizing a picture dictionary

Activity centers arranged in the classroom provide another type of experience in which children can engage during
the independent work period.

The conference period. Conferences for the reading
period are scheduled during the planning session. These conferences can be scheduled on a voluntary basis, with children
indicating their desire to meet with the teacher; they can be
scheduled on a partly voluntary basis with all children given
the opportunity to volunteer, but with the teacher also adding
names of children who have not had a conference the previous day(s); or the conferences can be scheduled by some
predetermined basis--pupil needs, alphabetically, by tables,
or by rows. Regardless of which procedure is employed,
care is taken to make sure that all children have conferences,
and that a few children are not getting the major portion of
the conference time. Keeping a record of the number of
times each child has had a conference assures the teacher
that each child is getting his "reading turn."

Each conference lasts from five to ten minutes; therefore, it is impossible for all pupils to meet with the teacher
each day. The conference schedule is planned in such a way
that each pupil meets individually with the teacher at least
every three days and possibly every two days. On the days
when pupils are not scheduled to meet individually with the
teacher, they engage in some type of teacher-directed activity during the reading period (either small group situations
or total group situations).

The physical setting for the conference is in one corner of the room. Either the teacher's chair and a chair for
the pupil are located here, or a reading table is provided
where several children meet at the same time. Regardless
of which arrangement is selected, a certain degree of privacy is maintained during the individual conference in order
that each child may get the important feeling that "this is my
special time with the teacher."

The individual conferences are definite teaching situations, and as such, three aspects of a child's reading are
investigated: (1) his understanding of and reaction to the
story; (2) his ability to deal with the mechanics of reading;
(3) his ability to read orally. [14] Skillful questioning is needed in order to investigate the first two aspects; good listen-

ing and careful observation are called for in evaluating the
third aspect.

Although the kind of questioning pursued is determined
by the specific material read, questions such as these can
be used for investigating the pupil's understanding of and reaction to a story:

1. Why did you choose this book?
2. Which character did you like best? Why?
3. Did you like to read this story? Why?
4. Can you tell me what happened in the story?
5. What part of the story did you like best? Why?[15]

Questions such as these can be used for investigating the pupil's ability to deal with the mechanics of reading:

1. Was the book hard for you, easy for you, or just
   right? How can you tell?
2. How do you know that you are reading better than
   you did?
3. With what words did you have difficulty?
4. Were there any words that you didn't know at first
   but later figured out? How did you do it?[16]

In evaluating the child's ability to read orally, the
teacher watches for such things as smoothness of reading,
expressiveness of voice, indications that the story is meaningful to the child (for example, laughing at a funny part),
rate of reading, and use of word recognition skills.   The
Reading Inventory gives a more complete listing of items for
the teacher to observe.   At intervals a tape recording is
made of each child's oral reading.   Then it is possible for
the teacher to make a careful analysis of certain aspects of
each child's oral reading at a time when the class is not
present.

In ending the conference, plans are made for future
activities, such as working on a special weakness, developing an interesting way to share a story with the group, or
selecting a new book to read.

In order to be better prepared for the conference, the
teacher established a card file (5 x 8 cards) of all the books
available in her classroom.   On each card these items are
recorded: (1) title of book; (2) difficulty level; (3) comprehension questions suited to the book; (4) a listing of some of

the difficult vocabulary; and (5) pages or paragraphs which are well suited for oral reading. Then, when a child comes for his conference, the appropriate card is taken from the file and specific helps for investigating the child's reading are on hand.

Group Work. Since group work is discussed in relation to grouping and skill development, the topic is not considered here.

Sharing. The sharing period is a very valuable part of the reading period. Books which are shared enthusiastically by pupils become irresistible to other children; thus, teachers are not faced with the problem of trying to locate a book which will interest each child. Many of the children will have decided which book they want to read next after hearing about it during the sharing period.

Every effort is made to keep the sharing period interesting and stimulating. This goal can be achieved by taking time to help children plan different ways of telling about books. First grade pupils can use these ways to share their books:

1. Show an illustration from the book and tell why you like it.
2. Tell only the beginning of the story; let the class predict how it might end.
3. Read an exciting or funny page aloud.
4. Tell whether the story is true or make believe. Show a picture you made about the story to prove your decision is right.
5. Perform an experiment given in the book. (Especially good for science stories.)
6. Tell about the characters in the book. Then tell a riddle about one of the characters and have the class guess the answer.
7. Pantomime one of the characters in the story. Have the class guess who the character might be. (Good for animal stories--bears, ducks, rabbits)
8. Prepare a dramatization of part of the story. (Usable when two or more pupils have read the same story)
9. Show a painting which illustrates one part of the story.
10. Show pictures drawn of the main events in the story; have the class try to tell a story from the

pictures.
11. Make simple puppets and give a puppet show.

To add variety, some days the sharing situation can be planned as a television show, or a radio program.

Much of the sharing takes place in the total class situation. However, sharing also occurs in small groups. On these occasions, several small groups are formed, and one child is selected to serve as chairman in each group. The teacher then rotates among the groups.

Teacher-pupil evaluation of independent work. After an independent work period, the teacher spends a brief time informally evaluating the independent work completed. During this time, the teacher walks around the room observing the work of the children and making comments to each pupil or to small groups who have been working together. This type of informal evaluation is necessary in order that children realize the work in which they engage without close teacher supervision is important.

During the sharing period, opportunities are also utilized to evaluate independent work. For example, if a child shows a painting which illustrates a story he has read, teacher comments are directed to the quality of his work. (When making such comments with the total class as an audience, discretion must be used in giving criticisms.)

Evaluation of the reading period. At regular intervals, perhaps even daily in the beginning of an individualized reading program, time is taken for group evaluation of the reading period. Discussion centers upon such aspects as: (1) In what ways did the reading period go well?; (2) How could we improve it?; (3) Did we complete our independent work? If not, why not?; and (4) Is there any part that we should especially try to improve?

In addition to a general evaluation, specific parts of the period can be thoroughly appraised. For example, if the sharing period did not proceed smoothly, specific ideas can be enumerated on ways of working to make it better. Through careful evaluation sessions, children grow in self-evaluation and self-direction.

Evaluation of an Individualized Reading Program

Basic to the success of an individualized reading program is continuous use of evaluation procedures. All types of data are utilized in the evaluation process: intelligence tests, mental maturity tests, standardized reading tests, teacher-made tests, workbook exercises, teacher-made exercises, Individual Reading Conference Records, Cumulative Book Lists, Reading Inventory Records, Running Log Records, samples of children's reading papers, comments made by each child about his reading, and comments made by parents about their child's reading.

From appraisal of these data, each child's strengths and weaknesses in reading are noted and plans made for providing the types of experiences best suited to each child's stage of development. Thus, evaluation gives direction to learning and can rightly be considered an integral part of teaching reading in an individualized reading program.

Notes

1. The term sight vocabulary refers to words that are memorized or recognized as a whole.

2. Russell, David H. and Karp, Etta E. Reading Aids Through the Grades (New York, Columbia University Press, 1951).

3. Minneapolis Public Schools, Minneapolis, Minnesota Independent Activities for First Grade Minneapolis, Department of Elementary Education, 1956.

4. Indianapolis Public Schools, Indianapolis, Indiana Purposeful Activities for the Primary Grades (Indianapolis, Division of Curriculum and Supervision, 1958).

5. Darrow, Helen Fisher and Allen, R. Van Independent Activities for Creative Learning Practical Suggestions for Teaching, Number 21, Alice Miel, editor (New York, Bureau of Publications, Teachers College, Columbia University).

6. Let's Play a Game. Suggestions for Games Independent Activities for Developing Reading Skills (Boston,

Ginn and Company).

7. Gray, William S. On Their Own in Reading (Chicago,
   Scott, Foresman and Company, 1960).

8. Monroe, Marion Growing Into Reading (Chicago, Scott,
   Foresman and Company, 1951).

9. Hildreth, Gertrude Readiness for School Beginners
   (Yonkers-on-Hudson, World Book Company, Inc.,
   1950).

10. Harrison, M. Lucille Reading Readiness (Boston,
    Houghton Mifflin Company, 1939).

11. Reeve, Olive R. "The Vocabulary of Seven Primary
    Reading Series" Elementary English, 35 (April,
    1958), p. 237-39.

12. Veatch, Jeannette, 583, p. 48.

13. Dickinson, Marie 137, p. 157.

14. Veatch, Jeannette 583, p. 52-53.

15. Ibid.

16. Ibid.

Chapter 6

Individualized Reading Procedures

Teacher-Pupil Conferences

At the very heart of the individualized reading approach is the concept of the teacher-pupil individual conference during which the major aspects of evaluation and instruction take place. It is here that the individual attention given to the pupil helps him with his tasks and enables the teacher to assess his progress.

In Gertrude M. Sullivan's master's thesis, the information given by 47 Rhode Island teachers who responded to an inquiry about their use of individual teacher-pupil conferences is set forth. A summary of this information has been excerpted from her thesis and is presented as the first passage in this chapter.

A conference check-list, found to be useful by Sylvia W. Roston in her primary classroom, is taken from her thesis and included next.

This is followed by a discussion by Doris D. Roettger of the way in which conferences can be used to develop specific reading skills.

Obviously a teacher must keep some sort of records of his conferences. The excerpt from Anna M. Hune's master's thesis suggests record keeping procedures and is the final selection in this section.

Sharing

It has been said that individualized reading procedures eliminate all group activity. The fact is that there are many opportunities for group work in this approach. One of the most frequent whole-class activities engaged in during the individualized reading period is "sharing." Here children tell their classmates about their reading in a wide variety of ways

Amy E. Jensen and Auline L. Bailey include in their masters' theses lists of possible ways in which sharing can take place.

Record-Keeping

The success of an individualized reading program depends in part on an adequate system of record-keeping. Since children are working on individual tasks and reading different books, it is essential that a record of some kind be kept. It is equally important that the record-keeping not be so demanding and so time consuming as to interfere with reading activities.

The passage taken from Dorothy L. Donahue's master's thesis discusses procedures in record-keeping.

Combining Programs

In Chapter 4 a selection by McKay is included, which reports on a survey of teachers who were combining individualized reading and basal reading procedures in their classrooms. In this section an excerpt is presented from an article by Gudelia and Raymond B. Fox, who advocate such a combination.

How 47 Teachers Used Teacher-Pupil Conferences in
the Individualized Reading Program

by

Gertrude M. Sullivan

(This material is excerpted from the author's 1966
Rhode Island College master's thesis, A Study of
the Conference Technique in Reading Instruction
Among Elementary Teachers of Rhode Island.)

Source of Reading Material

Source	Number
Room library	42
School library	35
Home	29
Public Library	11
Teacher's personal book supply	5
Book clubs	5
Bookmobiles	4
Exchange with other pupils	3

Activities During Independent Reading Period

Activity	Number
Reading silently	46
Select a book	34
Ask teacher for help with words	22
Ask other pupils for help	18
Write reports of reading	15
Read orally to other pupils	11
Read orally to teacher	10
Illustrate stories	2
Oral sharing	2

Grade Level of Use of the Conference

Grade	Use of conference		
level	Yes	No	Total
6	3	3	6
5	3	2	5
4	2	3	5
3	4	3	7
2	6	2	8
1	10	5	15
Remedial	4	0	4

Note: Some teachers reported teaching plural grades

Time, Length, and Frequency of Conferences

Total weekly time	Frequency	Minutes per conference	Indi-vidualized	Grade
10 hours	varies	30	Yes	3
7.5 hours	2 days	20	Yes	1
5 hours	2 days	5	Yes	1-2
5 hours	2 per week	5	Yes	1
4.5 hours	3 per week	3	Yes	1
3.75 hours	daily	2-3	Yes	1
3 hours	2 per week	10	No	4
3 hours	3-4 days	5	Yes	1
2.5-3 hours	weekly	5-10	No	1
1-1.5 hours	varies	--	Yes	6
1-1.5 hours	weekly	5-10	No	2
1.5 hours	varies	10	Yes	3
1 hour	weekly	2	Yes	5
1 hours	daily	few	No	3
1 hour	weekly	5-6	Yes	2
45 min.	2 days	3-5	No	5-6
30-45 min.	monthly	5	No	4
20 min.	bimonthly	1-2	Yes	1
15-20 min.	varies	few	Yes	1
15 min.	2-3 per week	5-10	Yes	3

Conference Activities

| | Number of |
Activity	teachers
Diagnosis of reading problems	24
Vocabulary check and development	24
Discussion and questioning	22
Development of word attack skills	21
Oral reading	20
Recording of pupil progress	16
Planning for future reading	14
Development of study skills	13
Silent reading	8
Going over book reports	4
Comprehension check	1
References	1
Checking on returned library books	1

Rank Order of Importance of Conference Activities

Rank	Activity
1	Vocabulary check and development
2	Diagnosis of reading problems
3	Development of word attack skills
4	Discussion and questioning
5	Oral reading
6	Development of study skills
7	Silent reading
8	Planning for future reading
9	Recording of pupil progress
10	Going over book reports

Greatest contribution of the conference. The outstanding advantage of the individual pupil-teacher conference
over group teaching of reading, as reported by teachers, is
the one-to-one relationship between pupil and teacher.   Although variously expressed by different teachers, the same
underlying thought was found in all responses.   All stress
the importance of the child as an individual.   The conference's contributions to the teaching of reading, as expressed

by various teachers, are:

1. The conference allows an exclusive personal relationship between teacher and child. The guarantee of the teacher's individual attention is of special benefit to the retarded reader.

2. The individual attention helps the child to assess his own particular problems, strengths, and weaknesses. It helps the teacher to get to know better both the child himself and his reading needs and abilities.

3. The success or failure of the child is private.

4. The assurance of exclusive teacher interest helps the individual child to develop greater self-confidence and he is stimulated to greater effort in reading.

Weaknesses.   There was little disagreement among the respondents as to the conference's weaknesses.   The major disadvantage is lack of time.   Giving adequate attention to all the areas of reading which belong in the conference is time consuming and poses a serious problem to teachers who use the conference technique.

Another difficulty, which is especially hard for the first grade teachers, is planning for the rest of the class so that the conference may proceed with a minimum of interruptions.

Teacher skills.   "The teacher who uses the conference technique," reported one respondent, "needs the same skills as any good teacher of reading."   More specifically, a teacher must have the following qualities:

1. He must be patient, understanding, kind, friendly, interested in the child, and considerate of the child's feelings.

2. He must have a thorough knowledge of the stages of developmental reading and of the reading skills needed at each level.

3. He must be familiar with many books.

4. He must be able to establish rapport (a calm, re-
   laxed child and a teacher who is not easily dis-
   tracted by the rest of the class constitute the first
   step).

5. He must have the ability to diagnose a child's
   reading problems, to clarify his skills and weaknesses, and to work with him at his individual
   reading level.

6. He must have skill in questioning. The right kind
   of question will bring forth the child's ideas and
   stimulate discussion.

7. He must have the ability to listen and to guide by
   suggestion rather than by direct order.

A Checklist for Teacher-Pupil Conferences

by

Sylvia Willner Roston

(This material is excerpted from the author's 1962 National College of Education master's thesis, <u>An Individualized Reading Program in a First and Second Grade.</u>)

I come to a reading conference

1. _____ to learn more about what I am reading.

2. _____ to tell the teacher about what I have read.

3. _____ to get help in sounding out words.

4. _____ just because I like to read to the teacher.

5. _____ to let the teacher know what I have read.

6. _____ to tell about the book I read.

7. _____ because I like help in choosing a book.

8. _____ because I get more attention than reading by myself.

9. _____ because I like to answer the questions the teacher asks.

I do not come to reading conferences often because

10. _____ I like to read a lot before I come.

11. _____ It takes such a long time to read a book.

12. _____ I don't like to answer the teacher's questions.

13. _____ I don't like to read to the teacher.

14. _____ I don't read very much.

15. _____ the teacher may think that the book I'm reading is too hard.

16. _____ the teacher may think that the book is too easy.

I take books home at night because
17. _____ I enjoy reading them.
18. _____ it will make my parents happy.
19. _____ it will make my teacher happy.
20. _____ I like to read to my parents.

I do not take books home at night because
21. _____ I would rather do other things.
22. _____ I don't like to read.
23. _____ I am afraid I will lose the book.
24. _____ my parents don't want me to bring them
             home

When I take a book home
25. _____ I read aloud to my parents most of the time.
26. _____ I read to myself most of the time.

Using Teacher-Pupil Conference to Develop
Reading Skills

by

Doris Dornfeld Roettger

(This material is excerpted from the author's 1964
University of Tennessee master's thesis, <u>The Effectiveness of an Individualized Reading Program
in Developing Reading Skills and Interest in Reading.</u>)

Individual Conferences

Teachers held conferences with each child once or
twice a week. Although it is impossible to state precisely
the length of these conferences, they tended to be from five
to ten minutes in duration. In addition, the teacher talked
briefly each day to a number of children at their desks about
their books.

The individual conferences involved diagnosing, teaching, listening, sharing, evaluating, discussing and planning.
The plan of the conferences was flexible and was determined
by the needs of the child and the immediate purpose of the
teacher. In each conference the teacher and the child engaged in only one or two activities such as (1) checking a
child's comprehension of the meaning of a specific chapter or
passage, (2) singling out words to check the child's word attack skills, (3) exploring a child's feeling toward the main
character, (4) teaching the child a specific skill, or (5) making an assignment to reinforce a skill. In each conference,
however, the child read orally a section which he had chosen
and prepared in advance. During the conference the teacher
noted the child's strengths and weaknesses, skills developed
or to be learned, and similar data.

How One Teacher Kept Records on Her Conferences
with Pupils

by

Anna Marie Hess Hune

(This material is excerpted from the author's 1959
Ohio State University master's thesis, The Organization, Implementation and Evaluation of an Individualized Program in an Upper Socio-Economic
Community.)

Teacher-Pupil Conference Records

Date

2/12 Reading Salute. Seems to understand and enjoy
book. Help given in pronouncing proper names and multi-
syllable words. Tendency to read too fast; some repetition
of words; occasionally overlooks periods.

Provide opportunity to select and read a short story
to group. Reviewed oral reading goals. Suggested pupil locate on map places mentioned in stories he reads. Assigned
seat-work in syllabication--p. 39 and 59 in Friends Far and
Near Workbook.

2/21 Commented on work done with syllabication.
Would rather just read. Preparing for oral reading The Lob-
ster Roast by Amy Wentworth Stone. Read one page. Set
up date for same. Has finished Dr. Trotter and His Big
Gold Watch and now reading The Lucky Baseball Bat. Needs
to think more about sharing his reading interests.

2/27 Read from Whitey and the Rustlers. Discussed
book. Recommended more difficult reading. Assigned "Lou
Gehrig, Yankee Hero" from Believe and Make-Believe, for
study. Use glossary for word meanings; explain batting averages; compare batting averages of other famous ball players.

218

3/6 Read aloud from Here Comes Kristie. Hesitant
about proper names. Still a tendency to read too fast.
Wanted more baseball stories. Asked how teacher knew he
liked sports and horses. Discussed ways of locating materials. Will arrange to have child help librarian.

3/11 Discussed Buddy and the Old Pro. Located
material to suit his interest. "A neat story!" Displeased
with poor sportsmanship. Beginning to understand that win-
ning the game might not be the most important thing in school
sponsored sports. Would be unlikely to admit this to his
peers. Suggested locating and reading other sports stories--
try basic reading series.

3/21 Discussed Penny Goes to Camp. Book chosen
because he was going to camp next summer. Excited about
it. Commented "Funny how your parents know better than
you what you will like." Used High Roads (Grade 4 reading
text) to check ability to locate materials.

3/25 Discussed Freddy. Displayed well-developed
sense of humor. Commented, "Easy to confuse grown-ups.
This make-believe story is good; fairy tales mostly silly;
like funny stories." Suggested that he find name by which
"make-believe" stories were known and then to locate, read
and list such stories. Work to be completed by 3/28.
Check during reading time.

4/3 Read aloud last three pages of Horace, the Happy Ghost which had been previously assigned. Read with obvious enjoyment. Planned to read entire story to friends
who had expressed interest. Remarked--"Hard to keep from
repeating words when your mind is three or four words a-
head of what you are saying. Pronouncing words can't be as
important as getting the sense." Assigned story The Bird
Woman. He is to keep list. Use glossary and dictionary
for pronunciation and meaning. Reviewed "key to pronunciation." To be completed 4/7.

4/11 Discussed Hominy and His Blunt-nosed Arrow.
"Not enough time to read as much as before; more time
spent on social studies and arithmetic. Need that worse.
Just almost hate arithmetic anyway." Encouraged self-evaluation and wise use of time.

4/7 Spent entire time in evaluating last book report.
Compared Ossie and the 19th of April with the four previ-

ous reports, re: handwriting, spelling and the composition of summary statements. Spelling needs were: "decided, caught, nobody, woman, trucks, broken." To learn words and use them in sentences which would tell something about the story in which they were found.

4/25 Discussed the Sword and the Tree. Puzzled about knights and all the fighting. Meager background of understanding. Satisfactory interpretation of literal meaning, though. Suggested encyclopedia for further information. Librarian could probably help. Supplied some information myself but need to "bone up," too.

4/30 Read silently Equal Pay for Equal Work and interpreted figure of speech accurately. Read Little Nuisance and successfully applied word attack skills (with teacher guidance) to the following words: "terrier, mongrel, insisted, patience, protector, favorite, anxiously, excitedly." Word meanings from context--"cowboys wheeled their horses," "brought his horse squarely to a stop in front of the girl." "'We'll see what Day says,' Clint shot back."

5/7 Read the story The Saving Sneeze at sight. No problem with words. Comprehension excellent. Further encouragement with respect to book selection that requires sustained effort.

Fifty Ways of Sharing in an Individualized
Reading Class

by

Amy Elizabeth Jensen

(This material is excerpted from the author's article, "Attracting Children to Books," which appeared in <u>Elementary English</u> in October, 1956.)

To have children become acquainted with a wide variety of books, the teacher might encourage her class to
share them with and advertise them to one another in the
following interesting ways, thus stimulating them to read
more books of good quality and, incidentally, giving them opportunities to show their ingenuity and creative ability in art,
writing, dramatic arts, and other fields:

1. Making a poster is an excellent way to advertise
    a book. For such posters, paint, crayons, chalk,
    paper sculpture, ink, cut-out pictures, real ma-
    terials, and other things can be used, depending
    upon what is available for making flat or two- or
    three-dimensional ones.

2. Constructing a miniature stage setting for part of
    a story is a delightful experience. For such set-
    tings, pupils can make a miniature stage or use a
    cardboard, wooden, or metal box. Discarded ma-
    terials and odds and ends can be used for the back-
    ground and props. Small dolls of various kinds,
    wire or pipe cleaner forms, papier maché figures,
    or any other suitable ones can be employed as
    characters. Toys of various kinds are useful in
    creating such settings.

3. Decorating a jacket in any desired manner and
    writing an advertisement to accompany it may at-

tract children to a book even more than the original covering.

4. Children enjoy preparing a monologue from a story, and such a performance gives them the ability to put themselves in others' places.

5. Writing a book review for a room, school, or town newspaper not only requires careful reading but gives a real purpose for using language arts.

6. Creating a series of original illustrations for a story, using any medium desired, requires good judgment in the selection of incidents to picture and in the choice of suitable materials for executing them.

7. Writing a movie script for a good action story is an experience that helps children to arrange events in sequence and to see how necessary movement is in certain types of stories.

8. Children who read the same play or story (which lends itself to dramatization) can give a performance, such a group project being an excellent one for socialization, sharing ideas, and giving the children an opportunity to participate in dramatic arts, an activity which they need and enjoy.

9. Books on how to make or how to do things can be shared by having the readers give oral or written directions, bring in something made at home, or demonstrate step-by-step procedures to the group, thus increasing the ability to follow and give directions.

10. Stating real reasons for liking or not caring for a book, not from a snap judgment but after a thorough examination of it, requires critical thinking upon the part of children and helps them to evaluate other books.

11. If a travel book is read, an illustrated lecture, using postcards, photographs, slides, pictures clipped from magazines or from other publications, can be shown to young armchair travelers who are interested in people like themselves from near and

far, and it is an excellent way to promote good in-
tercultural relationships.

12. Children can use the following mechanical devices
and others which they may ingeniously devise to
make a "movie" of a book:

   a. Drawing a series of pictures on a long sheet of
      paper, the ends being fastened to rollers, which
      are turned to move the pictures into view.

   b. Making a double frame so that while one picture
      is being shown in one frame, a second one is
      fed into the other frame.

   c. Quickly flashing on the screen a series of pic-
      tures.

   d. Binding together a series of action pictures to
      flip for motion.

   e. Actually using a motion picture camera.

13. A vivid oral or written description of an interesting character in a book makes other children want
to become better acquainted with such a person.

14. Although an author's purpose in writing a story
should be more or less accepted, writing or telling different endings or making other changes when
they are not satisfied helps children to develop
such attitudes as fairness, justice, and other desirable ones.

15. Writing or telling the most humorous incident,
the most exciting happening, the most interesting
event, the part liked best, or the saddest part helps
children to seek certain types of materials from a
book and make a suitable selection.

16. Marking beautiful descriptive passages, interesting conversational sections, or other particular
parts for oral reading gives the reader a real audience situation, provides an opportunity for the
group to appreciate excellent writing, improves
imagery, and enlarges the vocabulary.

17. Telling a story to a musical accompaniment of some kind gives twofold pleasure to an audience if planned carefully for the kind of music selected, volume, and synchronization.

18. The child who likes to make lists of new, unusual, and interesting words and expressions to add to his vocabulary might share such a list with others, using them in the context of the story, thus giving the children the feel of the book and adding words to the store they already possess.

19. A pantomime cleverly acted makes children guess about the story and then want to read the book to really find out more about it.

20. Writing a letter to a friend or the librarian to recommend a book spreads the good news about it.

21. Giving a synopsis of a story is an excellent way of gaining experience in arranging events in sequence and learning how a story progresses to a climax, showing the importance of the surprise element, and giving a knowledge of all the other structure phases of a good book.

22. Using information in a book to make a scrapbook about a subject or a collection of things satisfies the desire to collect, and when shared with others, stimulates them to work on a similar project.

23. A puppet show planned to illustrate a story is sure to interest all children. The puppets can be wooden or papier maché ones, string-manipulated ones, paper bag puppets, hand or finger figures, cardboard shadow puppets or commercial ones, depending upon the child or children presenting the show and the materials available.

24. A historical book or similar type of story lends itself well to the making of a large, colorful, pictorial time line or map, which can be executed by using any materials and medium the individual or group may wish.

25. Children reading the same book can check each other's comprehension or the story by writing a

set of questions which they think readers should be able to answer after reading the book.

26. Broadcasting a book review to a radio audience over a school program requires careful reading and work in speech, and this experience gives an opportunity to use ingenuity in planning sound effects, background music, etc.

27. Dressing as one of the persons in the story and telling what role he plays provide valuable, vicarious experience in giving a live interpretation of a character.

28. Preparing a book review to present to a class at a lower level is an excellent experience in storytelling and gives children an understanding of how real authors must work to prepare books for children.

29. Having the pupils find out about a favorite author and present a brief biography of him with sketches of his books makes such books more understandable and personal.

30. Cutting a piece of paper in the form of a large thumbnail and placing it on the bulletin board with the caption, "Thumbnail Sketches," and letting the children put up drawings and sketches from books give brief acquaintance with many books.

31. Stretching a cord, captioned "A Line of Good Books," between two dowel sticks, with paper cloths on which is written or drawn something about various books hanging from it, attracts children.

32. Clay, soap, wood, plaster, or some other kind of modeling is purposeful when it is done to make an illustration for a book.

33. Constructing on a sand table a diorama, using creatively any available materials to represent a scene from a story, can be an individual project or one for a group of children who have read the same story.

34. Dressing paper, cardboard, wire, rag, or other

handmade dolls or costuming ready-made ones and
writing or printing descriptions of the characters
they represent make an interesting display.

35. Children like to watch someone give a chalk talk
done with white chalk on a blackboard or with colored or black chalk on paper, employing sketching
or cartooning techniques to develop the story.

36. Creating a detailed, colorful mural on a blackboard, paper, or cloth not only calls attention to a
book it represents, but makes a beautiful decora-
tion for the book corner as well.

37. Planning a living book by making a large frame
to represent a volume and having a tableau for favorite books, with a commentator to weave the
threads of the stories, is a project that can be
shared with the whole school.

38. Writing and drawing a rebus for a story requires
skill in interpreting words into pictures and gives
those who have difficulty with spelling an opportunity to create a piece of work with few errors.

39. A bulletin board with a caption about laughter or
a picture of someone laughing at excerpts from
funny stories rewritten by the children from material in humorous books is sure to be a popular spot
in the book corner.

40. Comparing one book read with a similar one is an
excellent experience in evaluating.

41. Making an original reference book from factual
materials read is a worthwhile experience in organizing such materials, and the perusal of such a
work by others gives them additional information.

42. Thinking up new adventures, experiences, or incidents to add to a book is fun, furnishes opportunities for oral and written expression, and gives a
feeling of authorship.

43. Writing to the library board to request that certain books be purchased for the children's collection adds books that pupils really like and is a way

of tying together the school and this particular community service.

44. Writing and executing an original play about the magic of books calls attention to books in various fields and makes children realize how much joy they can experience through reading.

45. Arranging with the director of visual aids for the showing of pictures to acquaint the children with some of the good books that have been dramatized in the form of movies gives them an opportunity to see professional interpretations.

46. Listening to excellent radio reviews of children's stories not only acquaints the children with a number of books but helps them with story-telling techniques.

47. Preparing an attractive book fair gives children an opportunity to browse among good books, encouraging many to read.

48. With the fad for television, children enjoy making a miniature set to present a performance, using the theme of an interesting book.

49. Visiting a book store or library gives children a speaking acquaintance with many books, and some are stimulated to read the new, attractive books displayed in these places.

50. Books of poetry can be shared in the following ways:

   a. An experience in the joy of sharing choral reading is live, eager group participation with freedom and spontaneity, and through such recitation, the timid child can be helped (even if just through a line) to realize his powers.

   b. Writing a composite poem after reading a book of verse gives each child an opportunity to make a contribution, either a word, phrase, or line.

   c. Dramatizing poetry furnishes an outlet for children's love of acting.

d. Collecting pictures to illustrate verses selected from books builds appreciation of poetry and art.

e. Accompanying poetry with various rhythmic activities is an enjoyable experience.

f. Setting a verse to music is a delightful aesthetic experience.

g. A poetry parade in costume gives the children an opportunity to participate in dramatic activities.

h. Adding original stanzas to a poem gives the children an understanding of poetry construction and encourages them to write.

How Children Can Share Their Reading Experiences

by

Auline Lowery Bailey

(This material is excerpted from the author's 1961
Central Missouri State College master's thesis,
A Comparative Study of the Grouping Method of
Teaching Reading with the Individualized Method.)

1. Writing a summary of a book on a 3" x 5" card
2. Telling the story to the class
3. Discussing the book by panel
4. Dramatizing the story
5. Pantomiming the story
6. Making a shadow box, both individually and with a group
7. Reading the story to the lower grades
8. Telling the story, using a flannel board
9. Reading excerpts to the class
10. Drawing pictures illustrating the story
11. Sharing a phonograph recording of a story read
12. Making posters to sell the book
13. Constructing stage props for a story, using corrugated
    cardboard
14. Writing advertisement jingles for books
15. Making original illustrations for a book
16. Writing character sketches of book characters
17. Giving illustrated lectures for travel books

18. Competing with class in vivid oral descriptions of characters

19. Reading dialogue orally using the voice to reflect meaning

20. Reading funny parts to the class

21. Making a list of words used in conversation synonymous for "said"

22. Sharing interesting words with the class

23. Writing to authors of stories

24. Writing letters to friends about books

25. Giving a book review to our room over the school inter-communications system

26. Creating interesting bulletin boards about books

27. Making up questions to ask children about books

28. Telling a story or reading a poem to music

29. Making a map of legends of the United States

30. Having "Story Book Character Day," all dressing as their favorite character

31. Making murals of books

32. Presenting a biography of an author

33. Giving a chalk talk of a story

34. Dressing dolls as characters

35. Comparing two books

36. Giving a character sketch of a villain in a story

37. Making a class booklet of poetry collected from magazines, newspapers, etc.

38. Working on a list of books to be purchased

39. Making a wrapping-paper costume depicting a character

40. Making an authentic back-drop for a dramatization of a story

41. Giving demonstrations from science books or social studies books

42. Writing original stories as an individual and sharing with the class

43. Writing original stories with a group
44. Preparing a hall demonstration of books
45. Reading chorally
46. Writing composite poems
47. Reading a book and sharing it with a "pal"

Record Keeping in an Individualized Reading Program

by

Dorothy L. Donahue

(This material is excerpted from the author's 1961
Central Connecticut State College master's thesis,
An Experiment in Individualized Reading in an Un-
selected Heterogeneous Sixth Grade Class.)

Pupil's Notebook

A. The Table of Contents - This is a complete and current
list of the books read by the pupil in the reading program.
Its purpose is to indicate to the teacher how wisely the
pupil is choosing his books, and whether the pupil is growing in his reading interests and ability. The following
criteria should apply.

   1. All the books should be approved.
   2. The books should generally be on the level of the
      pupil's reading ability.
   3. The books should be varied to meet the widening
      interests of the pupil (fiction and non-fiction of all
      types).
   4. The books should increase in difficulty to corre-
      spond with the growth in reading ability.

B. Vocabulary - The purpose of this section is to stimulate
interest in new words, to increase the pupil's vocabulary
and thus raise the reading level, to improve the pupil's
word recognition skills (context clues and dictionary
skills). The criteria for judging this section should include the following:

   1. Words listed should be those which he may have
      heard before but did not clearly understand.
   2. Rare or unusual words should not be included.

232

3. The number of words entered should indicate that the book being read is neither too difficult nor too easy.
4. The context in which the word was found should be given to make the word more meaningful.
5. The synonym, given by the pupil, should indicate the meaning of the word as used in the text.

C. Daily Log - The purpose of this section is to provide a check of the reading done by the pupil and enable him to put into practice the reading skills he is being taught. The following criteria should apply.

1. Entries should be on the level of the pupil's ability.
2. Entries should be varied to meet the different needs of the pupils.
3. Entries should be varied in accordance with the material being read.
4. Entries may include listing of details, summaries, predictions, sequence of events, character description or analysis, etc.

D. Evaluation - This section will contain the ratings of the teacher given after periodic inspection of the book as well as pertinent comments and suggestions for improvement.

Teacher's Notebook

This book will contain all the information obtained by the teacher which will help in planning a program of instruction. This information will be obtained from records, from formal and informal testing, from diagnostic observations in the individual conferences as well as in all reading activities throughout the day. Diagnosis and recording of reading needs is a continuous process.

A. For each Pupil

1. List of books - This will indicate
   a) the reading level
   b) "   "   interests
   c) "   "   growth
   d) "   "   needs

2. Record of contacts - This will include, with dates, a record of all individual conferences or group lessons

and the material used, the assignments given or suggestions made, the excerpts or reports read to the class.   This section will enable the teacher to note the degree of participation of each child and to plan to give equal time to all children.

3. Errors or needs in oral or silent reading.   This will be the basis for plans for individual conferences or group lessons.

    List:
    a) Reading errors - not other language arts errors
    b) Specific errors - not mere generalizations
    c) Typical not occasional errors

4. Progress noted.   Remarks here should be based on the needs and lessons indicated in the previous 3 sections.

B. Class Diagnostic Sheet

A list of all reading skills with a check under the name of each pupil who needs help in that particular skill. This will provide the basis for organizing group or class lessons.   Formal and informal tests may be used for diagnostic purposes or for noting improvement.

C. Source Material for Drill in Skills

A reference page noting specific materials (book and page) designed to meet the instructors' needs to the specific skills should be prepared.   This can include exercises from texts, workbooks, independent exercises, etc.

Should Individualized Reading and Basal Reading
Be Combined?

by

Gudelia Fox and Raymond B. Fox

Available evidence does not justify the claim that individualized reading instruction produces greater gains in reading achievement than a basal reading program, nor does it support the contention that a basal reading program is superior to an individualized program. Both approaches seem to have distinctive advantages. Therefore, the most prudent course of action for the teacher would seem to be to utilize a combination of the two approaches.

Several writers have criticized the "either individualized reading or basal reading" approach. They believe that although there are some elements of individualized reading that are desirable, there are other factors which a program of basal reading provides that cannot be met by an individualized approach. Consequently, they favor a combination of the two approaches. They contend that such a combination provides many and varied reading opportunities for children and at the same time, provides them with a systematic program of skill development.

Stauffer enumerated several advantages to be gained by using a combination of the two approaches, and he also gave insights into what the teacher must do if he adopts a combination approach. Veatch recommended that teachers who are uncertain of the individualized approach or who lack adequate materials for an entire class should begin by having

one child choose his instructional materials and then gradually extend this approach to a group.

Unfortunately, there is no panacea for the difficulties
which teachers encounter in attempting to teach children to
read. The teacher who is concerned only with the development of reading skills will not achieve the objectives of a
good reading program, nor will the teacher who is concerned only with development of favorable attitudes toward
reading. For that reason, a good reading program should
consist of both individualized reading and basal reading instruction. It will be interesting to see what future research
has to say on the subject.

Chapter 7

Individual Differences and Individualized Reading

The idea of individualized reading would not be likely to survive if there were not a growing realization that differences between individual children are very great. This realization grows out of a recognition that children differ not only in mental ability but in rates of learning, in ways of learning, in interests, in experiential background, in physical endurance, in emotional attitudes, in social skills, and in degree of motivation as well.

The first two passages in this chapter, taken from articles by Edgar S. Farley and Roy P. Wahle, respectively, discuss the nature of the individual differences between children which provide the rationale for such programs as individualized reading.

The third passage deals with the desirability of the individualized reading approach in the teaching of disadvantaged children. This is taken from an article by Beverly M. Keener.

How Children Differ from Each Other

by

Edgar S. Farley

Most persons with even limited experience with children and youth will agree that each differs in some measure from every other. The research data attesting to the fact are imposing and convincing. However, even if these data did not exist, the harried mother, trying to cope with the problems, desires and needs of her three or four children, would need no convincing of the unique nature of each. Nor would the elementary school teacher, facing each day 25 or 30 children and recognizing her responsibility for the learning and behavior of each, demand proof that differences exist among children.

Children Differ

Children differ in a multitude of ways. However, for purposes of reinforcing the theme of this editorial, it may be worthwhile to review briefly some of the areas of difference among children.

Perhaps the most prominent difference is that of sex. In addition to the obvious physical differences, it is generally recognized that girls, in a wide variety of ways, mature earlier than boys. For example, they mature earlier than boys in total physical development and develop an interest in the opposite sex at an age when most boys are primarily concerned with sports and outdoor life. Though evidence exists that sex differences are sometimes overemphasized, the fact remains that such differences have real significance in the

learning situation for the individual child. Girls tend to be
almost a year ahead of boys in total maturity when they enter school, and most girls gain another year in maturity by
the age of 13 or 14.

Children also differ in intelligence. Although much
remains to be learned about the exact nature of intelligence,
for practical purposes anyone dealing with children recognizes that some children react more quickly, learn more rapidly and seem to understand more thoroughly than others.
Recognition that children of the same chronological age will
vary widely in mental age is wide-spread. Acceptance of the
reality that this has implications for teaching and learning is,
however, less general.

Children differ in cultural background. In a nation
such as the United States, made up of a wide diversity of
races, nationalities and religions, cultural diversity is as
real as St. Louis. The farm boy from Nebraska, the girl
from Westchester, the child from the heavily industrialized
Gary are culturally different and that fact has bearing on the
way that they learn and the way in which they may best be
taught. Religious differences, social-class differences, eth-
nic differences, race differences and almost limitless combinations and mixtures of these differences affect the teaching-
learning situation in almost any classroom in the United
States.

Children are different in state of health, both physical and mental. This statement seems so obvious--indeed
so trite--as to be hardly worth writing. And yet, what significance it has for teaching and for learning! Except in
terms of understanding the individual child, how can the effect of chronic illness upon learning be assessed? Can the
heartsick child from the broken home react to a classroom
situation in the same way as the happy youngster from a
"normal" home? Who can measure the cumulative effect of
regular frustration upon a child's readiness to learn?

It would be possible to go on for many pages detail-
ing the differences that exist among children. However, as
was stated earlier, the case hardly needs proving. Children
are different and most people recognize the fact.

Putting Difference to Work

What difference does such recognition make in the

teaching-learning situation in the American classroom? Unfortunately, in many--perhaps most--it makes little or no
difference. Day after day, week after week in many classrooms children are "taught" as if they were all exactly alike.
All receive the same assignments. All are measured by the
same standards. If the teacher happens to be kind of heart,
she may say, "Johnny has an I. Q. of only 90. He cannot be
expected to do as well as the others. Even though he hasn't
earned it, I'll give him a D because he tried."

Perhaps it actually never occurred to the teacher that
Johnny should not have had the same assignments, been
taught by the same methods or had his work measured by the
same standards as his classmates. Or perhaps the teacher
did recognize the need for dealing with Johnny differently,
but drew back because "I can't possibly prepare individual
lessons for 30 children--I don't have the time," or "I know I
should teach each child as an individual, but I don't know
how." In any case, far too often Johnny is treated as part
of a group and is lost.

There is, of course, grouping for instruction. This
practice is based on the hope that if sufficient care is used
and if sufficient data for selection exist, it is possible to as-
semble a group of children who are alike--or sufficiently so
to obviate any need for varying the way the individual members of the group are taught. Groups are assembled in many
ways. Children with similar intelligence quotients are
grouped. Sometimes similar scores on standardized reading
examinations are used as the basis for the group. Whatever
is the criterion, the idea is to bring together children sufficiently alike so that they may be taught alike.

It would be unfair to condemn this practice as unwork-
able. Certainly grouping children according to likeness with
respect to some reasonable criterion is more likely to be
successful--or to be successful for more children--than is
forming a group at random and treating the members as if
they were all alike. However, it must be said realistically
that grouping according to likeness is not the answer to the
problem of dealing with the differences among children. Perhaps not as many children are lost when intelligent grouping
practices are utilized, but some certainly are lost.

In the last analysis, the only answer to dealing with
the individuality of a child is to teach him as an individual.
Teach him as an individual with as complete a knowledge of

his problems, strengths and weaknesses as it is possible to attain.   There would seem to be no other solution that would assure every child an opportunity to learn in accordance with his ability and desire.

Quite obviously, to teach in this manner would involve many changes in the educational pattern.   Problems of numbers of children assigned to a teacher, traditional grade level structure, and of evaluation and grading--to name only some of the more serious matters--certainly would be involved. Such changes come about by gradual evolution and not by sudden revolution.   It is not likely that the schools of this year or next will abandon group teaching methods for the individual approach.

However, progress is being made.   Many elementary school teachers are teaching reading to boys and girls through the individualized approach and are enthusiastic about the results.   Many secondary teachers are attempting to adapt their teaching to the individual through assignments tailored according to the needs and abilities of each student. If study in depth of each student has not become a widespread practice at least some teachers are trying it.   In short, many teachers recognize that learning takes place only within an individual and that individuals reach eagerly for those learnings that are in keeping with their individual development, disregarding whatever else is offered.

Principles of Individualization of Instruction

by

Roy P. Wahle

(This material is excerpted from the author's article, "Methods of Individualization in Elementary
School," which appeared in <u>Educational Leadership</u>
in November, 1959. Copyright (c) 1959.)

We believe that when a child first learns to relate in
a social circumstance we should provide him with an understandable and manageable situation. Why, then, do we continue to generalize that six-year-old boys are as ready to read
and do the work that schools expect as are six-year-old
girls?

Bellevue found, in a comprehensive study of its elementary children, that many of the boys who were above
average in intelligence persisted in low reading groups through
all six elementary grades! Surely, the grouping criteria
needed to be examined. They were then examined and, consequently, the Continuous Growth Program was introduced as
an experiment.

Two years have elapsed. Evidence is accumulating
which indicates that if children are allowed to proceed at
their own rate through the primary grades, reading problems
are reduced and individual self-confidence is enhanced. No
longer need children sit next to children simply because nature decreed that they would be born in the same year. Human growth is related to a calendar, but not as intimately
as our elementary graded classifications might imply. There
are better criteria for grouping than birthdays.

In the primary grades, a single criterion for grouping might be the level of demonstrated ability to read. The
ability to read is not singular. Rather, it appears to be a
reflection of complexities captured, in the primary years

242

at least, by the multiple phenomena of maturation and growing self-realization.

Democracy may be affected by our methods for individualization in the elementary schools.

A class is a group of human beings. Unfortunately,
the exigencies of mass education have tended to equate a
class to a cubicle in a building. The four walls of the classroom must become unlimited if quality instruction is desired.
A class is a vital social group with important subgroups. It
is a miniature society which the alert teacher quickly per-
ceives and utilizes.

Teachers must recognize isolates, subgroups, the total group and all the internal interactions. Attitudes toward
school, toward vocational choice, and toward life and its purpose may be affected by these interactions. The teacher of
a group of human beings must be as eager about each child
individually as he is about what is being planned and
learned.

Guidance nourishes curriculum and curriculum serves
guidance. There is a unity between guidance and curriculum
which thwarts attempts at separation. The changing nature
of society and its shifting demands are consequential but
surely subtle. An elementary school will study the varying
degrees of knowledge acquired by pupils outside the school,
the impact of TV, travel, community displays and events.

Methods of individualization in the elementary school
must be feasible, applicable and appropriate. Individualization of the guidance and instructional program is more a
matter of spirit and atmosphere than it is pronouncement and
rule. But there are marks by which one may discern the
elementary school and the school district which are more
concerned about children than about things.

Marks of Individualization

Let us examine some of these marks which denote
that individualization is paramount: (a) the library is the
center of learning, (b) there are numerous approaches to
similar learnings or conceptualizations, (c) there is flexible
grouping based upon defensible criteria, (d) attention is directed to the exceptional, (e) a class is a group of separate
human beings, (f) guidance nourishes curriculum and cur-

riculum serves guidance, (g) classes or instructional groups
tend to be small, (h) informed generalists direct the school's
administration, (i) a respect for scientific inquiry and experimentation prevails, (j) parents and patrons help define
the goals and purposes of education, but professional educators define and designate the methods and techniques.

The library is the center of learning. The printed
symbol is the most efficient device ever invented by man to
transmit his culture and to broaden personal experiences and
understandings. Better elementary schools early establish,
by symbol, facility and practice, the central importance of
books and their contents. Individualization in reading and
research is a basic necessity of our times. Full-time year-
around library service at each elementary school is a practical goal.

But a library is more than books. It should encom-
pass all instructional materials and devices which will enrich meanings. A librarian is the essential member of the
teaching staff whose knowledge of books and instructional materials will enhance the motivational and learning quality of
any lesson or individual searching which children must pursue in order to grow in understanding.

There is flexible grouping based upon defensible criteria. Wherever children gather together there will be grouping. Good elementary schools concern themselves with the
criteria used for determining the varying instructional groups
which are inevitable in mass education. Old forms are consistently questioned in the light of deeper knowledge about human growth and development. There is nothing sacred about
25 or 30 or 10 within a group. Neither chronological age
nor the intelligence quotient taken alone offers a legitimate
basis for grouping, yet we persist with the graded structure
of the elementary school or select "gifted children" by a
score on a test! Research again and again supports the negative value of retention, but we maintain a blind faith that
repetition of unlearned material will guarantee its comprehension!

It appears possible that some form of an ungraded
program, when maturation and its manifestations of reading
readiness and reading ability are major concerns, will better
answer the perplexing problem of grouping in the primary
school. Does it automatically follow, however, that an ungraded program necessarily provides a sound structure for

grouping at the intermediate level?

Individualized Reading and the Disadvantaged Child

by

Beverly M. Keener

(This material is excerpted from the author's article, "Individual Reading and the Disadvantaged,"
which appeared in the Reading Teacher in February,
1967.)

A visit to a depressed urban area classroom during
a typical reading period usually reveals a group of children
holding the same book in front of them as they are seated in
a circle with the teacher. At the same time, children not
in the reading circle are likely to be engaged in seatwork
activities of the usual sort, such as the completion of workbook exercises or reproduction of work from the blackboard.
Upon closer examination of the situation, the observer notes
a vacant expression on the faces of all children in the reading group, with the exception of the child who is reading a-
loud. When the youngsters are questioned about the passage
read, they sometimes offer no response, or one unconnected
with the material. Meantime, the children at their seats are
staring aimlessly into space, doodling on little scraps of paper, handling small toys or talking with neighboring children.
When asked to comment on this situation, the teacher will
often shrug and say, "It's very difficult to keep those not in
the reading circle constructively occupied." Further probing
into reasons for the lack of vivacity in the reading group itself brings an even less clear-cut explanation.

While the above observations can be made in thousands
of classrooms throughout the country, they are particularly
disturbing when found in the inner-city, for the most difficult task facing teachers of the disadvantaged today is that
of raising achievement levels in the area of reading. Over
the past five years public and private organizations have
spent millions of dollars to provide staff and materials for

scores of special reading projects in city school systems
throughout the country.   In addition, vast numbers of tutorial
programs manned by enthusiastic volunteers are underway in
the same target areas.   The federal government, as part of
the war on poverty, is the latest source of staggering sums
of money for remedial reading.   The major thrust of most of
these programs is aimed at providing children with more of
the same instruction in reading, rather than a different type
of instruction.   In spite of this massive assault, the problem
persists.   Disadvantaged children almost invariably are not
scoring as well as their suburban counterparts on standardized reading tests.

It is time to re-think the ways in which reading is
taught to these children.   Although the individualized approach has yet to gain widespread acceptance as an effective
way to teach reading, the possibility of its use with deprived
youngsters deserves careful consideration.

Inherent in this method are the selection of reading
matter by the student himself, based upon interest and ap-
peal, and the teaching of reading skills when a need is shown
for them, rather than at a moment arbitrarily selected by
the teacher.   The use of self-selected material is an excellent means of reaching the disadvantaged, for it is well known
that the typical basal reader featuring stories about unreal
children who speak in clipped sentences and live in a middle-
class utopia does little to kindle a love of reading in any
child, let alone one whose world is very different from that
portrayed in most readers.   By providing youngsters with a
wide range of books for, about, and by minority groups as
well as those that feature the urban environment, the teacher
immediately removes some barriers to reading.   As one
child engaged in an individualized reading program put it, "I
like reading this way because now I can read about people
like me. "

Teachers are frequently concerned about the best ways
in which to organize a class for individualized reading.   This
is particularly true of teachers who work with the disadvantaged, for they often find that these children have little inner-
direction, possess short attention spans, and need a clearly
defined sequence of classroom activities.   The most successful organization seems to involve the total class of youngsters
working simultaneously on the same phase of the program;
all children read at the same time in their self-selected
books while the teacher holds conferences with individuals.

Following this, time is then given for all children to work on
skills materials organized around individual weaknesses.
During the skills session, the teacher may instruct a small
group of children who have demonstrated a common need for
certain skills, circulate among the children as they work on
individual assignments, or give instruction to the poorest
readers. Since many disadvantaged children demonstrate a
need to become physically involved in the learning process,
self-manipulated audio-visual aids such as earphones and tape
recorders, individual filmstrip viewers, or reading games
can be used to advantage during the skills time. In addition
to providing incentive, these materials reinforce skills learning. The pairing of students to work in skills teams is another means of stimulating interest and promoting involvement.

In attempting to create an atmosphere in which growth
of reading power will flourish, it is important that each
small degree of progress made by youngsters be recognized.
This is easier to accomplish in an individualized program
than in a basal reader program, for in the latter situation
progress is usually signalled by movement into a "higher
group," an event that does not occur frequently for most children of the poor. Too often they develop an image of themselves as always being in the "low group," be it in the reading situation or life itself. Individualized techniques give
back to the child a sense of importance and worth. He knows
that whatever he selects to read will meet with the teacher's
approval.

Further strengthening of the child's self-image occurs
when he is able to make a contribution to the class which is
uniquely his own--the sharing with others of a book that has
delighted him. Such sharing can take the form of art projects, dramatizations of characters, or simply the reading
aloud of a particularly interesting passage. It provides a
creative outlet for youngsters as individuals, whets the reading appetite of other class members, and is much more
warmly received by all involved than a typical book report.

Educators must reach into the realm of the new and
different for solutions to the complex problems of human
deprivation and its effect on learning. In an era when great
need exists for a high level of education for all persons
there is no better place to begin than in the field of reading
instruction.

Chapter 8

Books! Books! and More Books!

Basic to the success of individualized reading is an ample supply of appropriate reading materials. The amount of reading material consumed by an individualized reading class is always amazing even to those quite conversant with this approach. A very adequate and extensive discussion of ways of procuring books for an individual reading program is found in the literature but space does not permit a full treatment of this subject here. An especially good treatment of this subject is found in Larrick's writings. [1] Lists of books helpful to individualized reading teachers can also be found in a number of references. [2]

In this chapter the first selection by Professor Charlotte S. Huck of Ohio State University deals with the effective use of children's literature in the classroom.

The second selection is excerpted from the master's thesis of Robert G. DeLisle. Mr. DeLisle prepared study guides and activity sheets for each of fifty children's books. Three of these guides are reproduced here.

Notes

1. Larrick, 311, 312 and 313.

2. Dees, 127; Ellard and others, 151; Gunderson, 222; Lazar, 315; Loken, 326; Michalek, 369; New York, 387.

Using Children's Literature Effectively

by

Charlotte S. Huck

(This material is excerpted from the author's article, "Planning the Literature Program for the Elementary School," which appeared in Elementary English in April, 1962.)

Elementary school teachers have all but forgotten that the most important reason for teaching boys and girls to read is to help them become readers. Controversies continue to be waged over methods of teaching reading, the most appropriate age for beginning instruction, and machines versus basic materials. Many primary teachers report that they spend over one-half the total school day on reading instruction alone. Teachers proudly point to the results of reading achievement tests to prove the effectiveness of their teaching. As a nation we take pride in the 98% literacy rate of our population. Recent criticism to the contrary, the majority of the evidence points to the fact that our schools are teaching children the skill of reading. And yet our schools have failed miserably in helping boys and girls develop the habit of reading. In many instances we have developed an illiterate group of literates--adults who know how to read but do not read. In one study, nearly one half (48%) of the adults in the United States had not read one book during the year. Another study which contrasted American reading habits with that of adults in other countries revealed that only 17 percent of the Americans had been reading from a book the previous day whereas 55 percent of the English sample had been engaged in this activity. Despite the rising educational level and the high standard of living, a large proportion of the American public expresses little interest in reading.

Although there are many factors which are responsible for the small amount of book reading in the United States, one major factor may well be the overemphasis of the instructional or basic reading program to the neglect of the literature program in the elementary school. In fact, some elementary school teachers would maintain that literature was something one studied in high school, not the elementary school. Others would say that reading and literature are synonymous. Still others would claim that the literature program is cared for by the "free reading" period on Friday afternoon when teachers are free to complete their attendance records while the children are free to develop appreciation and discrimination for fine literature by reading a Nancy Drew mystery! We have no literature program in the elementary school when we compare it with our carefully planned developmental programs in reading, spelling and arithmetic. All our efforts are directed towards teaching children to read --no one seems to be concerned that they do read or what they read. The means have become the end. We have developed better and better basic readers, we have even cut some of them apart and boxed them! Yet few children ever developed a love of reading by reading a basic reader or by progressing from one colored reading card to another. It is almost as if we had put our children in link trainers for reading, and then focused our attention on producing bigger and better link trainers and methods of using them without ever giving the children a chance to use the skill they have developed by discovering the thrill of flying. Link trainers do play an important role in training pilots; basic readers play an important role in helping children to learn to read. However, the ultimate goal of both of them should be self-elimination.

Teachers and children must not prize the skill of reading as an end in itself; they must see it as a beginning of a life-time pleasure with books. There are no values in knowing how to read; only values which are derived from reading. As teachers recognize the values which result from wide and varied reading, they will see the need for a planned literature program in the elementary school.

The first major value of literature is enjoyment. Personal enjoyment of reading is a respectable activity and should be encouraged. Adults read for pleasure and not to produce a book report. Children too should discover the joy of just reading for fun. They may want to share their enjoyment in many different ways but children should not feel that they always have to do something with a book to celebrate its completion. Reading books should be a natural part

of children's lives and not such a momentous occasion that
we must shoot off firecrackers in the form of book reports,
mobiles, or dioramas each time a book is completed. This
practice is a remnant of the past when books were scarce
and precious and reading ability was limited to a few. A
wide variety of experiences in interpreting children's literature may deepen children's appreciations, but they should
never become the required penalty for reading a book. Alert
teachers know when children's needs have been met through
reading; they do not ask for tangible verification. One fourth
grader, whose mother had just died, was introduced to Cor-
bett's The Lemonade Trick. This book contains some delightful spoofing of boys' and dog's behavior. You may remember the part where Waldo, the dog, drinks some of the
magic lemonade and immediately becomes so good that he
goes out in the backyard to fill in the holes which he had dug
the day before. For two days, this fourth grader was completely absorbed in this book. Once he was observed reading
it while he walked to the coat closet. Escapism, yes, but he
had found an acceptable way to contain his problem, and in
the midst of sorrow, a book had been able to make him
laugh.

Personal-social growth may also be influenced by what
children read. Probably many of us first experienced death
and its accompanying feelings of loss and separation as we
read of Beth's death in Little Women. American children today may realize some of the personal horrors of war as they
identify with Tien Pao in De Jong's starkly written book, The
House of Sixty Fathers. Some of our over-protected white
children may experience the hurts of prejudice for the first
time as they read and identify with Mary Jane, the main character in Dorothy Sterling's fine story by the same name which
tells of desegregation in our public schools in the South. Or
books may help children with the developmental task of grow-
ing-up and fulfilling their adult roles. They discover as they
read such books as Nkwala by Edith Lambert Sharp that this
is a universal experience and they identify with the Salish In-
dian boy whose "childhood itched him like a goatskin robe."
Books help children to explore living, "to try on" various roles
and accept or reject them as they search for their own identity.

Children may satisfy their desire for information and
intellectual stimulation through wide reading. Willard Olson
has identified what he calls the "seeking behavior" of boys
and girls. Certainly this is revealed in children's response

to the recent flood of factual books.   Informational books are
no longer disguised by the fictional trappings of a trip to the
farm with a favorite uncle.   Children are hungry for knowledge about the physical and social world in which they live.
Many well-written informational books contribute to the thrill
of helping children discover specific facts by presenting them
clearly and in a meaningful way.   These books satisfy but
they do not satiate; they supplement and extend texts in science and social studies.   Such fine books as the special edi-
tion of Rachel Carson's The Sea Around Us widen children's
vision and open new vistas of beauty and mystery.

Only as children are exposed to much fine writing will
they develop an appreciation for a well-chosen phrase, rich
descriptive prose or convincing characterization.   After a
story has been finished, the teacher and children may take
time to reread and relish particularly enjoyable words or
paragraphs.

The period of childhood is limited.   If children miss
reading or hearing a book at the appropriate age for them,
it is missed forever.   No adult catches up on his reading by
beginning with Peter Rabbit or Homer Price.   There is no
one book which must be read by all children, but there are
many fine books which we would hate to have children miss.
These include some of the classics also, but many of our
modern books which may become the classics of tomorrow.
There is a body of children's literature which is worthy of
a solid place in the curriculum.

Finally, the true value of the effects of the literature
program for today's children will be seen in the reading habits of adults in 1985.   The explosion of knowledge makes it
essential that our children become readers.   The natural ob-
solescence of materials has so increased that adults must
become constant readers if they are to stay abreast of new
developments.   The mark of the informed man is no longer
whether he can read, or what he has read, it may be based
upon what he is currently reading.   Our sociologists are predicting amazing increases in the amount of leisure time for
the average person (not in our profession).   The acid test of
the reading program in our schools will be the use which
children and adults will make of books in this increased leisure time.

Obviously, these six values of literature will not be
fulfilled by an instructional reading program or by a Friday

afternoon recreational reading period. As teachers, librarians, and administrators become committed to these val-
ues--to the worth of literature in children's lives--they will
plan a comprehensive literature program for every elementary school. The planning must start with teachers who read
themselves, who enjoy reading and recognize its value for
them. Their first task will begin with making books, many
books and fine books, available for boys and girls. The recent recommendations in the Standards for School Library
Programs suggest that all schools having two hundred or more
students need well-organized central libraries and a qualified
librarian. In 1958-59 some two-thirds of our elementary
schools did not have central libraries and the ratio of qualified school librarians to pupils was one librarian to some
4, 261 pupils! When may we look forward to the day that
parents and educators will begin to view libraries as being
as worthy of school funds as multi-purpose rooms and
$40,000 cafeterias! Books are the tools for learning, the
very bread of knowledge. Must our children continue to be
like Alice at the Mad Hatter's party, prepared to feast at the
table of reading with no room and no books?

We must do more than make books available for boys
and girls, we will want to create a climate which will encourage wide reading. While visiting schools during Book Week
this year, I observed several classrooms that had small displays of new books on the window sills. I watched and I
waited for two whole mornings and I never saw a single child
have time to look at or read any one of those books. Like
the mathematician counting his stars in the Little Prince,
they were too busy with "matters of consequence" to take time
to enjoy reading. A planned literature program does take
time. It provides time for children to read books of their
own choice every day. It allows time for children to share
their experiences with literature in many ways. In the
planned literature program time is provided for the daily
story hour regardless of the age of the group. For we know
that most children's reading ability does not equal their appreciation level until sometime in the junior high school.
During the daily story hour, the teacher will introduce the
various kinds of literature which children might miss otherwise. Certain books need to be savored together in order to
heighten children's appreciation. This seems to be particularly true of such fantasy as The Gammage Cup, The Bor-
rowers and even that most American of all fantasy, Charlotte's Web. Teachers will not want to read books which
children themselves will ordinarily read. It is fun to read

a chapter of <u>Henry Huggins,</u> but children will eagerly finish
this book themselves once they have been introduced to it.
A variety of books should be presented in order to at least
expose boys and girls to different types of books.   Children
in the middle grades go on reading jags--they read series
books with the same avidity with which they collect bottle
tops.   This is characteristic of their developmental patterns
and should not be a cause for concern.   If fifth grade girls
only want to read horse stories, let them.   Could you fill in
a balanced wheel for your reading pattern this year?   A life-
time of reading will show a certain balance, but even an a-
dult follows particular reading interests, completely absorbed
in biography for a while or perhaps plunging into theology for
the first time, or avidly reading everything which has been
written by a newly discovered author.   Can't we extend children the same freedom of selection which we allow ourselves?

In planning a literature program, teachers will not
only provide for separate times for literature experiences
but they will make wide use of certain trade books to enrich
and vitalize learning experiences in <u>all</u> areas of study.   Children should be encouraged to verify, extend, or contradict
the presentation in their textbook by contrasting it with facts
found in other books.   Social studies are greatly enriched by
the many excellent books about children in different lands,
by biography, and by fine historical fiction--those books which
clothe the factual bones of history and make it come alive.
Children who read Fritz's <u>The Cabin Faced West</u> or <u>The</u>
<u>Courage of Sarah Noble</u> by Dalgleish will have a better un-
derstanding of their historical heritage than the children who
are limited to a single textbook approach.   History, by its
very nature, is interpretative.   Children need to read books
with many different viewpoints in order to become critical
assayors of the contemporary scene.   The flood of factual
books in science has been gratefully received by children
and teachers.   Future space pilots can find the most recent
information in trade books rather than texts.   For example,
Beeland and Wells' book <u>Space Satellite, the Story of the</u>
<u>Man Made Moon</u> came out in a third edition, three years af-
ter its first printing!   Very few texts can be that up-to-
date.   Arithmetic, art, and music may all be enriched
through the use of exciting books in children's literature.
The day of the single text for all is gone, as many fine books
find their rightful place in the curriculum.

The planned literature program will only be as effective as the teachers who make it.   This means teachers will

have to know children's literature; it means they will want
to keep informed of the new developments in the field.   A
continuing in-service study group might read and review some
of the 1500 juvenile titles which come off the press yearly.
Some faculty meetings might well be devoted to discussions
of the place of children's literature in the curriculum and the
development of lifetime reading habits of boys and girls.

Vertical planning of teachers from kindergarten through
grade six might result in a guide for a literature program
either as an integral part of the total curriculum or as a
separate program.   Such a guide might include purposes,
plans for selection of books, recommended books for reading
to children and by children, suggested experiences with literature and evaluation procedures.   Texts in children's literature and such journals as Elementary English, The Horn
Book and the School Library Journal should be a part of every school's professional library.   Teachers and librarians
might prepare recommended buying lists for Christmas and
birthday gifts.   Lists of books for reading at home could also be prepared, for children who become enthusiastic about
books at school will want to continue their reading at home.

Finally, we may agree as to the values of a planned
literature program but unless we evaluate that program, it
probably will not be included in our curriculum.   Provision
should be made for a staff evaluation of the total literature
program--values of it, time devoted to it, and the success
of the program.   Children's reading habits should be evaluated as well as their reading skill.   Interest in reading is
not as intangible as it may sound; it can be measured, not
in terms of how many books boys and girls have read, although that is a part of it, but in terms of the depth of understanding and new insights which they have gained from
their reading.   Reading achievement tests do not measure
this nor do city-wide comparisons of grade level standings.
But teachers, librarians, and parents know if children are
reading.   Hopefully, we would wish that all children might
echo the feelings of this child in the third grade who wrote
about her world of books.

My Own World

When I open up my book I go into a world all
    my own
Into a world of sorrow or joy,

but wherever it is I don't hear the things
about me.
I could be reading in a busy noisy factory,
but my world keeps me away, My world of
books.

This then is the acid test of our literature program--not do
children know how to read, but <u>do</u> they read, <u>what</u> do they
read, and more important, do they <u>love</u> to read.

This enthusiasm for books doesn't just happen. It results from an effective instructional program which is well-
balanced by a literature program that has definite purposes
and a definite place in the curriculum. It requires a teacher
who is dedicated to the values of literature and it demands
that we lift our sights from our basic reading programs in
the elementary school to a planned literature program for
all!

How One Teacher Prepared Reading Guides

by

Robert G. Delisle

(This material is excerpted from the author's 1966
University of New Hampshire master's thesis, A
Study of an Individualized Reading Program in
Grade Six.)

Afraid to Ride
by C. W. Anderson

Book Talk

1. Why was Judy afraid to ride?
2. What favor did Mr. Jaffers ask of Judy?
3. What happened to make Judy ride Lady?
4. How was Lady acquired by Mr. Jaffers?
5. Why had this particular horse been bought?
6. Why do you think Judy finally rode?
7. Why do you think Lady allowed Judy to ride her?

Word Talk

A. Many times you can tell the meaning of a word from
   other words in the same sentence.   This is called getting the meaning from the context.
   Directions: Write the word that means the same as the
   underlined word in the sentence.

   1. A deer sailed in a most amazing leap.
                a. flue
                b. flew
                c. flu

2. He watched her long swinging stride.
        a. parse
        b. peace
        c. pace

3. He reached for a hoof and picked it up.   There was no resistance.
        a. oppressive
        b. opportune
        c. opposition

4. There was a tang in the air despite the sunshine.
        a. nip
        b. nap
        c. bun

5. Dinner that evening was a happy occasion.
        a. eventual
        b. eventide
        c. event

B. The letters ea may have the sound of short e as in bed or they may have the sound of long e as in beet.
Directions: If the letters ea have the sound of short e write short beside the word. If the letters ea have the sound of long e write long beside the word.

  6. team
  7. increased
  8. ease
  9. breakfast
10. dreams
11. mean
12. head

C. When two or three letters come together and make one sound, the letters are called a blend.
Directions: Circle the blends in the words.

13. glow
14. proper
15. stable
16. speed
17. bridle
18. stirrups
19. trotted

D. A syllable is a part of a word which usually contains a
    sounded vowel.
    Directions: Divide the following words into syllables.

    20. paddock
    21. stable
    22. rider
    23. jumper
    24. broken
    25. lying

E. When two letters come together and make a third sound,
    the letters are called a <u>digraph</u>.
    Directions: Circle the <u>digraphs</u> in the words.

    26. shone
    27. breath
    28. chill
    29. hush
    30. wish

KEY   Afraid to Ride

Book Talk

1. She had fallen from a horse and broken her leg.

2. Mr. Jaffers asked Judy to care for Lady.

3. She had to go for help. A person had been injured in a
    fall.

4. Mr. Jaffers bought her from a man who was dissatisfied
    with Lady's jumping.

5. Both Lady and Judy were afraid of riding and riders.

Word Talk

    1. b. flew
    2. c. pace
    3. c. opposition
    4. a. nip
    5. c. event
    6. team---long
    7. increased---long
    8. ease---long
    9. breakfast--short
    10. dreams--long

11. mean---long
12. head---short
13. (gl)ow
14. (pr)oper
15. (st)a(bl)e
16. (sp)eed
17. (br)i(dl)e
18. (st)irrups
19. (tr)otted
20. pad/dock
21. sta/ble
22. rid/er
23. jump/er
24. bro/ken
25. ly/ing
26. (sh)one
27. brea(th)
28. (ch)ill
29. hu(sh)
30. wi(sh)

The Big Wave
by Pearl Buck

Book Talk

1. What was the big wave?

2. Why were there no windows facing the ocean?

3. What did Old Gentleman want to do for Jiya?

4. What signal was used to tell of a big wave?

5. What other danger was there on the island?

6. Why did Jiya decide to rebuild his house on the beach? Why did he have a window facing the ocean?

7. What was learned about the lives of the Japanese fishermen and farmers?

Word Talk

A. Many times you can tell the meaning of a word from other words in the same sentence. This is called getting the meaning from context.
Directions: Write the word that means the same as the underlined word in the sentence.

1. The dark water was often <u>phosphorescent</u> and gleamed as though lamps were lighted deep beneath the surface.
   a. incandescent
   b. luminescent
   c. transparent

2. The earth <u>yielded</u> to the fire and split open.
   a. gained
   b. gave up
   c. trained

3. The fields were <u>terraced</u> by walls of stone, each one of them like a broad step up the mountain.
   a. shaped
   b. sharpened
   c. shoved

4. He <u>bade</u> them good night and climbed the hill to his home.
   a. cold
   b. told
   c. sold

5. A school of fish was going to go through the <u>channel</u>.
   a. clearing
   b. usage
   c. passage

B. When two or three letters come together and make one sound, the letters are called a <u>blend</u>.
   Directions: Circle the blends in the words.

   6. strong
   7. springs
   8. clean
   9. sweeping
   10. scroll
   11. sliding
   12. instead
   13. mattress

C. When two words come together and make a third word we say that we have a compound word.
   Directions: In Column I there is a list of words. In Column II are the words which are to be added to those in Column I. Write the compound words.

	I	II
14.	farm	man
15.	noon	foot
16.	man	servant
17.	mountain	house
18.	gentle	day
19.	bare	side

D. A syllable is a part of a word which usually contains a sounded vowel.
Directions: Divide the following words into syllables.

20. earthquake
21. channel
22. motioned
23. boiling
24. ocean
25. signal

E. When two letters come together and make a different sound, the letters are called a digraph.
Directions: Circle the digraphs in the words.

26. untouched
27. fishing
28. earth
29. fathoms
30. ashore

KEY   The Big Wave

Book Talk

1. The big wave was the tidal wave which often hit the island.

2. The fisherman did not wish to see the wave if it came.

3. The Old Gentleman wanted to educate Jiya.

4. The Old Gentleman raised a flag.

5. There was also an active volcano on the island.

Word Talk

1. b. luminescent
2. b. gave up
3. a. shaped
4. b. told
5. c. passage
6. (str)ong

   7. (spr)ings
   8. (cl)ean
   9. (sw)eeping
 10. (scr)oll
 11. (sl)iding
 12. in(st)ead
 13. mat(tr)ess
 14. farmhouse
 15. noonday
 16. manservant
 17. mountainside
 18. gentleman
 19. barefoot
 20. earth/quake
 21. chan/nel
 22. mo/tioned
 23. boil/ing
 24. o/cean
 25. sig/nal
 26. untou(ch)ed
 27. fi(sh)ing
 28. ear(th)
 29. fa(th)oms
 30. a(sh)ore

Big Red
by Jim Kjelgaard

Book Talk

1. What animals did Big Red fight to save Danny's life?

2. Why was Danny training Red?

3. Why can Red no longer be shown?

4. What was Danny's father's occupation?

5. Why did they wish to kill Old Majesty?

6. Where did this story take place?

7. What makes you think the author knew about dogs?

8. Why did Danny's father's attitude toward dogs change?

9. Why did each of the characters feel as he did about dogs?

Word Talk

A. Many times you can tell the meaning of a word from
    other words in the same sentence. This is called get-
    ting the meaning from context.
    Directions: Write the word that means the same as the
    underlined word in the sentence.

    1. The red-faced man <u>lunged</u> forward.
        a. dashed
        b. slashed
        c. slipped

    2. Melted snow filled every ditch and <u>depression.</u>
        a. hallow
        b. hollow
        c. tallow

    3. Red had an <u>ecstatic</u> time chasing a chipmunk.
        a. enjoyable
        b. enviable
        c. energetic

    4. He heard a dog bark, then a <u>succession</u> of hurried
        barks.
        a. recurrence
        b. renewal
        c. reappearance

    5. In one mighty leap Red <u>bridged</u> the distance between
        them.
        a. collared
        b. covered
        c. collected

B. The suffixes <u>-er</u>, <u>-or</u>, <u>-an</u>, <u>-eer</u>, mean "one who does
    something."
    Directions: Add one of the above suffixes to each of the
    following words. Write the words.

    6. conduct
    7. pursue
    8. prison
    9. hunt
    10. manage

C. Many words are related in a particular way.
    Directions: In each line there are four words. Three
    of the words are related and one is not. Write the word
    that is not related.

    11. beaver, mink, partridge, martin
    12. birch, beech, bovine, pine
    13. hammer, rifle, trap, knife
    14. collie, greyhound, basset, varmint
    15. leash, paw, collar, muzzle

D. The dictionary often gives several meanings to words.
    Read the meanings for pass. Write a phrase for each
    of the meanings.

    ex. pass a car
    pass the salt

KEY   Big Red

Book Talk

1. He fought a wolverine and a bear.

2. He was trying to train him to be a partridge dog.

3. He was badly mauled by Old Majesty.

4. He was a trapper.

5. Old Majesty was killing a great deal of livestock.

Word Talk

        1. a. dashed
        2. b. hollow
        3. a. enjoyable
        4. a. recurrence
        5. b. covered
        6. conductor
        7. pursuer
        8. prisoner
        9. hunter
       10. manager
       11. partridge
       12. bovine
       13. hammer
       14. varmint
       15. paw

D. Check with your dictionary

Chapter 9

The Teacher of Individualized Reading

In a sense, this whole book is about the teacher of individualized reading, but the two selections in this chapter are focused particularly in this direction.

The first passage is taken from the monograph series "Improving Reading Instruction" prepared by the staff of the San Diego County Department of Education. In preparation for the research project described in this series a scale was developed to measure teachers' attitudes towards various approaches to reading instruction. The scale and an explanation of its purpose is included in the excerpt reproduced here.

The second selection is a description of the excellent series of films prepared for the training of individualized reading teachers by Professor Lyman C. Hunt, Jr., now of the University of Vermont, while he was at Pennsylvania State University.

A Teacher Inventory

by

San Diego Board of Education

(This material is excerpted from Teacher Inventory
of Approaches to the Teaching of Reading, Improving Reading Instruction, Monograph No. 3, 1961.)

A Teacher Inventory of Approaches
to the Teaching of Reading

Systematic evaluation of a reading program is essential for its improvement. Such evaluation may be classified
into three general areas. These areas are: (1) evaluation
of pupil achievement in reading, (2) evaluation of the instructional materials used, (3) analysis of the teacher's approach
to reading instruction. Considerable attention has tradition-
ally been given to the first two areas, but little has been
done in the area of analysis of teacher approaches. This
monograph deals with a method of teacher self-evaluation of
three selected approaches to the teaching of reading and provides an instrument to assist in the evaluation process.
This instrument, "A Teacher Inventory of Approaches to the
Teaching of Reading," was developed and used by elementary
school teachers participating in the San Diego County Reading
Study Project during 1959-60. The sixty-seven teacher-re-
searchers in this study rated the use of the inventory between good and excellent, which were the top two ratings on
a five-point scale. An explanation of the organization of the
inventory is presented in this monograph, together with suggestions of how the inventory may be used, directions for
scoring and interpreting results, and a copy of the inventory
with its scoring sheet. Persons wishing to reproduce the inventory and scoring sheet may do so giving appropriate recognition to the Department of Education, San Diego County.

I. ORGANIZATION OF THE INVENTORY

The inventory consists of thirty-three items categorized into three approaches to the teaching of reading--namely, the Basic, Individualized, and Language Experience Approaches as defined in "A Description of Three Approaches to the Teaching of Reading." The descriptive statements in the inventory relate to the following eleven elements of a total reading program:

> Purpose of Reading Instruction
> Basis of Plan for Reading Instruction
> Motivation for Reading
> Materials of Instruction
> Classroom Organization for Reading
> Provision for Direct Reading Instruction
> Provision for Supplementary Reading
> Place of Skill Development
> Place of Vocabulary Development
> Provision for Individual Differences
> Basis of Evaluation

Space is provided at the end of the inventory for the teacher's own written descriptive analysis of the approach he is using in reading instruction. The score sheet enables the teacher to evaluate the responses he has made to items in the inventory.

II. SUGGESTIONS FOR USE OF THE INVENTORY

There are two primary ways in which the inventory might be used:

1. A teacher might use it to analyze the approach he is presently using in his teaching of reading. Through analyzing his responses to the individual items on the inventory, he may be helped to systematically think through what he believes about reading instruction.

2. A teacher desiring to change his approach to the teaching of reading might use the inventory to measure the degree of change he is able to effect. He would first respond to the inventory in terms of his present methodology as it relates to elements

of the Basic, Individualized, and Language Experience Approaches.   After a period of study, in-
service education, and possible experimentation in
his classroom using the approach to which he wished
to change, he would again respond to the inventory.
By comparing differences in responses on the inventory taken at two different times, the teacher could
see whether, and to what extent, he has been successful in effecting change.

Teachers desiring to experiment with different approaches may wish to have other materials developed in the
original Reading Study Project.   These include "A Description of Three Approaches to the Teaching of Reading," "An
Inventory of Reading Attitude," and "Manual for Teaching the
Language Experience Approach."   Copies of these materials
can be secured from the Department of Education, San Diego
County.

III.   DIRECTIONS FOR SCORING AND INTERPRETING
RESULTS OF THE INVENTORY SCORE SHEET

After a teacher completes the inventory, he can use
the score sheet to determine how closely he is following one
of the three approaches to the teaching of reading.   Some
teachers may find that the approach they are using includes
elements from more than one approach.

Two factors should be examined in interpreting the
scores of the inventory: (1) the pattern of the total scores
in the Basic Approach, the Individualized Approach, and the
Language Experience Approach; (2) an item analysis of each
of the eleven elements of the reading program and their in-
terrelationships.

Total Score Pattern

As a result of the use of this inventory in the Reading Study Project, it is believed that one of three basic patterns will emerge.

1. A high score in one approach and lesser scores in
the two other approaches indicates agreement with
the high scoring approach.   This agreement becomes more significant as the spread increases between the high score and the scores in the other

two approaches.

In Illustrative Example 1 on page 274 the high score of 51 on the Basic Approach is considered quite reliable because the scores on the Individualized and on the Language Experience Approaches fall in the disagree range. This pattern of total scores indicates to the teacher that his approach to teaching of reading is in agreement with the identified elements of the Basic Approach.

2. A second pattern which might emerge is one of relatively high scores on two different approaches and a lower score on the third approach.

In Illustrative Example 2 on page 276 a teacher scored 50 on the Individualized Approach, 51 on the Language Experience Approach, and 26 on the Basic Approach. This pattern of total scores would indicate that the teacher was successful in combining the Individualized and Language Experience Approaches or might be using elements of each of them with different groups in the class.

3. A third pattern is the scores for all three approaches falling in the same range of agreement or disagreement.

In Illustrative Example 3 on page 278 a teacher scored 47 on the Basic Approach, 47 on the Individualized Approach, and 44 on the Language Experience Approach. All of these marks fall in the "Agree" range. This third pattern of total scores could indicate two possible conclusions. First, the teacher may be using elements of each of the approaches with different groups in his class. Secondly, he may not have used the inventory with discrimination to analyze his method of teaching reading. There are some basic incompatibilities between the three approaches, especially when each approach is considered in totality. If the third pattern of total scores appears, the teacher should carefully reconsider each of the eleven elements of his reading program. Such consideration should help him to better understand his approach as it relates to the three defined approaches. Study of Monograph 2 of this series, "A Description of

Three Approaches to the Teaching of Reading," and
its attached bibliography will give the teacher the
additional insights he needs to discern elements of
each reading approach and to differentiate between
the approaches.

Item Analysis of Elements of the Reading Program

The teacher should study each of the eleven elements
of his reading program as indicated on the score sheet. He
should analyze each element in reference to his total score
pattern of approaches.

In Illustrative Example 1 the teacher's total score
pattern indicated a strong agreement or acceptance of
the Basic Approach. Element H, "How I Include Skill
Development in My Reading Program," shows a possible inconsistency with the total score pattern. The
teacher's score of 1 on item 23 indicates a disagreement with the skill development element of the Basic
Approach. The score of 5 on items 2 and 7 would
give further indication of inconsistency. In this case
the teacher should reconsider numbers 23, 2, and 7
to make sure that this rating of these items is actually in agreement with his reading approach. If the
items are scored accurately, the teacher should further analyze this aspect of his reading program. He
might gain help in referring to Monograph 2, "A Description of Three Approaches to the Teaching of
Reading," previously indicated.

In Illustrative Example 2 the teacher's total score pattern indicated strong agreement with the Individualized
and Language Experience Approaches. In item analysis of the elements of the program there appears to
be an inconsistency in item F, "How I provide for Direct Reading Instruction." In this case, the teacher
should again consider items 5, 6, and 32. He has
indicated strong agreement with the statement that he
does most of his direct teaching of reading as pupils
discuss with him, and the reading group, the story or
selection to be read. This agreement is compatible
with the Basic Approach, which in the total score he
tends to reject. In this case a more careful analysis
of the elements of the three approaches is advised.

In Illustrative Example 3 there is a pattern of agreement with all three approaches. In analyzing the individual elements there is no total disagreement on any of the items. In this case the teacher should strive to develop a deeper insight into each of the elements of the three approaches to the teaching of reading.

The Written Description of Approach

The teacher's written description of his approach at the end of the inventory will prove useful for comparison with the individual items of the eleven elements as the teacher continues his self-evaluation.

By carefully describing the manner in which he carries out the various elements of his approach, the teacher provides himself with a means of assessing the accuracy of the ratings he has given each element in the inventory. In addition, he may be helped in determining which of those elements that should be contained in a total reading program are not present in his own teaching.

Illustrative Example 1

Elements of the Reading Program	Basic		Individualized		Language Experience	
	Item	No.	Item	No.	Item	No.
A. My Purpose for Reading Instruction	28	5	33	1	3	1
B. The Basis for My Plan of Reading Instruction	27	5	24	1	21	1
C. How I Motivate for Reading Instruction	12	5	9	1	18	1
D. Materials of Reading Instruction Which I Use	1	5	16	1	11	1
E. How I Organize My Classroom for Reading	19	5	25	1	4	1
F. How I Provide for Direct Reading Instruction	5	5	6	1	32	1
G. How I Provide for Supplementary Reading	15	5	17	1	22	1
H. How I Include Skills Development in My Reading Program	23	1	2	5	7	5
I. How I Incorporate Vocabulary Development in My Reading Program	31	5	30	1	10	1
J. How I Provide for Individual Differences in My Reading Program	14	5	13	1	8	1
K. My Criteria Evaluation	20	5	26	1	29	1
Total	51		15		15	

Scale of Scores	11	22	33	44	55
Basic					
Individualized					
Language Experience					
Degree of Agreement	Disagree	Tend to Disagree		Tend to Agree	Agree

Illustrative Example 2

Elements of the Reading Program	Basic		Individualized		Language Experience	
	Item	No.	Item	No.	Item	No.
A. My Purpose for Reading Instruction	28	1	33	5	3	5
B. The Basis for My Plan of Reading Instruction	27	2	24	5	21	5
C. How I Motivate for Reading Instruction	12	3	9	5	18	5
D. Materials of Reading Instruction Which I Use	1	2	16	4	11	5
E. How I Organize My Classroom for Reading	19	1	25	5	4	5
F. How I Provide for Direct Reading Instruction	5	5	6	1	32	1
G. How I Provide for Supplementary Reading	15	4	17	5	22	5
H. How I Include Skill Development in My Reading Program	23	3	2	5	7	5
I. How I Incorporate Vocabulary Development in My Reading Program	31	1	30	5	10	5
J. How I Provide for Individual Differences in My Reading Program	14	1	13	5	8	5
K. My Criteria Evaluation	20	3	26	5	29	5
Total	26		50		51	

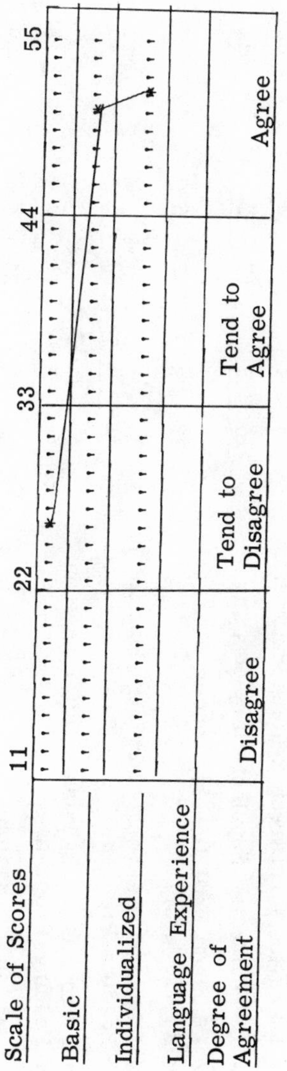
Scale of Scores
11
22
33
44
55
Basic
Individualized
Language Experience
Degree of Agreement
Disagree
Tend to Disagree
Tend to Agree
Agree

Illustrative Example 3

Elements of the Reading Program	Basic		Individualized		Language Experience	
	Item No.	No.	Item No.	No.	Item No.	No.
A. My Purpose for Reading Instruction	28	2	33	5	3	5
B. The Basis for My Plan of Reading Instruction	27	5	24	5	21	5
C. How I Motivate for Reading Instruction	12	5	9	4	18	5
D. Materials of Reading Instruction Which I Use	1	4	16	5	11	4
E. How I Organize my Classroom for Reading	19	5	25	5	4	4
F. How I Provide for Direct Reading Instruction	5	4	6	2	32	2
G. How I Provide for Supplementary Reading	15	5	17	2	22	4
H. How I Include Skill Development in My Reading Program	23	2	2	5	7	3
I. How I Incorporate Vocabulary Development in My Reading Program	31	5	30	5	10	5
J. How I Provide for Individual Differences in My Reading Program	14	5	13	4	8	2
K. My Criteria Evaluation	20	5	26	5	29	5
Total		47		47		44

Scales of Scores

Basic

Individualized

Language Experience

Degree of Agreement

11 22 33 44 55

Disagree | Tend to Disagree | Tend to Agree | Agree

The chief purpose in using this inventory is to assist the teacher, through self-evaluation, to improve his insight and understanding of the teaching of reading. It should be remembered that there is no single approach considered to be the best or the only one for all teachers. Each teacher should develop an approach to the teaching of reading that is in harmony with his most effective teaching style. This can best be accomplished by the careful analysis and study of his approach to the teaching of reading. It is possible that a combination of various elements of the different approaches will prove to be most effective for some teachers in achieving success in reading instruction. An eclectic approach to the teaching of reading, however, should not contain incompatible elements.

Since the teaching-learning situation is a dynamic one, the teacher is continually evaluating the effectiveness of his approach to teaching and is constantly striving to develop his own most effective plan of teaching. It is hoped that the inventory discussed here will assist the teacher in this very important task of self-evaluation.

Teacher Inventory of Approaches
to the Teaching of Reading

Prepared by
Reading Study Project Committee
Department of Education, San Diego County

Instructions: Here are 33 statements regarding the teaching of reading as different teachers would approach it. These statements should be read carefully and then judged in terms of their accuracy for describing your approach to the teaching of reading. Your judgment will be indicated by using the following key:

Place a "5" beside the item if it is entirely accurate.
Place a "4" beside the item if it tends to be accurate.
Place a "3" beside the item if it is neither accurate nor inaccurate.
Place a "2" beside the item if it tends to be inaccurate.
Place a "1" beside the item if it is entirely inaccurate.

Please read all 33 statements at least once before you attempt to make final judgments.

_____ 1. I provide a systematic program of instruction in reading for my class primarily through the use of a single main source of printed materials.

_____ 2. In my class, attention is given equally to reading skills, interests, and attitudes.

_____ 3. The basic purpose of reading instruction in my class is to extend use of all of the language arts by using each child's thoughts, ideas, and experiences in language activities.

_____ 4. My classroom is organized so far as reading instruction is concerned for the production, sharing, and reading of graphic and written materials based upon the child's own thoughts, concerns, and ideas.

_____ 5. I do most of my direct teaching of reading as pupils discuss with me and their group the story or selection to be read, and as they participate in reading group activities.

_____ 6. In my class, the individual pupil receives most of my direct instruction in reading during individual conferences. This direct instruction is based upon the reading selections he has read or is reading on his own.

_____ 7. In my class, reading skill development follows naturally from each child's oral and written expression and is therefore dependent upon each child's unique language development rather than upon a predetermined sequence.

_____ 8. In my class, I utilize materials which are in the pupil's language based upon his thoughts and experiences. This material serves as a major source of reading material for himself and other pupils. This serves as a primary means for providing for individual differences in my class.

_____ 9. In my class, I feel that the best motivation for reading is stimulated through provision of a wide variety of reading materials which meet the interests and maturational needs of the pupils.

_____ 10. I introduce words (new reading vocabulary) to the children as they find a need to use them in their writing and reading of material. Dictionaries, word lists, and other sources of new words are a- vailable and the children are encouraged to use them as needs arise.

_____ 11. The reading activities of the pupils in my class are based primarily upon many other language experi- ences, especially oral and written language of the individual pupils.

_____ 12. In my class, children are motivated to read by be- ing helped by me to see the relation of the story or selection to be read to their experiences, and by being helped to acquire the vocabulary and skills necessary for success in each new reading task.

_____ 13. I try to provide for individual differences in my class by providing and encouraging the use of a wide range and variety of printed materials.   I provide for individual conferences with each pupil in which we discuss his reading problems and his progress.   (I am also able to do individual instruc- tion in these conferences.)   Group conferences are used for the same purposes when this is appropriate.

_____ 14. In my class, provision for individual differences is made mainly through the use of flexible ability groups.   This allows me to give attention to the common problems of each of the groups.   I can al- so give attention to individual student's problems as a part of the group instruction.

_____ 15. In my class, free reading of library table materi- als is allowed while other pupils are being in- structed in reading groups, or on special days des- ignated for free reading, or when pupils have fin- ished assigned work, or any combination of these possibilities.   Free reading time is included to as- sist children in strengthening their reading skills and for personal enjoyment.

_____ 16. I try to provide for and encourage many language activities based upon the self-selected reading material read by individual pupils or by several pupils. Handwriting, spelling, written expression and usage are given attention when they apply to the reading selections which have been chosen by individual pupils.

_____ 17. In my class, most reading by children is "free" reading in that the children generally select their own material to read and are encouraged to read this material for purposes apparent to them, one of which is to become a better reader.

_____ 18. I believe that motivation for reading in my class is stimulated through the child's realization that his oral language expression based upon his own experiences and thoughts as well as the ideas and thoughts of others can be written and thus read.

_____ 19. I have a regular reading period set up to take care of direct teaching of reading and other reading activities. Handwriting, spelling, written expression and usage are taught at another time and are given attention during the reading time when they directly apply to the reading lesson situation.

_____ 20. I evaluate pupil progress in my reading program in relation to material he [the student] is able to read and his achievement of the skills necessary to read successfully a given level of reading material.

_____ 21. I base my plan for reading instruction upon the oral and written expression and identified needs of the children.

_____ 22. I encourage children to use free reading time to read materials prepared by other pupils, books of special interest to them, and materials which will help them develop ideas for their own written productions.

_____ 23. Skill development is the primary objective of my reading program.

_____ 24. My plan for reading instruction is determined by and follows the reading needs of individual children as they meet reading problems which require my guidance and help.

_____ 25. My classroom is organized to facilitate many and varied activities relating to reading. I set up time for individual pupil conferences, small group reading situations, and provide for silent reading of self-selected materials for individual students.

_____ 26. I evaluate children's growth in reading in terms of the quality and quantity of materials read, skills acquired as well as interests and attitudes developed.

_____ 27. I group the pupils in my room in terms of reading ability (generally three groups). I try to gear my instruction in reading to the needs of each of the groups.

_____ 28. Reading instruction in my class is designed, for the most part, to develop the skills and mechanics of the reading process.

_____ 29. I evaluate the reading growth of the pupil in terms of his ability to express himself in oral and written form, in terms of his skill in reading, comprehending and interpreting written material of all types.

_____ 30. I provide for pupil growth in vocabulary through individual pupil-teacher conferences, encouraging pupils to seek assistance from other pupils in the class, silent reading of a variety of printed materials, group conferences, and through encouraging the use of resource materials (dictionaries, word lists, etc.).

_____ 31. I introduce new vocabulary to each reading group prior to their silent reading of a new selection.

_____ 32. I base my direct instruction in reading primarily upon material produced by the children themselves. This direct teaching, depending upon the situation, is done through group activities, total class activities, or through sessions with individual pupils.

_____ 33. The main purpose of reading instruction in my class is to develop wholesome reading interests and attitudes as well as the development of adequate skills through the child's desire to discover, select, and explore a wide variety of reading materials.

In your own words, describe briefly the way you feel you teach reading. You might include statements concerning your purposes for reading instruction, place of skill development, vocabulary development, plan for instruction, evaluation of pupil progress, classroom organization, provision for individual differences, etc. Give examples of methods, techniques, and procedures if you wish.

_____

_____

_____

_____

_____

_____

_____

Scoring Sheet for Teacher Inventory of Approaches to the Teaching of Reading

The scoring sheet consists of three columns. Each of these columns contains an item number which is directed to an element of the reading program.

<u>Directions for scoring:</u>

Step 1. The score (1, 2, 3, 4, or 5) which a teacher gives to each item should be recorded in the item space provided on the scoring sheet.

Step 2. Total the numbers recorded in the Basic Approach column, the Individualized Approach column and the Language Experience Approach column.

Step 3. Mark with an X the total score of each approach at the appropriate spot on the profile scale.

Elements of the Reading Program	Basic Item No.	Individualized Item No.	Language Experience Item No.
A. My Purpose for Reading Instruction	28	33	3
B. The Basis for My Plan of Reading Instruction	27	24	21
C. How I Motivate for Reading Instruction	12	9	18
D. Materials of Reading Instruction Which I Use	1	16	11
E. How I Organize My Classroom for Reading	19	25	4
F. How I Provide for Direct Reading Instruction	5	6	32
G. How I Provide for Supplementary Reading	15	17	22
H. How I Include Skill Development in My Reading Program	23	2	7
I. How I Incorporate Vocabulary Development in My Reading Program	31	30	10
J. How I Provide for Individual Differences in My Reading Program	14	13	8
K. My Criteria Evaluation	20	26	29
Total			

Scale of Scores	11	22	33	44	55
Basic					
Individualized					
Language Experience					
Degree of Agreement	Disagree	Tend to Disagree	Tend to Agree		Agree

Training Individualized Reading Teachers
Through the Use of Films

by

Lyman C. Hunt, Jr.

(This material is excerpted from An Experimental
Project Appraising the Effectiveness of a Program
Series on Reading Instruction Using Open-Circuit
Television, Report on Grant No. 736059.00
N. D. E. A., 1961.)

The characteristics of an individualized reading program used as the basis for developing the measures are described here.

1. Children select their own reading materials depending on their interests, purposes, and facility in reading.

2. Children read their books at a rate which their
purposes, preferences, and proficiencies permit.

3. Children must be responsible for learning gained
through reading. Each individual shows to what degree he
has become involved in learning from his reading and can be
helped, guided, and taught by the teacher. This can be done
by means of the personal contacts the teacher makes through
conferences: A) with an individual child on a very close personal basis; B) with a small group about the same book;
C) with a small group in which each child has read a different book; D) with the individual reporting to the whole class.

4. Skill development takes place at the time it is
needed with the children who need it. As it becomes evident
that a child is ready to be taught or helped to improve or re-
fine one he has already developed partially, the teacher provides for such learnings on the spot or by assigning the child
to a small group which will meet soon for such a purpose.
In this way, skills which the child learns by himself natur-

ally are not belabored in the group and valuable time can be used for those skills in which the child needs help.

5. Many kinds of creative expression come as outgrowths of this kind of a reading program. Creativity may take the form of a picture, a diorama, an original story or poem, or a mobile. The degree of a child's involvement in the story, the form of expression he elects may in part determine the creative effort the child makes in responding to material read.

The Basal Textbook Reading Program

It is assumed that there is a common understanding of the policies, principles and practices which give identity to the basal textbook program. Its basic features may be described in terms of material, classroom organization, and instructional practices.

1. Materials usually consist of short story episodes and anthology type books. The textbooks are developed by series or sequence and are designated as appropriate for a particular grade level.

2. Classroom organization usually consists of several so-called ability subgroups which are met by the teacher on a rotation basis. Children work on assigned tasks at their seats when they are not involved in direct group instruction. Group instruction is developed by the teacher according to the progress of the particular group through the textbook sequence. Each member of the group moves ahead at the pace established for the group.

3. Instructional practice demands that each textbook selection be developed with the group in the order of its occurrence in the series according to the following steps:

      A. Creating interest
      B. Study of vocabulary new to the series
      C. Reading
         a. Directed silent reading
         b. Rereading or oral reading
      D. Skill development and practice
      E. Follow-up work (usually workbook)

As plans developed, it became evident that four major

areas would form the foundation of the TV program series:

1. a variety of ways of using books with children:

In a reading program in which each child selects
a different book to read, there are various ways in which he
may choose books and react to them. He may know exactly
what he wants next or he may ask the teacher's guidance in
locating books about his interests. (Whatever he reads has
an influence on what he chooses to read later.) He may
read just for what the author of the book says to him. He
may want to talk about his book with others--the teacher, a
friend, a group of classmates. He may be moved to respond
to his reading through an art form or in creative writing.
An infinite variety of responses and combinations of responses
is possible.

2. the reading-writing, writing-reading interaction:

Reading is possible because someone has written
down his thoughts, his ideas, his reactions to surroundings
and to particular situations. Reading which is stimulating
encourages readers to write down their own reactions and
thoughts. Children write about what they read and read stories they have written.

3. the development of skills:

Within the framework of the individualized reading
program, skills are developed at the point and at the time
when they are needed by the child. Growth in skills is an
individual matter just as are the other phases of learning.

4. the ways in which to help the child who finds reading difficult;

Such a child finds himself in a unique position for
learning. With group pressure removed he receives help
which is geared especially to his needs.

The content of each of the 15 weekly programs is
described here briefly.

READING INSTRUCTION: INDIVIDUALLY OR IN A GROUP -
GRADE LEVEL 2

Idea of children reading in a small group or individually;

how children may be helped to gain confidence in group work and then move to individualized reading; book sharing by individuals with the group.

FROM UNIT STUDY INTO INDIVIDUALIZED READING - GRADE LEVEL 2

Unit work developed by a group as it leads each member through different avenues of interest into an individualized reading program. Children and teacher discuss the unit which they worked out together. Each child then branches out on his own independent reading.

THE INDIVIDUAL CONFERENCE IN INDIVIDUALIZED READING - GRADE LEVEL 6

Individual conference between teacher and pupil is the heart of the individualized reading program. Here the teacher helps the child discover deep and personalized meanings of the book he is reading, detects and alleviates specific reading needs, and gives attention to oral readings in a natural situation. Teacher does all these things as he meets several of his students individually.

GLIMPSES OF INDIVIDUALIZED READING - GRADE LEVEL 1

First grade teacher shows several phases of individualized reading. Use of chart to develop meaningful reading material and word recognition. Examples of the individual conference at the first grade level. Two children work on word learning activities through a word game.

CHILDREN CHOOSE BOOKS TO READ - GRADE LEVEL 4 & 5

Children's selection of their own reading material as influenced by their interests, goals, and reading facility as well as by actions of their own classmates and teachers. Creation of a mobile, a picture, and an oral summary as resultant activities and outcomes from their reading.

CHILDREN SHARE WHAT THEY HAVE READ -
GRADE LEVEL 3

Children sharing with others their reactions and responses to books read. Making of a simple diorama; increasing of children's vocabularies through the study of "puzzling" words; examples of both individual and group work in reading.

READING COMPREHENSION THROUGH GROUP DISCUSSION -
GRADE LEVEL 5

Teacher demonstrates teaching reading comprehension through discussion in depth with a small group; develops a way of helping children to become so deeply involved in what is read that each takes from this reading something that touches his or her own personal life.

FROM CHART TO BOOKLET
GRADE LEVEL 1

Teacher writes a story on a chart as some first graders tell of a trip to the television studio. She allows children to point out words and sentences on the chart to help develop their word recognition and then writes each sentence on a separate paper. Children choose which sentences they will illustrate. The finished "illustrated sentences" are stapled together into a booklet for the classroom reading table. Boy reads the finished booklet for the group.

CLASSROOM ORGANIZATION FOR INDIVIDUALIZED READING
GRADE LEVEL 3

Four parts of the individualized reading program developed through conversations between the children, the teacher, and the program hostess. Children show steps of choosing books, independent silent reading, individual teacher conferences, and sharing books through oral reporting and creative activities. Child-centered, book-centered program shown. Responsibility which teacher develops in children so that she can be free to work with individual children stressed.

DISCUSSING IDEAS IN BOOKS -
GRADE LEVEL 6

In order to discuss books with children it is not necessary
for a teacher to know every detail in the books the children
read. Teacher invites a group of boys and girls to come
together to discuss the ideas in the books they are reading
or just have read. Importance of discussion questions asked
by the teacher.

THEY WANT TO READ ABOUT EXPERIENCES -
GRADE LEVEL 2

Children's natural interests in living things (chicks) and in
planning a trip to the poultry plant were responsible for a
fine chart which was used to develop word recognition and
word attack skills through games with words from the chart
story. Children become engrossed in reading independently
a variety of stories related to what they anticipate seeing at
the poultry plant. They tell each other about the stories.

HELPING WITH WORD RECOGNITION -
GRADE LEVEL 4 & 5

Group of games is in process for children who need further
help with developing word recognition vocabularies. Group
disbands when its purpose is served. The teacher helps one
child to develop relationships between familiar and unfamiliar
words (phonics). Girls who have read one of the Madeline
books play it as a puppet show before the class.

WORD GAMES TO DEVELOP RECOGNITION SKILLS -
GRADE LEVEL 5

Learning word recognition skills and building vocabulary
makes a happy and profitable occupation, rather than a deadly
one, by playing games some of which the children devise
themselves. A study of varied types of games teaches the
philosophy underlying the use of games in developing word
recognition skills.

EVALUATING CHILDREN'S PROGRESS IN AN INDIVIDUALIZED PROGRAM OF READING - GRADE LEVEL 3

What he gains from his reading is a measure of the child's reading progress. Answers given to questions, performance in oral reading, and involvement in reading as determining factors when teachers and children work together. Other measures of child's reading emerge through discussion, criticism of others, and self-criticism. Records kept by teachers and children on a card or in a notebook, as well as other culminating activities, show us what a child learns from his reading.

READING AND WRITING THROUGH STORYTELLING - GRADE LEVEL 1

Children have always loved to be told stories. A teacher tells a folk story to which the children listen with delight. After talking about the folk tale, they ask to write an original story. Creative writings in action.

USE OF THE TEACHER-PUPIL CONFERENCE GRADE LEVEL 6.

Stress placed on both the individual and group conference where each child is reading a book of his own choice. The teacher talks individually to two students questioning each to develop a deeper understanding of his reading and giving help as it is needed. Group meeting of students with teacher who guides the discussion of their books around interesting ideas common to the children or emerging from the books. Values of each kind of conference with children.

USE OF CHARTS IN INDIVIDUALIZED READING - GRADE LEVEL 2

"A trip to the woods" as an experience base for learning to read, learning activities which grew out of the trip include a chart story, an original story by one child, a diary, and discussion of books about things seen. Illustration of two important principles, namely: that our most important reading is derived directly from living and thinking and that word learning is most effective when meaning is developed prior to the study of the whole word and the study of parts common to many words.

CHILDREN SELECT THE BOOKS THEY READ -
GRADE LEVEL 4 & 5

The child's selection of his own reading material capitalizes on his interests. One child tells about a book he has read, two others play a ball game with words, the teacher helps locate Paul Revere's ride, two girls are doing research on message sending, several children tell about books they have read. Importance of freedom of choosing books to this reading program.

READING-WRITING INTERACTION -
GRADE LEVEL 3

Teacher reviews with her children the important ideas in the part of an exciting dog story which she has just read to them. Each child then reads to the group the ending for the story which he composed. The teacher then reads aloud the author's conclusion. Watch children think.

SHARING BOOKS AND STORIES -
GRADE LEVEL 1

A teacher and her children share some of their favorite books. Each child, as well as the teacher, shows a particular part liked best. Presentation of lists of favorite children's books at other grade levels, ways to keep informed about them, and sources of information.

The following summary conclusions seem justified:

1. Theoretical differences between the basal textbook program for reading instruction and the principles of the individualized program for reading instruction can be precisely defined and described.

2. On the basis of theoretical differences so defined, evaluative measures can be constructed for purposes of detecting differences in the application of these described principles within the setting of the classroom reading program.

3. The evaluative measures can be used to discern

differences which exist among teachers in the classroom instructional program in reading. Each of the three evaluative measures for teachers and the one measure for parents was sufficiently precise to reflect differences in performance or in attitudes.

4. Principles basic to the individualized reading program can be demonstrated through a TV program series and carried to a widely dispersed audience of teachers and parents through open-circuit TV.

5. A TV program series carrying content of this nature has a measurable effect on teacher performance within the classroom reading instruction program. The influence of the TV program series can be seen in terms of observed teacher performance. In addition, a self-report of teacher performance, and teacher attitudes toward reading instruction reflect the impact of the TV program series.

6. Attitudes of parents can be similarly affected and measured following the viewing of the TV series.

7. The TV program series apparently does not have a direct, measurable influence on children's performance when measured in terms of reading achievement and attitudes toward reading.

The generalization is made that open-circuit television can be used to influence the performance and attitudes of teachers and the attitudes of parents with respect to a particular educational concept, namely individualized reading instruction. Of great value in this specific project was the use of open-circuit television in an area of relatively sparse population density. It was possible to convey ideas demonstrated on TV over a wide geographical area to teachers and parents remote from the originating source of the ideas.

Chapter 10

The Librarian's Role in Individualized Reading

Individualized reading provides a good opportunity for cooperation between classroom teachers and librarians. An excellent discussion of their respective roles is given in West.[1]

In this chapter the first selection is excerpted from an article by Professor Patrick J. Groff of San Diego State College.

The remaining two selections are written from the librarian's viewpoint and are excerpted from articles by Marguerite P. Archer and Jean E. Lowrie, respectively.

Note

1. West, 612.

How the Librarian Can Help
the Individualized Reading Teacher

by

Patrick J. Groff

(This material is excerpted from the author's article, "The Librarian and Individualized Reading," which appeared in the Wilson Library Bulletin in January, 1960.)

The crucial difference between individualized reading and the teaching of children in a group using a single book, is essentially the adapting of the reading material to the child rather than the other way around.   Teachers well know that no child learns to read at the same rate as another, nor are his interests exactly the same.   By permitting him to select the material he will read, individualized reading allows the child to learn at his own individual pace and to read materials that are interesting to him.   Remedial reading is seldom necessary in classes using this method because there is no group standard for any child to fall behind, thereby becoming a remedial reading case.   There is less opportunity for a child to feel inferior because he is not held up to a group standard.   Bright children, on the other hand, are not held back and spurt ahead at an astonishing rate.

The idea of individualized reading is hardly a new one. Annie E. Moore wrote in 1916:

> The question may fairly be asked whether many children might not pass almost unconsciously into the art of reading and largely through their own spontaneous effort if they were surrounded by the right stimuli and freed from subjection to highly specialized, closely regulated methods, applied by overanxious adults who are determined that nothing shall interfere with the particular scheme in vogue. [1]

Individualized reading in this country in the passing
years has received much of the same kind of opposition as
do Anna Vorontosov's fictional efforts, however. There is
a passive agreement by many with it in theory, but a strong
feeling that it will not work for practical reasons. The support for the method is gaining momentum, nevertheless. Although only one textbook on the teaching of reading freely encourages the use of the plan--in fact, defends it as the primary method by which reading should be taught--two other
books totally devoted to describing the practice are now a-
vailable. Edward Dolch, a long-time specialist in the teaching of reading, is one of the few authorities who sees a strong
future for the method. He believes that because of the mental health emphasis in today's schools, supplementary reading
in the future will become of first importance, replacing basic
reading textbooks as the main body of reading material. He
remarks, "Many teachers have 'felt it in their bones' that
this is what the reading program needed..."

Children's librarians are well aware of the surge in
the publication of very-easy-to-read books for beginning
readers. The writer has compiled a list of over 300 books
published recently that the first-grade child can read independently or with a minimum of help. It seems likely that
such materials will become increasingly available. The suit-
ability of these materials for individualized reading is obvious, and speaks, at least indirectly, for the expanding acceptance of this method.

The published reports of individualized reading indicate that children learn to read as well and often better under
this method than under group instruction. There is the added
satisfaction for the child of being able to choose which books
he wants to read and to read them at a pace comfortable for
him. The ideas of freedom and reading books tend to become synonymous concepts in his mind. This observation by
the child, in itself, has manifold implications for our domes-
tic society. Parents, also, seem to be enthusiastic about the
plan, frequently because of the changes in attitudes about
reading and books they notice in their children. In some
cases children have brought parents to the library rather
than vice versa.

Some of the implications or points of significance for
librarians of individualized reading need to be pointed out.
Probably librarians by and large subscribe in principle to
this method of teaching reading. At least they long have pro-

tested the practice of classifying children as certain types of readers, a practice they have felt tends to restrict the child to reading materials of a relatively unchanging nature in both difficulty and interest, but does not take into sufficient consideration the inherent interest of specific reading material, or the effort on the part of the child to read highly motivating materials.

Individualized reading, of course, makes no absolute judgment for the child as to what material he can or should read. He makes the decisions under a process of self-selection, with the teacher acting as a guide and a counselor. This process, in fact, reminds one very much of the work of a librarian. The teacher must go beyond this point, obviously, and gives the child systematic help in word recognition, study skills and other reading abilities. Because the teacher actually does function much as a librarian at the same time, knowledge of children's books and their contents becomes as important for him as for the librarian. The help librarians can give in providing in-service education for teachers using this method should not be overlooked.

Librarians often have been shocked at the paucity of reading materials available in some schools. They should realize the advocates of individualized reading also find such conditions deplorable. The success of individualized reading depends upon the immediate availability of numerous and varied books and other reading materials at many reading-difficulty levels. One of the major objectives of individualized reading, therefore, is to increase the number and variety of books in schools. These prerequisites indicate the need for a school library in every elementary school as well as in every secondary school. Some advocates of individualized reading believe that the teaching of children to read in groups, using a single book at a time, actually has hindered the growth of school libraries. They believe if individualized reading were widely accepted, school libraries would be established as a natural consequence. This in turn might very well stimulate the education of more school librarians.

There is conclusive evidence in the reports of teachers using individualized reading that children who are taught to read by this method read many times more books than those taught by group methods. Also there is some evidence that the books they read during their leisure time are of better literary quality.

Some public libraries already have felt the effects of
schools, with no libraries of their own undertaking individualized reading programs. Because individualized reading as
yet is not widespread, the calls from schools for visits by
the librarian to explain library procedures and to describe
the juvenile book collection can usually be met.

Librarians among others have become distressed by
the increasing tendency in education to place a premium upon reading which is aimed at enabling the individual to get
along with others, or to more readily find group acceptance.
The child must "average out" in his reading interests so as
to become very much like every other child. He must, by
and large, read what other children read. Private aims in
reading are looked upon as non-utilitarian, and, therefore, are
suspected of having little value in satisfying group objectives.
The bookish, "lone-wolf" child becomes a source of disturb-
ance for his teacher, while the conformist child who smoothly meshes any individual purposes he may have into the
larger group framework is given much approval. The child,
in other words, is constantly required to read for external,
outer-directed reasons. Individualized reading disagrees to
a great extent with these objectives for reading. As far as
possible, under this plan the child defines his individual
reading goals and selects the reading material to satisfy
them. It is contended that more self-reliance and self-suf-
ficiency as well as a greater development of inner resources
are the result.

As the status of books in the minds of the general
public grows, so grows the stature of the librarian. It is
axiomatic that the person who reads little, or who reads materials of a decidedly low literary value, sees little need for
improvement of library service or the betterment of librarians' salaries and working conditions. One of the arguments
of the supporters of individualized reading is that by this
method the child will grow to adulthood with a more favorable attitude toward books, an increased sensitivity to the
value of libraries and library services, and a protective
point of view toward the inviolability of free expression and
the unhindered distribution of written materials.

Note

1. Moore, Annie E. "The Use of Children's Initiative in
    Beginning Reading." Teachers College Record 17:
    330-43, September, 1916.

A Librarian Views Individualized Reading

by

Marguerite P. Archer

(This material is excerpted from the author's article, "Individualized Reading," which appeared in
the Library Journal in October, 1961. Copyright
(c) R. R. Bowker, 1961.)

Librarians have often been adversely critical of regimented teaching practices through which children acquire
rudimentary reading skills but fail to develop a love of reading. Fortunately, many educators have also been concerned
about the same situation.

When the testing movement of 1910-1920 revealed
great differences among children within the same grade many
schools began to make adjustments in their reading programs. Most schools adopted a three-group system of instructional organization; in this system pupils were broadly
classified and taught according to their average reading ability as measured by standardized tests.

This type of achievement grouping, however, still did
not result in adaptation of teaching methods and materials to
the wide range of differences existing among individual children. Instead, the three-group pattern became a new lock-
step. Three groups were still inadequate to meet the needs
of children and the higher aims of conscientious teachers.

Teachers using the three-group lockstep found that in
many instances youngsters could sound out words, but they
still could not comprehend or interpret the ideas represented
by the words. In many more instances, children became
capable of comprehending and interpreting ideas but developed
a marked aversion to the reading process, particularly if
they had been stigmatized as poor or just fair readers over
a period of years.

The inadequacy of the three-group type organization was forcibly demonstrated to me when I began teaching a fourth-grade class. Having been trained in remedial reading, I soon found it necessary to expand the organization into five groups and four individuals. Then I began cutting across a-chievement-group lines to teach selected children certain skills such as consonant blends or syllabication. Concurrent-ly, children were volunteering to read a story to the class at milk time and choosing as helpers better-reading friends who liked the story as well as they did. Neither needs nor interests conformed to the standardized pattern of grouping.

In the 1920's, alternate plans of adjustment to indi-vidual differences such as the Winnetka and Dalton plans were attempted; these plans were still oriented to subject matter. Dr. Willard Olson's research in child development eventually led to the modern concept of individualization of instruction based on the seeking behavior of the learner, self-selection of materials, and pacing in accordance with the learner's development. Individualized reading was initiated in some schools, such as the Maury School in Richmond, Virginia. The new movement, however, received great impetus in the last decade as world crisis promoted "the urge to develop the special potentialities of each individual to the highest possible level." (Nila Banton Smith in Education, May 1961.)

Teachers using the new individualized approach hoped to shift the classroom emphasis from the mechanical to the thinking aspect of reading. They also aimed to help each child develop reading as both a useful and pleasurable com-ponent of his daily life.

With these broad purposes in mind, each teacher us-ing an individualized approach to reading attempted to devel-op less regimented practices. The following descriptions exemplify some of their approaches.

(1) The teacher obtained a wide range of reading ma-terials suitable to the span of reading purposes, interests, and abilities in his own classroom. These materials were kept flowing in and out of the classroom so that fresh read-ing matter could be readily available. With some guidance from the teacher, children selected individually appropriate reading material.

(2) The teacher noted each pupil's reading strengths and weaknesses and developed record-keeping systems

through which both the teacher and a particular child could evaluate his reading. These records (often written partly by the teacher and partly by the pupil) were used to note progress made, skills development needed, and breadth and quality of reading. Clues to all of these factors in the child's reading situation were obtained in whole class sessions, small group activities, and individual conferences.

(3) The teacher used a variety of organizational practices as well as a diversity of reading materials. Some teaching was done on a whole class basis, and some was done individually. Much was done through the formation of flexible groupings based on common interests, purposes, or needs.

Does the individualized approach to reading produce better results? There is considerable debate upon this point because most reports of experiments with this approach have not incorporated adequate controls. In addition, standardized tests do not measure the child's reactions to his reading experiences. Most studies show no statistically significant differences in comprehension and skills between experiment groups (using individualized programs) and control groups.

Can all teachers use the individualized approach successfully? The answer to this question is definitely negative. Incompetent and/or inflexible teachers could not use the individualized approach successfully since such teachers would also be unable to use more traditional methods successfully. To teach children to read by any method the teacher needs to know children; the many reading skills and appropriate methods and materials to use in teaching children these skills and a broad range of suitable reading matter. It is unquestionably a fact that far too many teachers do not have these qualifications. For the individualized approach to reading, the teacher also needs a reasonably adequate knowledge of fine children's literature. The recent survey of the National Interest and the Teaching of English made by the National Council of Teachers of English reveals that many teachers are inadequately trained for their profession.

Although a teacher may be sufficiently competent, flexible, and enthusiastic for the task of teaching children to read, he can not initiate an individualized program without a suitable supply of materials. Unfortunately, many American children are deprived of reading opportunity because of inadequate library services. The ALA has expressed its con-

cern over this deplorable situation and outlined specific goals
for greatly needed improvement in its Standard for School Library Programs. However, the general public must be a-
roused to demand adequate services before they will be provided in many communities.

Despite the aforementioned difficulties, will the individualized approach to reading be more widely utilized? It
will unquestionably spread to many more classrooms throughout the country. Even if the classroom approach is not utilized, the furor over individualization is currently at least
partially influential in producing some noteworthy improvements. Many teachers are attempting to employ other bases
than gross test scores for grouping in their classrooms.
Many teachers are also utilizing a much broader range of
materials than formerly. Trade books are being used far
more extensively in schools than they have been in the past.
Publishers of textbooks and workbooks are enriching their
products so as to make them more appealing, less prescrip-
tive and more worthwhile for children and teachers to use.
Traditionalists and "individualizers" seem to have mellowed
toward each other in the past year or so except for a few
militant extremists in both camps.

Will basal reader series disappear from elementary
classrooms? In all probability they will not because ready
access to various basal readers, diagnostic workbooks, phonic materials, word games, children's newspapers, magazines,
trade books, etc., facilitate the teacher's task of teaching
children needed reading skills and of helping children to develop desirable attitudes toward reading. In this respect, increased utilization of a more diversified group of classroom
materials can be anticipated.

Does diversification of materials endanger the child's
systematic acquisition of reading skills? The answer to this
question depends on the teacher's competence. Although a
thorough acquaintance with any one series may enhance a
teacher's feeling of security and confidence in his ability,
vested interests are probably also partly responsible for
much of the resistance to change. Even a cursory examination of a few basal reading series will reveal that there is
no unanimity of agreement on any one best sequence for
teaching reading skills. Regarding sequence in phonetic analysis alone, one cannot f nd concerted opinion.

Beyond this point, why should children needlessly be

subjected to time-consuming, interest-deadening, and pur-
pose-thwarting experiences? Are teachers deliberately trying to make children dislike reading? If the teacher is willing to take the time to select one basal reader series or one
textbook on the teaching of reading which he really likes and
then to check his pupils on the sequence of skills as described therein, he can ascertain each child's abilities and
disabilities. Then he can devote his energy to helping children to learn what they need and to develop a love of reading.

An individualized approach to reading implies a far
greater emphasis on library services than has heretofore existed. The librarian becomes a consultant, a guide, and a
greatly needed source of supply to classroom teachers and to
children. For this reason librarians should become well informed on the subject of individualized reading.

Another Librarian's View of Individualized Reading

by

Jean E. Lowrie

(This material is excerpted from the author's article, "Elementary School Libraries Today," which appeared in the Library Quarterly in January, 1960. Copyright (c) 1960.)

The elementary school of today is predicated upon the idea that all children, regardless of their native ability, should be encouraged to pursue knowledge as far and as fast as their background, interests, and intellectual potential will permit. The cultural heritage of the world belongs to all children. The freedom to explore nature, to become acquainted with beauty in all forms, to enjoy the best in literature, to understand the past and in turn relate it to the present--this is the inherent right of every child. Toward this end the school curriculum and, more specifically, for our purposes, the elementary-school library program are conceived. The selection, the availability, the organization, and the distribution of materials gathered together in the centralized library is designed to be of use and value to the kindergarten child and the sixth-grader, to the teacher and the administrator, to the gifted and to the slow learner.

It is the responsibility of the librarian to select materials which will challenge the intellectual capacities of the gifted child and will encourage the slow progression of a reluctant reader. These materials will be books, magazines, pictures, pamphlets, films, film-strips, slides, recordings, and other graphic materials, and they will be easily accessible to all members of the school population. For this instructional material is expendable. It is to be used. Youngsters come in to listen to recordings for a dramatization or story, to seek information for a classroom unit or to listen for fun; to preview filmstrips in the individual viewer for a

committee assignment; or to search for pictures to interpret
a report for the classes. This is in addition to the constant
use of books for all these purposes. Furthermore, the organization is not on the basis of first-, second-, or third-
grade level. Rather it is organized to capitalize on the interests of all students both in curriculum enrichment and in
reading for pleasure.

The librarian, therefore, must be a participant in the
curriculum development within the school. She must have an
understanding of the teaching approach used by the classroom
teacher and be alert to all opportunities to enrich the classroom program. It follows also that, if young people are ulti-
mately to become self-sufficient in locating the sources to
answer their questions, functional library instruction must become a part of the teacher-librarian planned program.

The library instruction program which is planned to
acquaint the entire school with the possibilities of the library
must be a most flexible affair. Its overall objective is to
stimulate and encourage enthusiastic use of all libraries
(school and public) through an informed handling of their resources. The general program which outlines the desirable
learning that an elementary boy or girl should possess before going into a junior or senior high school is planned by
the librarian and has been based on the needs and requests
of teachers and students over a period of years. But the
specific lesson on a particular tool or skill is dependent upon the immediate need of the individual or group. A formal
lesson in the use of the card catalog, for example, is usually presented at the request of the classroom teacher and in
direct connection with a unit of work in the room. When the
children have discovered that they must know how to find
many materials for class reports, they look for a tool which
will aid in organized searching. Thus the card catalog becomes important to them. This need usually develops in the
fourth grade, where the urge to gather additional information
is strong. On the other hand, there are many third-graders
who are capable of understanding the use of the simple card
catalog and are anxious to find books by themselves. A
good librarian capitalizes on both of these possibilities--the
classroom need and the individual curiosity--and two methods
of instruction are followed.

This is an aspect of elementary-school library service which requires close teacher-librarian co-operation.
Some teachers prefer to present the parts of a book, the

techniques of note-taking and allied skills in connection with the language arts programs. Others prefer to have the librarian introduce the skill or tool, with classroom activities planned to reinforce learnings. The significant point, however, is the break from the traditional prescribed list of skills to be learned in each grade in the direction of a presentation according to the needs of the particular library and its public, the interests of the children as excited by their own curiosities. Meaningful presentation results in more enjoyment in the use of library tools. The value of an organized arrangement where children easily learn to locate materials is immeasurable and is obvious, for the library must be constantly tapped in all phases of learning and becomes an extension of the classroom.

Reading guidance in all its aspects is an equally significant part of today's elementary-school library program. It may mean sharing of books and stories through the story hour in the library, or it may involve work in the field of teaching individual reading. It may expand reading interests beyond the narrow confines of "Another dog story, please," or it may stimulate creative dramatics and writing.

Sharing stories aloud, stories which present stimulating new worlds and evoke the imagination, is one vital aspect of reading guidance. But the stories which are presented, the books which are shared, must arouse an excitement for further exploration in recreational reading.

The introduction of good literature is a basic consideration in the entire educational program. Fairy tales, myths, fables, poetry, classics, and fine modern writing all appear in the library collection. They are good antibiotics for the inane, often poorly written stories of modern life which appear in many text and trade editions. Discriminating taste and recognition of sound writing can be developed in informational reading as well as in leisure reading. Furthermore, the plethora of informational books now being published makes it possible for the school librarian to evaluate all books for literary values as well as for accuracy and unbiased presentation of facts.

Individual reading guidance has been an important aspect of the elementary library program for many years. But the trend toward individualized teaching of reading in the classroom involves a new use of library books and new techniques of service by the librarian. This program is predi-

cated upon the availability of a large collection of books on
many reading levels and of varied interests. It is necessary
for both teacher and librarian to work closely together in
guiding the individual reading choices, choosing the books to
be used in the classroom, and providing supplementary materials. It necessitates that the librarian be conscious of
each individual child's ability; that she help him to be aware
of the fact that reading is pleasure, not drudgery; and that
books may be read both for individual delight and for the
satisfaction of personal curiosity. More and more teachers
are using library books for the teaching of reading to supplement or replace the basic text which all must read "before
passing." Such a program helps the youngster to move along
as rapidly as he is able to rather than limiting him by the
group's personnel or the book itself. Many of the new books
which we have today are inviting in both appearance and content. They are exciting and imaginative and may be read by
the beginning reader as easily as the traditional "See Puff
run." Teachers who are using this method for the teaching
of reading are united in their belief that it is absolutely necessary to have a good library before embarking on such a
program and a librarian who is interested in developing this
new technique.

The elementary-school library has its own particular
contribution to the needs of the accelerated or gifted pupil.
This is another area which has currently been receiving special attention from educators, parents, and interested citi-
zens. Schools where special programs have been developed
for these superior learners must have available materials
which will constantly stimulate exploration into many areas
and attempt to answer at least some of the questions posed
by the children as a result of wide reading. These accelerated readers, avid seekers of knowledge, need variety and
depth in their reading material. The children with special
interests and abilities in science need more detailed, more
advanced information than the average youngsters. The library presents an opportunity for the child to explore on his
own. It offers a time and a place for face to face conversation about books. It allows for the wide reading necessary
when text prepared materials are inadequate.

Gifted children need to be kept busy constructively,
and the library is the laboratory facility which provides this
opportunity. These children also require special guidance in
the area of recreational reading. More often than not their
direct interest is also their recreation. They make much

use of reference materials, but they need introduction to other interests, particularly in various forms, to literature. Whether these programs are carried on in the regular classroom or whether there is a special provision for this group, the elementary-school librarian is ready to secure the books which will be needed, and to assist in the expanded use of the materials.

The slow learners are not forgotten in the special services area, however. Displays of easy and picture books are prepared for class visits to the library. Many easy books are loaned to the classroom for the express purpose of arousing an interest in stories and encouraging the effort to read simple material independently. Books, filmstrips, and pictures which help in the teaching of the practical--food, clothing, shelter needs, newspapers, health and safety areas --are made available. A teacher checks out special airplane books for a second-grade problem child; a group which can be challenged by simple biographies of explorers and pioneers finds satisfaction in the library; a nine-year-old boy in the first grade becomes a library helper. These are experiences which may be found in elementary schools where the librarian is sensitive to the problems of this particular group.

It is evident that the kind of program which has been described cannot exist in situations where the scheduling of classes to the library is so restricted that no one may come into the library except at his particular time, once a week or even every other week. A situation where the scheduling cannot allow flexibility of teaching and the concomitant use of the library, or where the librarian is so afraid that someone may disturb her story-hour group that she locks the library door whenever a class is inside, defeats the purpose of the entire program. Granted that it is desirable to contact all children regularly, but, when the schedule becomes paramount and the service secondary, a modification is necessary.

It is unfortunate also that many elementary-school librarians or teacher-librarians retain too tight a control of the library materials. The fear of wide circulation of materials outside the library or of the development of the autonomous classroom collection rather than the fluctuating collection has deterred the program in elementary-school library service. Books and pictures should be available in such quantity that there will be a sufficient number for simultaneous use in the library or in the classroom as further expansion of the unit of study.

And then there is the librarian who talks about "my" library, "my" books, who does not let the teachers make suggestions about the material needed for teaching, or who sends the children away from the desk because the records will be all mixed up. If the library is to justify its existence, it does so on the service-to-all basis. This means that it is public domain, and the student and the teachers help in planning the program and enriching the collection. Unfortunately, there are also administrators who believe that the library must be administered as a traditional classroom program. Lesson plans must be devised for each period of the day with no deviation. Tests are administered regularly. The library becomes a formal situation. Children are restricted to library visits only after all their work is finished, or, worse yet, the library is a detention room, and a child is sent there only if he cannot behave in the class group. This is a way of thinking which is evident in far too many schools and calls for a revaluation of the function of the library in that school in terms of administration and services.

The scope of service must be increased to all the children in each elementary school. The library is not the sole property of the youngsters who can read. It belongs alike to the kindergarten child who is just being introduced to the delight of many picture books, to the second-grader who is still struggling with pre-primer material, and to the fifth-grade child who is pursuing a reading program which is designed for a slow reading group. The enjoyment of books and the delights of reading plus the understanding of the library as an information center begin to develop with the youngest child in the school program. The library must be open to serve all. Where programs are planned only at the third-grade level or above, re-examination of policy seems important.

Chapter 11

Reactions of Pupils and of their Parents

This chapter opens with a description of a means of ascertaining pupil attitude towards reading taken from the research report of the San Diego County Department of Education, which has been mentioned in several previous chapters.

The next excerpt taken from a thesis by Roettger is a suggested interview scale to be used in finding out about a pupil's reading experiences.

Rose A. Arkley lists eleven pupil evaluations of the individualized reading program which she conducted. The list is reproduced in this chapter.

A survey of parent opinion of individualized reading was conducted by Auline L. Bailey as part of her master's work. An excerpt from her thesis reporting the result of that survey is the fourth selection.

A description of children's reaction to her individualized program is presented in Anna M. Hune's master's thesis and is excerpted here.

Glenda A. Gray submitted a questionnaire to the pupils in her fifth grade class who had been taught reading through the individualized approach. The responses of her pupils are excerpted and constitute the sixth selection in this chapter.

Sylvia W. Roston prepared a "book motivation scale" which she administered to the 16 first and second grade children in her individualized reading classroom. The items used and the pupil responses constitute the next item presented.

Auline L. Bailey's master's thesis gives a list of responses from her fifth grade individualized reading group.

Ways in which parents can help their children in reading are briefly discussed by Amy E. Jensen. This excerpt concludes the present chapter.

Inventory of Reading Attitudes

by

San Diego County Department of Education

(This material is excerpted from An Inventory of Reading Attitudes. Improving Reading Instruction, Monograph No. 4, 1961.)

Uses of the San Diego County Inventory of Reading Attitudes

Exploration of pupils' attitudes toward reading offers rewarding possibilities for discovering how children feel about reading. We have much to learn about children's sentiments, interests, and innermost feelings relative to the broad field of reading and this instrument will only indicate surface responses to the way children feel. However, we believe that these surface responses should open doors which will allow teachers to gain new insights about children's reading attitudes and how they might be improved.

Elementary teachers are already taking attitudes into account in preparing learning experiences. This survey instrument will simply give them a more systematic look at reading attitudes in their classes in a form which will make comparisons with a larger sample possible.

Group Counseling

Once the teacher has used the Inventory to assess present attitudes toward reading, she can immediately use the results as a teaching tool. Informal item analysis whereby the teacher summarizes the class results on various items can lead to a discussion of individual preferences and tastes in reading, or she can systematically explore individual interests. Thus she can adjust her teaching to both the child's attitude toward reading and his pattern of interests.

Class discussion can verge on group counseling as students explore attitudes about themselves and discuss why they answered questions as they did. Simply making it "all right" for students to dislike what we do poorly, may help some to live more happily with themselves. It may also serve to motivate the teacher to make reading experiences more rewarding for the students.

Formation of interest groups has long been a practice in reading instruction. Children with similar interests enjoy getting together and sharing their likes whether it be writing poetry or telling stories.

The San Diego County Inventory of Reading Attitudes should provide information regarding children in a given class with similar interests or positive attitudes, i. e. , reading and sharing recipes, reading and sharing newspapers, etc. Through a class item analysis many such interest groups might be formed.

Similarly, children with common disinterests in a topic might be formed to study their area of disinterest and thereby discover the causal factors relating to these negative attitudes. With careful teacher guidance such students might discover that acting out stories with other novices in this skill area is fun or that catalogues contain much interesting content.

Counseling with Individual Students

In many classrooms reading programs provision is made for individual counseling with children. At this time the teacher helps the youngster to evaluate his reading progress, acquire skills and understandings, and plan for future growth. A child's attitude toward reading is a vital influence upon his reading success now and in the future; therefore, healthy reading attitudes need to be developed along with skills. However, before the teacher or pupil can attempt to improve attitudes, he needs to know what attitudes now exist and why. This then is where the reading attitude inventory can be of valuable assistance.

Much data can be gleaned from an individual discussion of why the student responded as he did--"I'm afraid they'll laugh at me if I read aloud," "We don't take any newspapers at our house," "Daddy says only sissies stay in the house and read," and "I can't read because I'm too dumb." Many avenues for helping the child may be opened as he tells his teacher how he feels.

Classroom Research

A standardized attitude inventory makes it possible for the classroom teacher to become a researcher within the four walls of her classroom. By administering the Inventory when she does her achievement and intelligence testing, she can study the relationships among reading achievement, ability to learn, and attitudes toward reading. She can explore the relationship between reading attitudes and social class, or test the possible effects of social adjustment or acceptance on reading attitudes.

In addition to a status survey, the teacher might wish to conduct a before and after testing program to examine changes that have come about over a period of a year or more. This before and after testing offers many possibilities in local school action research projects wherein two teachers or more may wish to establish control and experimental groups to test certain hypotheses pertaining to reading approaches, materials, techniques, etc.

Such concerns have practical application in the classroom as well as being of considerable theoretical interest.

In-Service Education

The San Diego County Inventory of Reading Attitudes offers rewarding possibilities for use in teachers' in-service betterment programs.

A principal and a group of teachers might wish to use the instrument as a vehicle for a child study activity related to students' reading problems. The group would hypothesize causes for certain negative reading attitudes and, in turn, attempt to validate these hypotheses through anecdotal record keeping of students' behavior.

Another in-service usage of the Inventory might simply

be a series of meetings wherein teachers would attempt to identify more definitively the nature of reading attitudes.

Regardless of the specific manner in which the Inventory is used in the in-service training of teachers, it should provide opportunities for viewing reading development in a broader scope and, in turn, teachers will discuss other means for using the San Diego County Inventory of Reading Attitudes.

Conferencing with Parents

Teachers have long known that the attitudes of parents toward reading influence the child's interests and performance. When a child comes from a home where reading materials are not available, the child is less likely to read or to be motivated toward learning to read. It would be quite useful to have a measure of a child's attitudes toward reading for use in parent conferences. If one can show the parents that they can help the child by demonstrating the value of reading at home, or through planning family activities which involve reading and language activity, it should be possible to enlist their help in changing the student's attitude.

It will also be possible to demonstrate the relationship of self-regarding attitudes toward interest in reading activities. We would be able to explain to parents that their child cannot be expected to enjoy an activity in which he is criticized or devalued. We can help them to see ways of making reading activities rewarding rather than frightening for the child. We can teach them that children will learn to read only if reading will bring them acceptance, or will serve some other purpose.

It might be quite interesting to administer the San Diego County Inventory of Reading Attitudes to a group of parents and thereby give them an opportunity to think through seriously their own attitudes toward reading.

San Diego County
Inventory of Reading Attitude

Name _____Grade ___ Boy   Girl
     Last   First   Middle

School_____ Teacher_____

Date of Test _____
                   Mo.   Day   Year

TO BOYS AND GIRLS:

This sheet has some questions about reading which can be
answered YES or NO.   Your answers will show what you
usually think about reading.   After each question is read to
you, circle your answer.

INSTRUCTIONS TO PUPILS

Draw a circle around the word YES or NO, whichever shows
your answer.

Sample A

      Yes   No   Do you like to read?

If you like to read, you should have drawn a circle around
the word YES in Sample A; if you do not like to read, you
should have drawn a circle around the word NO.

Sample B

      Yes   No   Do you read as well as you would like to?

If you read as well as you would like to, you should have
drawn a circle around the word YES in Sample B; if not, you
should have drawn a circle around the word NO.

Yes   No   1. Do you like to read before you go to bed?

Yes   No   2. Do you think that you are a poor reader?

Yes   No   3. Are you interested in what other people
                 read?

Yes   No   4. Do you like to read when your mother and
                 dad are reading?

Yes	No	5.	Is reading your favorite subject at school?
Yes	No	6.	If you could do anything you wanted to do, would reading be one of the things you would choose to do?
Yes	No	7.	Do you think that you are a good reader for your age?
Yes	No	8.	Do you like to read catalogues?
Yes	No	9.	Do you think that most things are more fun than reading?
Yes	No	10.	Do you like to read aloud for other children at school?
Yes	No	11.	Do you think reading recipes is fun?
Yes	No	12.	Do you like to tell stories?
Yes	No	13.	Do you like to read the newspaper?
Yes	No	14.	Do you like to read all kinds of books at school?
Yes	No	15.	Do you like to answer questions about things you have read?
Yes	No	16.	Do you think it is a waste of time to make rhymes with words?
Yes	No	17.	Do you like to talk about books you have read?
Yes	No	18.	Does reading make you feel good?
Yes	No	19.	Do you feel that reading time is the best part of the school day?
Yes	No	20.	Do you find it hard to write about what you have read?
Yes	No	21.	Would you like to have more books to read?
Yes	No	22.	Do you like to read hard books?
Yes	No	23.	Do you think that there are many beautiful words in poems?
Yes	No	24.	Do you like to act out stories that you have read in books?
Yes	No	25.	Do you like to take reading tests?

KEY: Questions 2, 9, 16, and 20 should be answered NO; the remaining questions should be answered YES.

What type of books
26. Do you like to read?
Fiction, etc. biography,
poetry

Asking Children About Their Reading Experiences

by

Doris Dornfeld Roettger

(This material is excerpted from the author's 1964
University of Tennessee master's thesis, The Ef-
fectiveness of an Individualized Reading Program in
Developing Reading Skills and Interest in Reading.)

Questionnaire Used in Interview With Children
Who Were in I. R. Programs

1. What is the best book that you have read in the last
several months?

_____

2. Which book would you put at the bottom of the list because it was not as good as the other books you have
read?

_____

3. Are there any books that you would like to have for your
own?

_____

4. Why did you select the book you are reading now?

_____

5. When do you usually read?_____

6. Why do you read?_____

_____

7. How do you feel about people who read a lot? _____

_____

8. What are you interested in that you like to read about in books?

_____

9. What books besides the dictionary have you used to look up things?

_____

10. How do you like to feel while you are reading a book?

_____

11. Do you like to read (very much) (some) (not at all)? Why?

_____

12. Do you like to read (more) (about the same) (less) now than you did when you were reading in your readers? Why?

_____

13. Do you read (more) or (about the same) than you did before?

_____

14. Are you going to read this summer?_____ Where will your get your books?

_____

15. Did you read last summer? _____ Where did you get your books?

_____

Some Features Children Like About
Individualized Reading

by

Rose Adatto Arkley

(This material is excerpted from the author's 1961 University of Washington master's thesis, The Analysis and Evaluation of an Individualized Reading Program for Third Graders Based on Contemporary Children's Literature.)

The following examples of student evaluations are taken from the files of this study:

1. I like going to the library table and getting any book I want to read.

2. Last year I didn't get any library time because my work was never finished fast enough.

3. Conferences give me a chance to talk to the teacher alone with no one else bothering.

4. I like reading this way because I can discuss any book with somebody. It's more quiet in the room too.

5. No one kicks people any more or bothers people.

6. I can keep all the words I didn't know before in my own word box inside my desk.

7. Last year the teacher would say, "Time for reading group one," and I just hated it.

8. I liked the authors we talked about and the letters we wrote them. I didn't know that authors were living people.

9. When I had to stay in the same reading group all year, it made me mad.

10. I can go ahead with my reading instead of waiting all the time like I used to.

11. Now I can get my own books instead of waiting for the
    teacher to give me one.

How Parents Feel About Individualized Reading

by

Auline Lowery Bailey

(This material is excerpted from the author's 1961
Central Missouri State College master's thesis,
A Comparative Study of the Grouping Method of
Teaching Reading with the Individualized Method.)

The parents of the children who received individual
emphasis in reading had been previously told to expect a
questionnaire as to their true feelings toward the reading
program. The questions that were asked and the responses
that were given are as follows (the number following the response indicates frequency of response):

1. Does your child ever complain of reading in the classroom?

   No--22   Yes--0

2. Does your child seem more or less interested in reading this year?

   More--21   Neither more nor less--1

3. What has your child done to indicate that he is more or
   less interested in reading this year?

   Does newspaper reading--1
   Goes to city library--2
   Checks out more books--1
   Reads more at home--5
   Talks more about what he (or she) had read--3
   Has begun a home library--1
   Understands what she reads--1
   Reads continually--1
   Reads every book he (or she) can get--2
   Reads now because she enjoys it--1

Reads of own will without prompting--1
Reads a great variety of material--1
Exchanges books with friends--1
Asked for permission to join a book club--1

4. Does your child read more or less at home this year?

    More--21   Same--1

5. Would you want your child to continue in a reading program of this kind?

    Yes--22   No--0

6. Do you like the grouping method used in the first four grades better than the method used this year?

    Yes--0   No--22

7. What features of the individualized method of teaching reading do you like?

    Reading alone--1
    Each child can read as much as he is able to
        read--2
    My child can choose her own books--1
    The opportunity to go ahead with other books
        rather than stay with the group--1
    The interest that has been created in my child
        for reading--2
    A child can read when he (or she) wishes to read
        and that way he feels more as if he isn't made
        to do something he doesn't want to do--2
    Special problems are more easily dealt with--1
    Reading silently--3
    It seems to stimulate more interest in the child
        and prompts her to use her own powers of se-
        lection and preference--1
    My child got to talk to the teacher more--2
    No response to this question--5

8. What feature of the individualized method of teaching reading do you dislike?

    No feature disliked--5
    When the children are grouped--2
    Oral reading--2
    No response to this question--13

Childrens' Feelings About Individualized Reading

by

Anna Marie Hess Hune

(This material is excerpted from the author's 1959
Ohio State University master's thesis, The Organization, Implementation and Evaluation of an Individualized Reading Program in an Upper Socio-
Economic Community.)

The children's enthusiasm for the new instructional
method can be inferred from the accounts listed previously
about the parent meeting and questionnaire.   An experience
characterized by the enthusiasm and happiness of the child
and one which bears the fruit of productive effort rarely
fails to elicit a like response from parents.   Such was the
case in the present study.

Anecdotes such as the following, will indicate how
some children felt about their reading.   One child was certain that he wanted to read just "horse stories."   He later
discovered a book in the classroom library about textiles
and told the teacher that everyone should read the book for
it was all about cloth--just what they were studying in social studies.   The outcome was that the story was read a-
loud to thirteen interested classmates, by the child who had
made the recommendation.   The writer observed the same
youngster as he was reading, one evening after school.   He
had placed his book on the seat of his chair and was kneel-
ing on the floor beside it, oblivious to all about him as he
peered at the book digesting its contents.   Finally, he
heaved a sigh of relief, turned to his teacher and remarked,
"Whee! I just had to see how 'The Mixed Up Twins' got out
of that one."

Another child, a reluctant reader, had never been
enthusiastic about printed material, but had seemed to be

gaining more reading skill as a result of the individualized procedures currently in use. The teacher was encouraged when the child volunteered this information, "You know, reading a book is just like taking a bath; you hate like the dickens to get started, but once you get in, it's not so bad. "

These words indicate one of those important "intangibles" mentioned before. "Every second, I'm learning more and more. " Self-revelation can be awe inspiring.

During a pupil-teacher conference, one child made these unsolicited comments, "I like this way to read. I can choose my book, and I don't have to wait for someone else to read. By the way, Kathy has a keen book. She read me the first chapter. "

During another teacher-pupil interview, guidance in book selection was under discussion. The child sensed the teacher's concern and took this means of reassuring her, "Sure, I just fiddled around at first, but now that we have so many books to choose from, I'll read a lot of them. "

In many instances the guidance functions of teachers operate naturally in personalized reading procedures. One child, when the classroom seating arrangement was changed, remarked to the teacher, "Do you think this is wise? You know that Anna and I are good friends and talk a lot. " The discussion about deferring talking (visiting) until all work was completed or until the recess period, helped to clarify a problem and offered suggestions for resolving it.

To another child, who tended to be impatient and intolerant of slow readers, the program meant, "More fun to read. I can pick out any book I like. I don't need much help with words. " When the same child met the word "traditional" during an oral reading check, the teacher asked to give the meaning. This she did with these words, "Sure I know what the word means. They were doing it a long time ago and still are. "

The teacher hoped that a reading program with no ceiling on achievement would prove a challenging experience, would tend to shatter the overdeveloped "X" concept and promote humility and tolerance. A planned program in terms of those objectives was initiated.

Several children indicated that they liked individualized reading because everybody could read for a longer time, and it was so much quieter.

A Survey of Childrens' Attitudes Toward
Individualized Reading

by

Glenda Arlene Gray

(This material is excerpted from the author's 1965
Marshall University master's thesis, <u>A Study of
the Individualized Reading Program at Holz Elementary School, Charleston, West Virginia.</u>)

1. When you went to the library to choose a book, did you
   feel that there were
   - 7   too many books
   - 13   just enough books
   - 7   not enough books

2. Did you feel that the library contained enough of the type
   of books that you like best?
   - 9   yes
   - 18   no

3. If you answered no to question two, write the type of
   book you felt that you needed more of _____

4. Did you feel that the books in the library were usually

   - 1   too hard
   - 24   just right
   - 2   too easy

5. Did you find it hard to choose a new book?
   - 17   yes
   - 10   no

6. Did you ever ask others (teacher or classmates) to help
   you find an interesting book?
   - 15   yes
   - 12   no

330

7. Do you think more magazines should be used in the reading program?
   <u>12</u>   yes
   <u>15</u>   no

8. Would you read the magazines as part of your reading if there were more in the library?
   <u>20</u>   yes
   <u>7</u>   no

9. Do you think that classic comic books should be used in the reading program?
   <u>19</u>   yes
   <u>8</u>   no

10. Would you read the classic comics as part of your reading if they were in the library?
    <u>20</u>   yes
    <u>7</u>   no

11. Do you think that the basic reader (<u>Sky Lines</u>) should be
    <u>15</u>   completed before starting individualized reading
    <u>12</u>   completed as part of individualized reading

12. This year we completed our workbook pages together. If you were to take part in individualized reading again and the workbook was used, would you
    <u>8</u>   want to complete the workbook before starting individualized reading
    <u>6</u>   want to complete the workbook as part of individualized reading
    <u>13</u>   complete the workbook as we did this year, with everyone working at the same time

13. Did you feel that the conferences were
    <u>14</u>   necessary
    <u>13</u>   sometimes necessary
    _____   not necessary

14. Did you feel that the conferences ever helped you in any way?
    <u>25</u>   yes
    <u>2</u>   no

15. Do you think the conferences should be scheduled by
    <u>10</u>   the teacher
    <u>17</u>   the student

16. Do you feel that the record book
      _18_   helped you with your reading
      _9_   did not help with your reading

17. Did the reading wheel help you read in different cate-
    gories?
      _16_   yes
      _11_   no

18. Do you think there should be
      _19_   more sharing activities
      _4_   less sharing activities
      _4_   no sharing activities

19. Do you like the individualized reading program?
      _27_   yes
      ____   no

20. Do you feel that you learn
      _20_   more in individualized reading than in groups
      _5_   about the same in individualized reading as in
             groups
      _2_   less in individualized reading than in groups

21. If you were to choose your reading program for another
    year, which would you choose?
      _27_   individualized reading
      ____   grouping

A "Book Motivation Scale"

by

Sylvia Willner Roston

(This material is excerpted from the author's 1962
National College of Education master's thesis, An
Individualized Reading Program in a First and
Second Grade.)

1. Which one of these three things would you like most to
do?
 (6) a. Read a comic book or the funnies
 (1) b. Make something out of clay
 (9) c. Read an interesting book

2. Pick the one you would most like to do from these three
things.
 (2) a. Put a jigsaw puzzle together
 (4) b. Draw a picture
 (8) c. Read a magazine for boys and girls

3. Which one of these would you choose?
 (7) a. Write a story
 (5) b. Cut and paste pictures in a scrapbook
 (3) c. Color in a coloring book

4. Take your pick from these three things.
 (1) a. Make something out of clay
 (9) b. Read an interesting book
 (5) c. Cut and paste pictures in a scrapbook

5. Which of these would you rather do?
 (8) a. Read a magazine for boys and girls
 (6) b. Read a comic book or the funnies
 (2) c. Put a jigsaw puzzle together

6. Pick the one you like most.
    (4) a. Draw a picture
    (5) b. Cut and paste pictures in a scrapbook
    (6) c. Read a comic book or the funnies

7. Which one of these three things would you like most to
   do?
    (5) a. Cut and paste pictures in a scrapbook
    (1) b. Make something out of clay
    (7) c. Write a story

8. Pick the one you would most like to do from these three
   things:
    (9) a. Read an interesting book
    (4) b. Draw a picture
    (1) c. Make something out of clay

9. Which one of these three would you choose?
    (6) a. Read a comic book or the funnies
    (7) b. Write a story
    (8) c. Read a magazine for boys and girls

10. Take your pick from these three things.
    (5) a. Cut and paste pictures in a scrapbook
    (3) b. Color in a coloring book
    (9) c. Read an interesting book

11. Which of these would you rather do?
    (1) a. Make something out of clay
    (7) b. Write a story
    (4) c. Draw a picture

12. Pick the one you like most.
    (3) a. Color in a coloring book
    (9) b. Read an interesting book
    (6) c. Read a comic book or the funnies

13. Which one of these three would you choose?
    (2) a. Put a jigsaw puzzle together
    (3) b. Color in a coloring book
    (4) c. Draw a picture

14. Take your pick from these three things.
    (9) a. Read an interesting book
    (8) b. Read a magazine for boys and girls
    (7) c. Write a story

15. Which one of these would you rather do?
    (3) a. Color in a coloring book
    (2) b. Put a jigsaw puzzle together
    (1) c. Make something out of clay

16. Pick the one you like most
    (8) a. Read a magazine for boys and girls
    (5) b. Cut and paste pictures in a scrapbook
    (2) c. Put a jigsaw puzzle together

Pupil Reaction to Individualized Reading

by

Auline Lowery Bailey

(This material is excerpted from the author's 1961
Central Missouri State College master's thesis,
A Comparative Study of the Grouping Method of
Teaching Reading with the Individualized Method.)

The children's responses to a questionnaire indicated
they favored the individualized method of reading. The pupils were given an "open-end" type questionnaire in an attempt to obtain their reaction to the individualized method of
teaching reading as related to previous experiences in group-
emphasis reading. The responses to the questions were as
follows (the number following response indicates the frequency of response):

   1. Reading this year has been
      more interesting to me--1
      fun--11
      very good--1
      a lot of fun to me because I could read--1
      fun because we could share it with others--1
      pleasant to me--2
      fun for the whole class--2
      fun to read what you want to read--1
      no response--1

   2. Next year I hope I can read
      more than this year--4
      all the books in the library--4
      good books like this year--3
      the way I did this year--5
      big books and read a lot of them--2
      by myself--1
      no response--3

3. Reading groups were
    good, but I like to read to myself--2
    not as much fun as reading what you want to
        read--1
    not fun at all--4
    not liked much by people--1
    the best kind of reading--1
    were nice--1
    not fun because nobody got to read the whole
        story--2
    too noisy for the ones who were not reading--2
    fun but I like our way better--2
    tiresome--2
    dull to listen to others read aloud--1
    disliked by most of the room--1

4. Next year I do not want to read
    in groups--12
    less books than I read this year--2
    little books that are "babyish"--3
    too many books--2
    books that I read this year--3

5. Reading groups made me feel
    bored--2
    stuffy with my books--1
    bad--1
    different from other people--1
    like a first grader--1
    embarrassed if I missed a word--1
    like I could read--1
    little--1
    crowded--1
    unable to read what other children did--1
    good because I got to read a lot--1
    bad or silly when I missed a word in the story--1
    like I was big and it still does sometimes--1
    tired--1
    silly--4
    like they don't trust you to read the book--1
    like a baby--1

6. I was always in the group that was
    Eleven children said they were in the best group
        in reading, including the two lowest ranking
        children on the achievement test scores. The
        remaining eleven said they were in the "good"

group, which was interpreted to mean either
the middle or top group.

What Parents Can Do

by

Amy Elizabeth Jensen

(This material is excerpted from the author's article, "Attracting Children to Books," which appeared in Elementary English in October, 1956.)

One of the greatest gifts a mother and father can give
to a child is a love of, and joy in reading. Every parent
needs to be convinced of the importance of each child's having books of his own, which should not be considered luxur-
ies but rather very necessary equipment; and every family
budget should provide for the purchase of wisely chosen
books at the child's level to satisfy his natural interest and
widen his wonderful world. Eaton stresses the importance
of such a possession when she says:

> ... an individual library of well-chosen books, all
> his own, will give a child more of a sense of val-
> ue, companionship, and individuality of books than
> sixty volumes hastily read and returned to the pub-
> lic library.

Parents should make the most of every opportunity to
share the reading interest of their children, thus enriching
their own understanding of childhood.

In selecting books, parents must keep in mind the
child's tastes and must realize that these tastes vary from
time to time. Since great changes take place in the rapidly-
moving world, parents must consider the need for getting rid
of the deadwood likely to collect, replacing certain books
with newer ones. Of great help to parents interested in
stimulating their children to read is Keckefoth's bulletin
entitled "Helping Parents Guide Children's Reading."

Besides buying books for their children and seeing that they use some of their own money for the purchase of them, parents can do the following things to interest children in good reading:

1. Read aloud to the children frequently.

2. Investigate the materials they have read and try in various ways to substitute good books for less desirable types.

3. Confer with their children's teachers to learn about the needs and interests of their children and to obtain suggestions for getting suitable books to answer those needs and interests.

4. Attend various book programs given by the P. T. A., librarians, and study groups to learn more about children's literature.

5. Use magazines, book sections of newspapers, and other sources to read reviews of approved books for children at various reading levels.

Chapter 12

Evaluation and Results

The acid test of any educational program is whether or not it "works." Do children learn what is intended to be taught? In individualized reading the aim is not only to teach children "how to read" but also to teach them "to read." Any fair evaluation of an individualized reading experience must take both these aspects into account. In reading evaluation there has been a tendency to overemphasize the value of standardized reading tests. Useful as they are, they do not give the whole picture. Equally important and often much more indicative of the success of a reading program is teacher observation. In individualized reading, evidence gathered from the children's reading activities is crucially important in any evaluation.

Doris D. Roettger, from whose master's thesis we have previously excerpted a passage, includes a scale for evaluating pupil performance on word recognition, comprehension, oral reading, work study skills, and pupil reading activities. It is reproduced here.

A scale with similar purposes by Marguerite R. Anderson is the second selection in this chapter.

Dr. Phylliss S. Adams' doctoral dissertation, from which a teacher orientation guide has already been included, describes evaluative procedures. The results given in her summary are included here.

Doris D. Roettger presents the results of pre- and post-testing of individualized reading classes using the Iowa Silent Reading Test.

Similar data are presented in Rose A. Arkley's thesis in which the California Reading Test was used both as a pre- and as a post-test. A table of results obtained is the fifth item in this chapter.

Data obtained from pre- and post-administration of
the Gates Advanced Primary Reading Tests are taken from
the thesis of Anna M. Hune.

Achievement scores in reading obtained by a longitudinal study of individualized reading are presented in
Frances V. Cyrog's thesis and are reproduced here.

A list of twenty indicators of desirable outcomes of
reading instruction compiled by Amy E. Jensen concludes
the present chaper.

How Does a Child Read?

by

Doris Dornfeld Roettger

(This material is excerpted from the author's 1964 University of Tennessee master's thesis, <u>The Effectiveness of an Individualized Reading Program in Developing Reading Skills and Interest in Reading.</u>)

Teacher Evaluation of the Individualized Reading Program

How Does the Child Read?

Word Recognition

To read effectively children should be able to use word recognition skills in their reading. To what extent does the individualized reading program help a child to:

	very great	great	some	limited	not at all
1. Develop a curiosity and an interest in words?	5	4	3	2	1
2. Acquire a large sight vocabulary?	5	4	3	2	1
3. Attack words independently through use of context clues?	5	4	3	2	1
4. Attack words independently through use of phonetic and structural analysis?	5	4	3	2	1

<u>Comments:</u>

343

Comprehension

To read effectively children must be able to understand sentences, paragraphs, pages, and stories. To what extent does the individualized reading program help a child to:

	very great	great	some	limited	not at all
1. Understand what he is reading?	5	4	3	2	1
2. Select main ideas and supporting details?	5	4	3	2	1
3. Distinguish between fact and fiction?	5	4	3	2	1
4. Understand the author's purpose?	5	4	3	2	1
5. Initiate his own thinking about the things he is reading?	5	4	3	2	1
6. Evaluate critically what he is reading?	5	4	3	2	1
7. Use ideas gained in reading toward solution of a problem?	5	4	3	2	1

Comments:

Oral Reading

In good oral reading children should be able to read aloud effectively. To what extent does the individualized reading program help a child to:

1. Read before an audience and hold their attention?	5	4	3	2	1
2. Choose appropriate selections for oral reading?	5	4	3	2	1

Comments:

Work-Study Skills

Children must have good work-study skills to find the information they need and seek. To what extent does the individualized reading program help a child to:

	very great	great	some	limited	not at all
1. Use reference books to locate information with increasing independence?	5	4	3	2	1
2. Develop skill in the use of pictures, glossary, table of contents, index?	5	4	3	2	1
3. Acquire techniques helpful in organizing materials, writing summaries and reports?	5	4	3	2	1
4. Choose pertinent references for information he wants?	5	4	3	2	1

Comments:

What Does the Child Read?

To what extent does the individualized reading program help the child to:

1. Use a wide variety of materials to satisfy his needs and purposes?	5	4	3	2	1
2. Read good literature both old and new?	5	4	3	2	1
3. Read a wide variety of books according to his interests, purposes and abilities such as biography, adventure, folklore, science, history, etc. ?	5	4	3	2	1

	very great	great	some	limited	not at all
4. Select reading materials which present an awareness of "good taste" in reading?	5	4	3	2	1
5. Refer to ideas, facts or stories to solve current problems?	5	4	3	2	1

Comments:

How Does the Child React to his Reading?

To what extent does the individualized reading program help a child to:

	very great	great	some	limited	not at all
1. Assume responsibility in his learning?	5	4	3	2	1
2. Gain independence in efficient means of study?	5	4	3	2	1
3. Recognize his reading strengths and weaknesses?	5	4	3	2	1
4. Feel free to go to the teacher for assistance with skills, for discussion, for interpretation?	5	4	3	2	1
5. Share and talk over his books with other children?	5	4	3	2	1
6. Give evidence of reacting emotionally to what he has read?	5	4	3	2	1
7. Appreciate the humor, suspense and pathos of the story?	5	4	3	2	1
8. Develop an appreciation of a favorite author?	5	4	3	2	1
9. Recognize different styles of different authors?	5	4	3	2	1

	very great	great	some	limited	not at all
10. Grow in appreciation of literary style?	5	4	3	2	1
11. Identify with the character of the book?	5	4	3	2	1
12. Become curious about interesting words and phrases?	5	4	3	2	1
13. Become completely absorbed in what he is reading?	5	4	3	2	1
14. Develop a love for reading?	5	4	3	2	1

Comments:

A Chart for Measuring Progress in
Reading Skills

by

Marjorie R. Anderson

(This material is excerpted from the author's 1964
Willimantic State College master's thesis, A Study
of Individualized Reading in an Ability Grouped
Sixth Grade Class at the Bolton Elementary
School.)

Name _____

A. GETTING INFORMATION							
1. Answering questions about details in the story							
2. Completing statements about details in the story							
3. Naming, listing, or describing specific facts in the story							
B. UNDERSTANDING IDEAS							
1. Recognizing main ideas and purposes							
2. Understanding specific references							
3. Recognizing plot							
4. Interpreting figurative language							
C. ORGANIZING IDEAS							
1. Arranging related ideas in logical sequence							
2. Classifying related details							

348

3. Summarizing								
4. Relating story development to outlining								
a. Selecting and writing main headings								
b. Selecting and writing subheads								
5. Using reference skills								
6. Following directions								
D. MAKING JUDGMENTS								
1. Drawing conclusions								
2. Recognizing implications								
3. Making generalizations								
4. Recognizing feeling, mood, emotions, character traits, etc.								
5. Giving reasons and evidence to support personal opinions related to the story								
6. Relating story to personal experiences								
7. Anticipating outcome								
8. Identifying and evaluating characters and their motives								
9. Comparing and contrasting								
E. STUDYING WORDS								
1. Recognizing the meanings of words								
2. Understanding inherent relationships between words								
a. Recognizing synonyms								
b. Recognizing antonyms								
c. Recognizing homonyms								
3. Classifying words as an aid to understanding								
a. Selecting words with associated meanings								
b. Locating or explaining descriptive phrases								

E. STUDYING WORDS (cont.)								
c. Determining word functions from context (parts of speech)								
4. Analyzing the structure of words								
a. Distinguishing root words								
b. Recognizing and using prefixes and suffixes								
c. Recognizing and analyzing compound words								
d. Listing and analyzing contractions								
e. Writing plural forms of words								
5. Using phonetic clues and pronunciation keys to recognize and pronounce words								
a. Determining and marking vowel sounds								
b. Recognizing single consonant sounds and blends								
c. Dividing words into syllables								
d. Noting accented syllables								
e. Using phonetic respellings								
6. Practicing dictionary skills								
a. Arranging words in alphabetical order								
b. Locating words by dividing the alphabet into four parts								
c. Locating words by using guide words								
d. Interpreting respellings								
7. Skimming								
F. SILENT READING HABITS								
1. Pointing								
2. Word by word reading								
3. Vocalization								
4. Speed								
5. Short attention span								
G. ORAL READING HABITS								
1. Pointing								

2. Word by word reading									
3. Limited sight vocabulary									
a. Lack of context clues									
b. Lack of phonics skills									
c. Endings									
4. Substitutions									
5. Repetitions									
6. Omissions									
7. Reversals									
8. Insertions									
9. Speed									
10. Poor expression									
11. Poor enunciation									
12. Actual speech defect									
13. Comprehension									
14. Hesitation									
15. Volume too loud									
16. Volume too soft									
17. Phrasing									

√ skill has been mastered

O needs more work

Guidelines for Teachers Planning to Use Individualized
Reading at the First Grade Level

by

Phylliss Stevens Adams

(This material is excerpted from the author's 1962
University of Denver doctoral dissertation, An
Investigation of an Individualized Reading Program
and a Modified Basal Reading Program in First
Grade.)

The purpose of this study was to determine the
strengths and weaknesses of two reading programs, the individualized reading program and the modified basal reading
program, in promoting the reading growth of selected first
grade children.

Three aspects were identified for exploration in each
of the reading programs: (1) determining the effectiveness
of each program in teaching the skills of beginning reading;
(2) determining the value of each program in promoting desirable reading habits and attitudes; and (3) determining the
extent to which each program fostered the development of
desirable work-study habits.

One hundred seventy-two first grade pupils in eight
classrooms in Englewood, Colorado, served as subjects for
the investigation. Of these pupils, 88 received reading instruction under the modified basal reading program and 84
were taught reading under the individualized reading program.
All of these pupils had attended kindergarten, were within
the normal age range for first grade, were enrolled in first
grade for the first time, had been enrolled in the class
since the beginning of the school year, and were regular in
school attendance.

Each of the teachers participating in the study had taught first grade for two or more years, had average or above average administrative ratings, and had expressed interest and desire in teaching beginning reading through the reading program they selected to follow.

Inasmuch as both reading programs were new to the eight participating teachers, program guides were developed by the researcher for teachers to use during the investigation. Also, monthly in-service meetings were held to provide additional assistance to the teachers.

The Metropolitan Readiness Tests and the Metropolitan Achievement Tests were used in the collection of data. In addition, three other instruments for gathering data were developed by the researcher: the Sight Vocabulary Test, the Reading Readiness Check List, and the Reading Check List.

Data concerning the initial reading readiness status of the pupils were obtained through the use of the Metropolitan Readiness Tests and the Reading Readiness Check List. The Metropolitan Readiness Tests results which were studied by using the t-ratio test revealed that:

1. The Individualized Reading Group was significantly higher in reading readiness status than the Modified Basal Reading Group.

2. The Individualized Reading Group exhibited less variability than the Modified Basal Reading Group.

3. There was no significant difference between the boys in both groups in reading readiness status.

4. The girls in the Individualized Reading Group were significantly higher in reading readiness status than the girls in the Modified Basal Reading Group.

The findings from the Reading Readiness Check List were in agreement with the Metropolitan Readiness Tests results.

Data concerning the reading progress of the two groups after 51 teaching days and after 102 teaching days were obtained through use of the Sight Vocabulary Test which was administered individually to each pupil; Form A of the Reading Check List, which was filled out by the teachers,

and Form B of the Reading Check List which was filled out
by the researcher who acted as an observer in each of the
classes. Also, at the completion of the second teaching
period, the reading tests included in the Metropolitan Achievement Tests were administered.

The findings from the Sight Vocabulary Test showed
that:

1. The pupils in the Individualized Reading Group
recognized more sight words than did the pupils in the Modified Basal Reading Group at the end of each teaching period.
While both groups more than tripled their sight vocabularies
from the end of the first teaching period to the end of the
second, the gain made by the Individualized Reading Group
was larger than that of the Modified Basal Reading Group.
However, these results could have been influenced by the
earlier finding that a significant difference existed between
the two groups in initial reading readiness status.

2. At the end of both teaching periods, the Individualized Reading Group did not have as wide a range of scores
on the test as did the Modified Basal Reading Group. Furthermore, the lowest score obtained by the Individualized
Reading Group was considerably higher than the lowest score
made by the Modified Basal Reading Group.

3. At the end of each teaching period, there was
little difference in the sight vocabulary achievement of the
boys in the Individualized Reading Group as compared to the
boys in the Modified Basal Reading Group.

4. The girls in the Individualized Reading Group recognized more sight words than did the girls in the Modified
Basal Reading Group at the end of both teaching periods.
However, the difference in sight vocabulary achievement between the two groups of girls was larger at the end of the
second teaching period than at the end of the first. Perhaps
the finding that the girls in the Individualized Reading Group
were significantly higher in reading readiness status than
the girls in the Modified Basal Reading Group influenced
these data.

The findings from the Reading Check List, Form A
and Form B, indicated that:

1. The Modified Basal Reading Group was superior
to the Individualized Reading Group in a majority of the

comprehension skills at the end of the first teaching period.
At the end of the second teaching period, the two groups did
not differ widely in comprehension. Thus, the gain made by
the Individualized Reading Group during the second teaching
period was larger than that of the Modified Basal Reading
Group.

2. After 51 teaching days, neither group was superior
in all of the skills of word recognition, although the Individualized Reading Group was more successful than the Modified
Basal Reading Group in phonetic-analysis skills involving visual discrimination abilities. At the end of 102 teaching days,
only minor differences existed between the two groups in
these skills of word recognition: use of context and picture
clues, perceiving words beginning with the same initial consonant sound, and substituting initial and final consonants to
unlock unknown words. Yet with regard to a majority of the
phonetic-analysis skills involving auditory and visual discrimination abilities (such as perceiving words beginning or ending
with the same sound and associating the sound with the appropriate letter symbol), the Individualized Reading Group
was superior.

3. For both teaching periods, the difference between
the two groups in oral and silent reading habits was small.
At the end of the first teaching period, the largest difference
was in the habit of reading with expression, with the Individualized Reading Group being better in this habit. By the end
of the second teaching period, the largest differences were
in relation to heeding punctuation marks and freedom from
finger pointing. The Modified Basal Reading Group was better at heeding punctuation marks. On the other hand, the
pupils in the Individualized Reading Group pointed to words
with their fingers less frequently than did the pupils in Modified Basal Reading Group.

4. At the end of both teaching periods, the two groups
differed widely in reading attitudes. The pupils in the Individualized Reading Group exhibited behaviors indicative of
desirable reading attitudes (such as selecting books to read
during free-time periods and displaying eagerness for sharing
reading experiences) much more frequently than did the pupils in the Modified Basal Reading Group. Also, the data
indicated that the poor readers in the Individualized Reading
Group showed behaviors associated with desirable reading attitudes (such as volunteering to read orally) more frequently
than did the poor readers in the Modified Basal Reading Group.

5. At the end of the first teaching period, the Individualized Reading Group had better work-study habits than did the Modified Basal Reading Group. The same was true at the end of the second teaching period; however, the differences between the two groups had become larger in the habits of following directions, accepting responsibility, and showing initiative in thinking of activities in which to engage. During the second reading period, the Individualized Reading Group generally showed improvement in work-study habits. In contrast, the Modified Basal Reading Group had large losses in the habits of accepting responsibility and completing independent work neatly, and small losses in other habits, i. e., completing independent work and following directions. It is possible that these data reflect the fact that teachers in the Individualized Reading Group were actually teaching work-study habits while not as much emphasis was being placed upon this type of teaching in the Modified Basal Reading Group. Perhaps the interest and enthusiasm of the pupils for the activities in which they are engaging also influenced these findings.

The findings from the Metropolitan Achievement Tests at the end of 102 teaching days revealed that:

1. A significant difference existed between the two groups in word knowledge, with the Individualized Reading Group being higher than the Modified Basal Reading Group. There was no significant difference between the boys in the two groups in word knowledge; however, the girls in the Individualized Reading Group were significantly higher in word knowledge than the girls in the Modified Basal Reading Group.

2. No statistically significant difference existed between the two groups in word discrimination. Also, there was no significant difference between the boys in the two groups in respect to this ability. A significant difference existed between the girls in the two groups, with the girls in the Individualized Reading Group being higher than the girls in the Modified Basal Reading Group.

3. No statistically significant difference existed between the two groups in reading comprehension. Likewise, there was no significant difference between the two groups of boys or between the two groups of girls in reading comprehension.

II. Conclusions

Interpretation of the data obtained during this investigation seemed to warrant these conclusions concerning the strengths and weaknesses of the two reading programs as carried out with the first grade pupils in this particular study.

1. Both an individualized reading program and a modified basal reading program were effective in teaching beginning reading to first grade children.

2. Word-recognition skills were taught effectively under both programs.

3. Both reading programs promoted the development of desirable oral and silent reading habits.

4. Although both reading programs were effective in developing sight vocabulary, an individualized reading program provided an especially desirable learning situation for sight vocabulary development.

5. An individualized reading program was particularly valuable for developing skill in the use of phonics.

6. During the early part of first grade, a modified basal reading program was advantageous for developing comprehension skills. Conversely, this was a weak feature of an individualized reading program.

7. An individualized reading program was especially valuable for developing positive reading attitudes and interest in reading among pupils, including those making slow progress. On the contrary, a modified basal reading program was weak in this aspect.

8. Desirable work-study habits were fostered in an individualized reading program. On the other hand, a modified basal reading program was weak in the development of desirable work-study habits and in the maintenance of such habits among pupils.

The findings from this study also seemed to support several other conclusions in addition to those pertaining directly to the strengths and weaknesses of the two reading programs. These conclusions were:

1. Basal readers were not essential to the development of sight vocabularies among first grade pupils.

2. A wider vocabulary with less stringent restrictions on the kinds of words used and the number of repetitions per word was indicated for beginning reading materials.

3. Materials at many different difficulty levels should be utilized in reading programs in order to meet the wide range of ability present among first grade children.

4. First grade pupils were capable of accepting responsibility and becoming self-directive when they were given instruction and sufficient opportunities to develop these behaviors.

Test Results

by

Doris Dornfeld Roettger

(This material is excerpted from the author's 1964
University of Tennessee master's thesis, The Ef-
fectiveness of an Individualized Reading Program in
Developing Reading Skills and Interest in Reading.)

Note: The tables giving test results are on pages 360-363.

Table III

Median Gains, Iowa Silent Reading Test, of Classes Using I. R. Thirteen Weeks

Group	No.	Median I. Q.	Rate Mar.*	Rate May**	Rate Gain	Compre- hension Mar.	Compre- hension May	Compre- hension Gain	Directed Reading Mar.	Directed Reading May	Directed Reading Gain	Word Meaning Mar.	Word Meaning May	Word Meaning Gain
Grade 4														
School E	36	106	4.9	4.9	-	3.7	4.6	+0.9	3.8	5.3	+1.5	4.8	5.5	+0.7
Grade 5														
School E	31	97	5.5	6.8	+1.3	5.7	7.8	+2.1	6.3	9.1	+2.8	6.4	6.9	+0.5
School F	24	98	4.3	4.1	-0.2	5.4	5.4	-	5.7	6.2	+0.5	5.4	5.9	+0.5

Table III (continued)

	Paragraph Comprehension			Sentence Meaning			Alphabetizing			Use of Index			Total Median Score		
	Mar.	May	Gain	Mar.	May	Gain	Mar.	May	Gain	Mar.	May	Gain	Mar.	May	Gain
Grade 4															
School E	4.8	5.6	+0.8	4.1	5.1	+1.0	5.0	6.3	+1.3	4.3	5.0	+0.7	4.5	5.2	+0.7
Grade 5															
School E	6.4	7.6	+1.2	6.9	7.9	+1.0	6.2	6.7	+0.5	6.1	7.5	+1.4	6.3	7.6	+1.3
School F	5.6	6.4	+0.8	4.6	5.2	+0.6	7.0	9.3	+2.3	6.0	6.8	+0.8	5.5	6.0	+0.5

* March 4 = sixth school month.

** May 28 = ninth school month.

Table VIII

An Analysis of Books Read According to Subject Areas for Classes Using I. R.

Group	No. in Class	Adventure	Animals	Biography	Fairy Tales	Frontier & Western	History	Humorous	Mysteries	Myths & Legends	People & Places in Other Lands
					Subject Areas						
		Classes Using I. R. 7.5 months									
Grade 4 (I) Sch. A	24	(18)*37	(21)131	(17)59	(16)34	(12)36	(20)46	(12)38	(17)40	(3)3	(10)26
Grade 4 (II) Sch. A	32	(27)78	(29)160	(29)142	(23)62	(18)40	(9)13	(27)58	(22)69	- -	(22)48
Grade 5 Sch. B	19	(12)36	(15)84	(12)89	(10)29	(14)45	(9)41	(9)38	(15)75	(8)11	(7)15
Grade 6 Sch. C	26	(10)26	(19)150	(11)39	(14)39	(1)1	(5)8	(23)109	(14)61	(5)7	(5)7
Sch. D	23	(18)54	(19)123	(22)156	(7)17	(7)17	(8)25	(21)102	(20)130	(6)13	(8)8
		Classes Using I. R Thirteen Weeks									
Grade 4 Sch. E	36	(19)76	(29)174	(22)63	(19)68	(13)34	(10)36	(18)67	(18)27	(10)15	- -
Grade 5 Sch. E	31	(21)58	(21)102	(8)15	(13)31	(8)39	(14)42	(17)55	(21)94	(4)21	(5)14
Sch. F	24	(14)22	(19)41	(15)54	(11)25	(4)7	(6)11	(3)4	(13)23	- -	(1)1

Table VIII (cont.)

	Poetry	Science	Science Fiction	Space	Sports	Stories About Boys & Girls	Total
				Subject Areas			
		Classes Using I.R.		7.5 months			
Grade 4 (I) Sch. A	(9)19	(17)37	(2)6	(3)6	(7)16	(12)40	514
Grade 4 (II) Sch. A	(16)22	(20)74	(11)40	(15)39	(11)24	(28)151	1020
Grade 5 Sch. B	(2)3	(12)62	(14)74	(12)31	(5)61	(12)38	710
Grade 6 Sch. C	(3)3	(5)10	--	(6)7	(11)36	(18)106	609
Sch. D	(3)3	(10)25	(10)16	(4)5	(6)13	(17)96	813
		Classes Using I.R.		Thirteen Weeks			
Grade 4 Sch. E	(8)19	(8)25	(5)8	(8)20	(15)143	(9)86	761
Grade 5 Sch. E	--	(3)6	(4)15	(8)21	(7)16	(21)117	645
Sch. F	(11)21	(7)25	(1)3	(3)4	(10)30	(14)44	315

*The number of pupils in each class who read books in a subject area is given in parenthesis before the number of books read in that area.

How Children Using Individualized Reading
Performed on Reading Tests

by

Rose Adatto Arkley

(This material is excerpted from the author's 1961
University of Washington master's thesis, The
Analysis and Evaluation of an Individualized Reading Program for Third Graders Based on Contemporary Children's Literature.)

Note: The tables giving test results are on pages 366-369.

Gates Advanced Primary Reading Tests Scores of Third Graders
September 1957 to May 1958

Boy Girl	IQ	Total Reading				Paragraph Reading				Word Recognition		
		Grade 1957	Grade 1958	Gain Grade Level	Gain Months	Grade 1957	Grade 1958	Gain Grade Level	Gain Months	Grade 1957	Grade 1958	Grade Level Gain
G1	112	2.9	5.0	2.1	25	2.5	5.4	2.9	35	3.4	4.6	1.2
B1	109	3.2	5.1	1.9	23	3.0	5.4	2.4	29	3.4	4.8	1.4
G2	130	3.1	5.0	1.9	23	3.3	6.4	3.1	37	3.0	3.7	.7
G3	116	2.2	4.0	1.8	22	2.9	4.2	2.0	24	2.3	3.9	1.6
G4	102	2.9	4.6	1.7	20	2.9	4.6	1.7	20	2.8	4.6	1.7
G5	114	2.8	4.4	1.6	19	2.9	4.4	1.5	18	2.8	4.5	1.7
B2	100	2.7	4.3	1.6	19	2.4	4.4	2.0	24	3.1	4.3	1.2
B3	125	2.2	3.8	1.6	19	1.8	4.2	2.4	29	2.7	3.5	.8
B4	133	2.8	4.3	1.5	18	2.5	4.0	1.5	18	3.1	4.6	1.5
B5	113	2.2	3.6	1.4	17	1.9	4.2	2.3	28	2.6	3.1	.5
B6	98	2.6	4.0	1.4	17	2.3	3.8	1.5	18	3.0	4.3	1.3
B7	102	3.7	5.1	1.4	17	3.1	4.8	1.7	20	4.3	5.5	1.2
G6	126	3.4	4.8	1.4	17	3.1	4.8	1.7	20	3.7	4.8	1.2
B8	93	2.5	3.8	1.3	17	1.8	4.0	2.2	26	3.3	3.7	.4
B9	94	2.8	4.0	1.2	14	1.9	4.0	2.1	25	3.7	4.1	.4

Gates Advanced Primary Reading Tests Scores of Third Graders (cont.)
September 1957 to May 1958

B10	118	2.8	4.0	1.2	14	2.2	4.2	2.0	24	3.4	3.8	.4
G7	98	2.8	4.0	1.2	14	2.1	4.2	2.1	25	3.6	3.8	.2
B11	113	2.9	4.0	1.1	13	2.8	3.8	1.0	12	3.1	4.3	.9
G8	118	3.1	4.1	1.0	12	2.8	4.0	1.2	14	3.4	4.3	1.2
B12	108	3.2	4.1	.9	11	3.1	4.0	.9	11	3.5	4.3	.8
B13	119	2.8	3.6	.8	10	2.5	3.8	1.3	16	3.1	3.5	.4
B14	108	2.8	3.5	.7	8	2.6	3.5	.9	11	3.0	3.6	.6
G9	119	3.0	3.7	.7	8	3.0	4.0	1.0	12	3.1	3.4	.3
G10	103	3.5	4.0	.5	6	4.0	4.0	.0	0	3.1	4.1	1.0
G11	124	3.3	3.8	.5	6	3.1	3.5	.4	5	3.5	4.1	.6
B15	112	2.2	2.7	.5	6	1.6	2.0	.4	5	2.9	3.4	.5

Gates Advanced Primary Reading Tests Scores of Third Graders
May 1958 to May 1959 Twelve Months or 1.0 Year

Boy/Girl	IQ	Total Reading Grade 1958	1959	Gain Years	Months	Paragraph Reading Grade 1958	1959	Gain Years	Months	Word Recognition Grade 1958	1959	Gain
B1	104	2.5	5.7	3.2	38	2.1	6.0	3.9	47	3.0	5.5	2.5
B2	117	2.9	6.1	3.2	38	2.4	6.8	4.4	53	3.4	5.5	2.1
G1	101	3.7	6.8	3.1	37	3.8	7.6	4.0	48	3.6	5.8	2.2
B3	117	3.5	6.2	2.7	32	4.0	6.4	2.4	29	3.0	6.0	3.0
B4	112	2.2	4.8	2.6	31	2.3	5.4	3.1	37	2.1	4.3	2.2
G2	118	3.2	5.7	2.5	30	3.0	6.4	3.4	41	3.5	5.0	1.5
B5	88	2.5	5.0	2.5	30	2.3	5.4	3.1	37	2.7	4.6	1.9
B6	105	3.4	5.8	2.4	29	3.8	7.4	3.6	43	3.1	4.3	1.2
B7	111	2.5	4.8	2.3	28	2.3	5.4	3.1	37	2.7	4.3	1.6
B8	109	3.1	5.4	2.3	28	3.1	6.4	3.3	40	3.4	4.5	1.1
B9	111	2.5	4.7	2.2	26	2.2	5.8	3.2	38	2.9	4.1	1.2
G3	106	2.5	4.7	2.2	26	2.2	4.8	2.6	31	2.8	4.6	1.8
G4	110	3.2	5.2	2.0	24	3.4	6.0	2.6	31	3.1	4.5	1.4
G5	128	3.5	5.4	1.9	23	3.8	6.8	3.0	36	3.3	4.1	.8
G6	114	3.0	4.7	1.7	20	3.1	5.4	2.3	28	2.9	4.0	1.1

Gates Advanced Primary Reading Tests Scores of Third Graders (cont.)
May 1958 to May 1959 Twelve Months or 1.0 Year

B10	112	2.7	4.4	1.7	20	2.0	4.4	2.4	29	3.4	4.3	.9
G7	113	2.9	4.5	1.6	19	2.8	5.4	2.6	31	3.0	3.7	.7
G8	107	3.4	5.0	1.6	19	3.8	6.0	2.2	26	3.0	4.1	1.0
B11	105	2.6	4.2	1.6	19	2.8	4.4	1.6	19	2.5	4.1	1.6
B12	100	2.0	3.5	1.5	18	2.2	3.7	1.5	18	1.9	3.4	1.5
G9	97	2.4	3.9	1.5	18	2.4	3.8	1.4	17	2.4	4.0	1.6
B13	92	3.3	4.5	1.2	14	3.3	4.4	1.1	13	3.4	4.6	1.2
G10	92	2.8	3.9	1.1	13	2.6	4.2	1.6	19	3.0	3.7	.7
B14	99	3.2	4.2	1.0	12	3.0	4.0	1.0	12	3.5	4.5	1.0
G11	94	2.4	3.3	.9	11	2.5	3.2	.7	8	2.4	3.4	1.0
G12	91	2.8	3.5	.7	8	2.5	3.5	1.0	12	3.1	3.6	.5
B15	92	2.9	3.6	.7	8	2.8	3.5	.7	8	3.1	3.7	.6

Reading Gains in Individualized Reading as Measured
by Standardized Tests

by

Anna Marie Hess Hune

(This material is excerpted from the author's 1959
Ohio State University master's thesis, The Organization, Implementation and Evaluation of an Individualized Reading Program in an Upper Socio-Economic Community.)

Note: The table appears on page 371.

Data From California Reading Tests, Primary Forms
AA (Jan.) and BB (May)

Average		Median		Range	
Jan.	May	Jan.	May	Jan.	May
4. 47	5. 54	4. 4	5. 2	3. 2-5. 0	4. 2-5. 8

Gains Made by Individual Pupils

Pupil	IQ	Grade Placement Jan.	Grade Placement May	Months Gained	Books Read Independently
1	134	4. 9	5. 4	5	25
2	128	4. 0	5. 0	10	10
3	122	4. 3	5. 2	9	12
4	122	3. 7	5. 2	15	14
5	122	4. 6	5. 2	6	18
6	119	5. 0	5. 5	5	20
7	118	4. 6	5. 2	6	39
8	118	4. 5	5. 0	5	40
9	117	4. 4	5. 2	8	17
10	117	4. 4	5. 4	10	33
11	116	4. 2	5. 8	16	14
12	116	3. 8	4. 5	7	18
13	105	4. 4	5. 5	11	18
14	105	4. 8	5. 8	10	17
15	100	4. 0	5. 0	10	14
16	100	4. 6	5. 0	4	36
17	99	4. 3	5. 2	9	22
18	99	3. 8	4. 7	9	21
19	99	4. 2	5. 2	10	17
20	97	4. 3	5. 2	9	16
21	97	4. 6	5. 2	6	33
22	97	4. 1	5. 5	14	13
23	94	4. 8	4. 8	0	20
24	84	4. 6	4. 8	2	29
25	83	3. 2	4. 2	10	10

Total Number of Books Read Independently 526.
Average Number of Books Read Independently 21. 4.
Median Number of Books Read Independently 18.

Reading Test Scores of Children Taught by the
Individualized Reading Approach

by

Frances Vanderhoof Cyrog

(This material is excerpted from the author's 1964
Claremont Graduate School master's thesis, A
Longitudinal Study of an Individualized Program in
Reading.)

Table 1

Norms Derived From Five Year Averages of Achievement
and Expectancy, 1949-54, Whittier Elementary Schools,
Whittier, California[a]

Reading Test Scores (In terms of grade placement)

Grade Level	IQ	Anticipated Reading Achievement	Actual Reading Achievement		
			Reading Vocabulary	Reading Comprehension	Total Reading
3	107	3. 5	3. 4	3. 0	3. 2
4	107	4. 6	4. 5	4. 2	4. 4
5	110	5. 8	5. 0	5. 2	5. 1
6	108	6. 6	6. 1	5. 9	6. 1

[a]Norms are based upon approximately 10,000
pupils test scores in reading.

Table 3

Comparison of Actual Reading Achievement of
Individualized Reading Groups with Their
Anticipated Reading Achievement

Grade Level	IQ	Anticipated Reading Achievement	Actual Reading Achievement		
			Reading Vocabulary	Reading Comprehension	Total Reading
3	108	3. 6	4. 0	3. 8	3. 9
4	107	4. 6	5. 9	5. 7	5. 7
5	108	5. 6	6. 8	6. 6	6. 7
6	109	6. 7	8. 1	7. 9	8. 0

Table 5

A Comparison Between the Anticipated and Actual
Reading Achievement of Individualized Group
(Grades 3-6) At Four Intelligence Levels

Grade		IQ Range			
		60-90	90-110	110-130	130+
3	Number of students	38	107	85	21
	Total Reading	3. 0	3. 7	4. 3	5. 3
	Anticipated Achievement	2. 6	3. 3	3. 9	4. 9
4	Number of Students	21	117	87	22
	Total Reading	3. 2	5. 2	6. 5	7. 2
	Anticipated Achievement	3. 5	4. 1	5. 1	6. 6
5	Number of Students	31	99	79	21
	Total Reading	4. 3	6. 3	7. 7	8. 5
	Anticipated Achievement	4. 4	5. 1	6. 5	7. 8
6	Number of Students	23	102	88	24
	Total Reading	5. 2	7. 0	8. 5	9. 4
	Anticipated Achievement	4. 9	6. 2	7. 5	8. 7

Desirable Outcomes of a Reading Program

by

Amy E. Jensen

(This material is excerpted from the author's article, "Attracting Children to Books," which appeared in Elementary English in October, 1956.)

1. Through a broad reading program, children are
   exposed to a variety of vital, interesting experiences, many of which help to unify the school subjects.

2. They are helped to understand and interpret life
   and are better able to face their own difficulties
   and appreciate their successes.

3. They gain an understanding of human relationships,
   their ability to feel and sympathize being height-
   ened by seeing deeply into people.

4. Character is developed, personalities are unlocked,
   ideals are set up, and the truths of life are presented, all these having a formative and lasting effect on children.

5. Their tastes are developed to the highest level
   compatible with their reading environment, standards of aesthetic appreciation being built up.

6. Different moods and feelings are satisfied.

7. Mental nourishment is provided, resulting in increased knowledge.

8. The natural desires for glamour, adventure, and
   romance are satisfied in wholesome ways.

9. The common culture of the various parts of the world is opened up to them through enchanting book journeys.

10. Escape from the humdrum activities and the necessary routine of daily life is offered.

11. There is improved quality of learning in all fields.

12. Latent talents and abilities are discovered, creative endeavor is challenged, ingenuity and imagination are stimulated, and satisfaction is provided in sharing creative experiences with others.

13. Sharing ideas, plans, and work with others teaches children an appreciation of and respect for others' contributions, thus developing desirable group relationships and resulting in better and fuller living.

14. Worthwhile interests are substituted for less desirable ones, and leisure time is profitably occupied, resulting in social and recreational values.

15. Through book therapy, personal problems are solved and . . . attitudes, such as tolerance, kindness, and consideration, are improved, resulting in emotional stability and the development of social consciousness.

17. In reading about the common, elemental things, children see the relationships between life and nature, and they perceive the greatness, wonders, and beauty of the simple things in life, thus enhancing their love of the natural.

18. Wholesome types of humor are substituted for less desirable ones, thus making children more discriminating.

19. The standards and quality of life are improved, and, in fact, the whole conception of life and society is broadened.

20. Through the reading and sharing of books, the spirit of children is freed, and the windows to a more beautiful and fascinating world than they might otherwise have known are opened to them.

Chapter 13

History of Individualized Reading

In this chapter on the historical background of individualized reading, the first two selections are by Frederic Burk and were written in 1913 and 1924 respectively. Burk taught at the State Normal School in San Francisco and was one of the early pioneers in the individualization of instruction. Actually the plan promulgated by him, which was so very influential in the movement away from whole class instruction, dealt with individual rather and individualized instruction. Burk believed in adjusting the pace of work to each student's particular capabilities but the idea of adjusting the material as well as the pace was to come later. The reader will be struck by the difference in style used half a century ago, but will, it is hoped, also recognize the innovative and imaginative proposals made by Burk.

The second selection is an excerpt from Frances M. Seeber's master's thesis. It is an excellent account of the development of individualized reading.

The final selection is excerpted from Jane A Goode's master's thesis. Her history of reading instruction is informative and sheds light on the inevitability of the development of individualized reading.

Breaking the Lock-Step

by

Frederic Burk

(This material is excerpted from the author's
monograph, "Lock-Step Schooling and a Remedy,"
published in 1913.)

During the present generation the efficiency of our
schooling, even in the best schools, has been repeatedly
called in question. There is a widespread conviction that
the results of our schooling are painfully disproportionate to
what is expected of it and to the tremendous amount of energy put into the cause. In many localities and institutions
no expense of money, energy and sincerity of purpose has
been spared, yet no appreciable improvement has been made.
Unquestionably something must be fundamentally and radical-
ly wrong. Naturally, suspicion has often turned upon the
teaching staff--upon the honesty and integrity of their purposes and upon the efficiency of the administrative machin-
ery. But those most initimately acquainted with facts have
generally become very thoroughly convinced that, aside from
sporadic instances, the fidelity of operators of the school
system is its strongest asset.

In the most recent years the cry has gone up that the
schools can be improved only by injecting into the course of
study a broader and richer curriculum. Many new studies
have been suggested and introduced. But this proceeding,
as a remedy, shows itself shortsighted, for if the schools
are inefficient in the teaching of the subjects which for gen-
erations they have been attempting to teach, efficiency is not
to be won by adding new and different subjects. The fundamental cause of inefficiency in the process must still remain. Further, however desirable and necessary it may be
to introduce certain new material, it would seem certain
that the same fate of inefficiency must befall the teaching of
the new subjects as now besets the teaching of the old. It

377

is no remedy for a disordered stomach to load it with more
and richer foods.

But there is one source of possible cause that has
been overlooked. It has been overlooked because it is so
manifest and so fundamental that it would seem idle to suspect it. This is the essential structure of the system itself.
In the following report I have laid bare certain impossible
assumptions which are imbedded in the foundation of the
school system by class instruction. These are appalling
facts which do not easily admit dispute, and which, once ad-
mitted, no longer justify further wonder that our schooling
should be inefficient. I also outline the plan of remedy
which the faculty of the school has been working out by experience during the past year. We are keeping accurate
records, and at a subsequent date, as time and trial justify,
we shall make other reports showing in a quantitative way
the measure of the efficiency of the remedy proposed.

                                                    Frederick Burk

                      The Millstone That Hangs About the
                          Neck of the School System

        Our school system represents the abiding faith of the
people that it is upon the efficiency of the schooling the State
must depend for the quality of its citizenship, for the integrity of its social institutions and for the material prosperity
of individuals. Yet despite the faith, despite the magnificent
equipment and administration and despite the fidelity of the
workers, an inexplicable canker of inefficiency somewhere
and somehow prevents the full and legitimate fruiting of our
school system. We have neglected to scrutinize what has
been handed down to us by the dead hand of tradition. We
are using as the chief operating tool a mechanism that makes
any reasonable degree of success impossible. The results
show it.

        The class system has been modeled upon the military
system. It is constructed upon the assumption that a group
of minds can be marshaled and controlled in growth in exactly the same manner that a military officer marshals and
directs the bodily movements of a company of soldiers. In
solid unbreakable phalanx, the class is supposed to move
through the grades, keeping in locked step. This locked
step is set by the "average" pupil--an algebraic myth born of

inanimate figures and an addled pedagogy. Under this fundamental assumption the following conditions necessarily must
be forced:

I. That all pupils in a given class shall be assigned,
and shall master with even thoroughness, exactly the same
length of lesson each day.

Otherwise there would be no class. Unless the length
of daily lesson is fixed, and even thoroughness of comprehension is assumed, the pupils would string out tandem, and
instruction would necessarily become individual.

In actual experience the requirement is impossible,
and uniformity is a threadbare semblance. While some pupils do prepare the lessons to the exacted length, others do
not do so, and, under any conditions, a uniform comprehension is always a mirage of stupid assumption. The class
system has no remedy for this state of affairs. All that
the teacher can do is to carry the class along over the established route, somehow, upon schedule time, and at the
end of the year, or half year, sort them out. Some are
sent on, and others, who have stumbled and lost step, must
be sent back to do the work of the year or half year over
again. The school has no right to assume what is manifest-
ly impossible--that all pupils of a class, despite physical
and mental differences, despite accidents and other exigencies which life constantly entails, can or will daily learn the
same length of lessons with even comprehension.

A debilitating by-product of measuring out of uniform
lessons is the establishment, early in the child's plastic
mind, that the thing to do in life is to do what is measured
out for one to do--never any more, under any circumstances,
and as much less as possible, under all circumstances.

II. The graded system assumes that all pupils during
the school exercise shall pay exactly the same degree of
attention, and shall reach comprehension by exactly the same
mental process, and shall reach it simultaneously.

We all remember that the first thing our first teacher
said at the beginning of the first day we ever went to school,
was, "Class! Attention!" She and her successors kept right
on saying the same thing, many times every hour of every
day, during all the years we ever went to school.

To force one pupil to give attention to a prescribed topic is a task worthy of any pedagogic steel. But reflect a moment upon the assumption of the system that a teacher can and shall force forty pupils to put themselves in this unnatural state, simultaneously, and maintain it for ten to forty minutes at a stretch, day in and day out. To maintain forced attention for more than a few seconds is impossible. What our minds really do is to slip and rest and then take a fresh grip to bring the state back again.

Our entire school system, from kindergarten through the university, both inclusive, is therefore operated with fearful waste of energy, and its undertakings are ever under the tremendous handicap of low-power and intermittent attention. These conditions necessarily mean slow and foggy learning and corresponding ease of forgetting. Nor, under the class system, is there any means whatever of remedying the situation. As long as we persist in a system which lays the condition as necessary that forty pupils must pay simultaneous, even, and continuous attention to an imposed subject of study we must content ourselves with a degree of attention of such low power that invention, originality and reasoning are impossible. All that we can ever get out of this system is just what we always have gotten--a feeble ability to memorize words and texts and a corresponding evanescence of memory of them. Is there any teacher in the land who will gainsay this truth?

III. The graded class system assumes that all pupils shall make exactly the same rate of progress and promotion, despite absences, despite illnesses, despite all variations in physical and mental conditions, despite all differences in ambition, in temperament, and in degrees of resulting application.

The class system, by its fundamental dogmas, is forced to ignore and deny the existence of these varying contingencies and to assume, in practice, the obvious absurdity that no pupil in the class will ever be absent, sick, or vary from the standard of application. The class system has no devices to meet any contingency. There is no alternative except to wait until the end of the term or year and turn the misfits back over the work with resultant over-age.

IV. Measuring one pupil according to the abilities of other pupils.

Under the class system the pupil is marked and rated by comparison with the mythical average pupil. The terms "excellent," "fair," "poor" upon the report cards mean not what the pupil has done, measured by his own abilities, but what he has done measured by other persons' abilities.

V. The class system does permanent violence to all types of pupils.

(1) It does injury to the rapid and quick-thinking pupils, because these must shackle their stride to keep pace with the rate of the mythical average.

(2) The class system does a greater injury to the large number who make progress slower than the rate of the mythical average pupil. Necessarily they are carried off their feet by the momentum of the mass. The class system has no right to set a pace which necessarily a large percentage, or for that matter any percentage, can not possibly maintain. This policy is of course as inhuman as it is stupid.

A Substitute for the Class Lock-Step

Well, then, what are we to do about it? The facts presented are self-evident. The black figures of over-age are a measure of the results. If we are honest, if we are responsible, we no longer can maintain the deceptive semblances of education under assumptions that are false and impossible. The alternative is to establish and find means of operating a system of schooling which rests upon the truths that no two pupils are alike physically and mentally, that no two can learn at the same rate, that the teacher does well who can direct the attention of one pupil instead of forty simultaneously. But the moment we cease forcing the lock-step and permit varying rates of progress, the pupils string out tandem. The class has disintegrated and the class methods also disintegrate. We are then confronted by the problem of how to instruct, efficiently, forty or more pupils directed by one teacher under the condition that no two pupils are identical physically or mentally, that each probably learns by processes and by virtue of motives peculiarly his own and at a different rate.

We hope we shall escape, at the outset, the misunderstanding that we have undertaken this work to promote

individual instruction.   The issue is not individual instruction, but to find some substitute for the lock-step.   It merely happens that we ourselves, in searching for some substitute, have come upon individual instruction.   We ask no one
to follow us, provided he finds some other adequate solution
of lock-step evils.

The issue is not whether the substitute we have outlined is sound or not.   If it is not, another substitute must
be found.   But no amount of attack upon our substitute in
any way bolsters up the lock-step system.   Its impossibili-
ties remain in as black type as ever.   We are not essentially concerned in making converts to our particular substitute.
We are concerned in arousing the energy to establish some
efficient substitute to replace the existing inefficiency of the
lock-step.   We will support any movement that accomplishes
this end, whether this movement uses our plan or any other
as good.   We have placed emphasis upon our solution because it is a habit of human nature, or superficial forms of
it, to shriek down as "destructive criticism" any attack upon
an established custom or institution, however iniquitous, and
to demand a constructive remedy.   We therefore have fore-
stalled this form of defense, but wish it clearly remembered
that the issue is the existing evil and not the proposed remedy.

Individual Instruction

by

Frederic Burk

(This material is excerpted from the author's article, "Breaking the Lock-step," which appeared in
the NEA Journal in April, 1924.)

An individual system of instruction was introduced into the Training Department of the San Francisco Teachers
College in 1913; to a certain degree, and with certain variations this system has been continued to the present--a period of ten years. Personally, I first began to cogitate upon
an individual plan nearly twenty years previous. Superintendent Preston W. Search, of Pueblo, Colorado, had e-
merged from the pedagogic darkness of those times and had
gone about the country uttering a message of strange device.
He questioned the class system in practice and upon principle. He was a clever expounder, clear-headed, sincere, a
forcible speaker and a man of presence. His experience
with the individual plan did not prove, in immediate outcome,
a particularly happy or successful one. But his experience
did unmask and expose to intelligent view a number of for-
midable difficulties which are embedded in any attempt to
supplant an ancient fallacy, preserved by tradition. He
found we must have an entirely different type of textbook,
and a body of teachers whose educational ideas were in complete opposition to what schoolmasters hold to be most true
and most dear. Mr. Search found these difficulties insurmountable and finally, in consequence, abandoned the educational service.

The San Francisco experience--The system undertaken by the San Francisco Teachers College did not com-
mence with a definite, worked-out plan, or, least of all,
a philosophy of education. In the beginning, there was no
intent to create an individual system. The efforts of our

faculty were directed simply to uproot a few obvious difficulties, which in a teachers' training school are apt to become much exaggerated. First was the difficulty that pupils
neglect to learn the prescribed tasks or lessons which the
student teachers laid out for them. Secondly, there was the
difficulty that the pupils easily became distrait, passé, blasé,
and they were constantly in mischief. Both of these diseases
were aggravated by the teachers' being young, inexperienced,
and naturally lacking in decision. We undertook to remedy
matters by announcing that thereafter no lessons would be
prescribed; each would pursue his own lessons and proceed
at his own rate.

     An unaccountable surprise--The result was electrify-
ing. It was surprising even to the most sanguine. Even the
poorest pupils, practically, maintained the former class rate
at least. The large majority went much faster, covering in
one term two, three, four, and five times the amount of
work by the class rate. At the same time the lack of interest and the disciplinary difficulties disappeared as mist before a rising sun.

     The Winnetka Plan--At present the most carefully
planned individual instruction is that now being carried out in
Winnetka, near Chicago, under the leadership of Superintendent Carleton W. Washburne and Assistant Superintendent Willard Beatty. Both these men, as well as some of their
teachers, were members of the San Francisco College staff
during the critical period. But a training department of a
Teachers College is not a suitable place to develop new educational projects. It must be done under the conditions of
a regular public-school system with a corps of teachers such
as has been developed in Winnetka.

     The Individual System is not a system having a mech-
anism, worked out in any adequate degree, anywhere. At
present it is merely a series of principles changing from day
to day in accordance with the changing development of modern science and civilization.

     The Individual System is not an expensive system--It
is in all probability cheap as compared with the class system. The class system holds a large percentage of pupils
in the lower grades, because it has no means of sending them
along when it is profitable to send them along. We do not
know how many the individual plan could profitably send a-
long. We do not know how many the class system holds

back profitably or unprofitably.   But we do know that thirty
to forty out of every one hundred pupils in the elementary
school are repeaters and it costs as much to send a pupil
the same road as to send him the first time--probably much
more.   We do not know the relative number of pupils who
are mentally maimed or permanently disabled by the spirit
and practice of the class system.   We are as ignorant concerning the class system of existing schools as we are concerning the non-existing individual system.

The Individual System is not a teacher's undertaking--
It is an administrative problem requiring a revolution of administrative mechanisms, a complete displacement of the
tools and mechanical processes of the class system, and the
substitution of new forms of books, new spirit, points of
view, and educational philosophy of life upon the part of
teachers, superintendents, boards of education, and instructors in teacher-training institutions leading to individual instruction.

It is not social or political Bolshevism--The individual system is not in any way related to, born of, or concerned by political Socialism, economic communism, irre-
ligious atheism, or philosophic individualism.   It is as unre-
lated to any one of them as it is to a cure for corns.   "Individual" instruction does not mean that pupils are to be con-
signed to solitary confinement in dungeon vile.   The school
under a system of individual instruction will be more social-
ized than under the class lock-step.   Lawyers, doctors,
artists, and candlestick makers are individualized special-
ists, it is true, but they do not withdraw from social experience by reason of their specialization.   In fact they live
by society.   No two pupils ever yet succeeded in learning
writing by two, to read, to spell, to figure--all of these require personal and individual attention in practice.   Yet it
is none the less true that the energy which furnished the
power to operate individually is generated by social activities, by the initiative to serve the group, and by the com-
munion of saints.   Further, the individual system differs
from the class system in that its activities call for real and
substantial purposes, not artificial contrivances.

Individual instruction is not a new ism--The individual system was invented by Adam.   For eons thereafter it
was the sole system of education.   The class system is the
new thing.   Up to a few centuries ago and for hundreds of
thousands of years previous the individual system only was

386   Individualized Reading

in current vogue. Less than a generation [ago] all rural
schools were individual. Indeed Oxford and other ancient
universities still visibly retain ancient individual customs in
the tutorial system.

What the Individual System is--It is as yet merely
an unmaterialized educational conception based upon the bio-
logical principle that no two individuals are enough alike to
be identically educated; that the chief business of schooling
is to stir into activity the personal initiative of dominant
native forces and has only little to do with putting information into cold storage as the class system does. While the
social group stimulates and furnishes the motives and purposes of education, the actual learning is always an individual process in which two cannot participate. The individual
system is not fixed and finally formulated because it deals
with the energizing of living data, not the preservation of
dead data. It will change as science changes, as new conditions demand, as varied purposes control.

Development of the Individualized Reading Movement

by

Frances Mangelsdorf Seeber

(This material is excerpted from the author's 1965 University of Kansas master's thesis, An Evaluation of Two Methods of Meeting Individual Differences in Teaching First Grade Reading.)

Historical Background

Individualized instruction is unique in that it is both one of the more recently important techniques of instruction, and probably the earliest form of instruction. The most primitive tribal education was handed down from father to son, as each generation was taught by father or older male members of the family or tribe what was deemed necessary for it to know.

The Greeks and Romans transmitted their culture through the individual tutoring of poets and philosophers. According to Eby and Arrowood,[1] Virgil said:

> The choice of studies will depend to some extent upon the character of the individual mind. For whilst one boy seizes the point of which he is in search, and states it ably, another, working far more slowly, has yet the sounder judgment and so detects the weak spot in his rivals conclusions. The former, perhaps, will succeed in poetry or in the abstract sciences; the latter in real studies and practical pursuits. Or a boy may be apt in thinking, but slow in expressing himself; to him the study of Rhetoric and Logic will be of much value. Again, some minds have peculiar power in dealing with abstract truth, but are defective on the side of the particular and concrete.

387

In the Middle Ages the concept of teaching changed
very little. The monastic schools were largely individual,
or at most a very small group because of the high selectiv-
ity and very small number educated. A. J. Harris[2] suggests
that the roots of individualized reading can probably be found
in the traditions of European universities, in which a student "read" individually for a degree, rather than accumulating courses.

A. D. C. Paterson states that it was notably the German universities of the nineteenth century which were based
on the view that the student was "a genuine seeker after
knowledge, capable of choosing his own way and directing his
own studies."[3]

With the coming of the Reformation, when Martin
Luther initiated education for the common man so that each
might read the Bible for himself, began the change from individual to group instruction, and various methods of teaching groups of people how to read appeared. Over a period
of time the German leaders developed their Volkschule into
one of the most highly organized and carefully graded systems of elementary education the world has ever known.
Some reaction to this appeared in the eighteenth century as
England developed the monitorial system in an attempt to
better provide for the individual.

In America, too, education changed from the small-
group dame schools. As the idea of the universality of education developed, large, graded elementary schools, with grade
levels, and established curricula developed, especially in
the larger cities. With them developed problems so universal, and so timeless that they might easily be dated 1963.
It was in 1873, however, that The Addresses and Journal of
the Proceedings of the Education Association for the Year
1872 published an article by W. T. Harris, titled, "The Early
Withdrawal of Pupils from School: Its Causes and Its Remedies,"[4] in which he challenged the validity of any instructional pattern based on the assumption that all pupils can do
a given amount of work in the same time. The suggestion
was that they should master the same subject matter, but
should have more time to do so.

In 1888, Preston Search, generally considered the
"first voice to be raised in protest,"[5] was vigorously de-
nouncing the lock-step method of instruction. His publication, An Ideal School[6] described his introduction of individu-

alized instruction in the schools of Pueblo, Colorado. By this time, however, the graded system was rigidly and firmly established, and as a result many children were failing because they couldn't meet the curricular standards.

In the early 1900's Frederic Burk established a program of complete individualization in experimental schools in San Francisco and Los Angeles, and in 1915 published his famous Monograph C, which was widely read and reviewed because it showed the results of two years of work toward individualized instruction. A feature of his plan was that while individual progress was provided for, there were also many opportunities for group work.[7] This program was described in the twenty-fourth yearbook of the National Society for the Study of Education.[8] Burk's ideas were later spread by Willard W. Beattie, Helen Parkhurst, and Carleton Washburne.

This movement was part of a growing awareness of individual differences. Originating with Darwin's 1859 study, Origin of Species,[9] the concept of individual differences developed through contributions from several countries. It was first applied to the human race in both physical and psychological characteristics by Galton,[10] of England. To study these differences, the British, under the leadership of Pearson, developed improved techniques for analyzing and describing them. Beginning in 1905, Alfred Binet and Theophile Simon[11] of France were developing ways to measure individual differences in intelligence and underscoring the realization of the wide range of mental abilities. During this same period James McKeen Cattell had brought a combination of the influence of Wundt, of Germany, and Galton, of England, to the United States, where he began his studies of individual differences in the simple sensory and motor performances in relation to academic success.[12]

Since then, psychologists have been finding marked differences in every measurable human trait, including that of ability to learn. With World War I came a shocking recognition of the illiteracy rate in our country, and a growing concern for teaching methods. New interest in experimentation developed.

In 1921 Laura Zirbes[13] experimented with independent reading activities and found that the brighter pupils, who had learned to read simple materials with ease and understanding, made more rapid progress with this independent reading than those of equal ability without it.

Lou LaBrant in the middle 1920's was exploring the values of a free reading program in the high school, reporting her findings in 1936 in "An Evaluation of the Free Reading in Grades Ten, Eleven, and Twelve, for the Class of 1925. "[14]

Carleton Washburne[15] was beginning to introduce individualized teaching methods into the public schools of Winnetka about this time. Washburne and Winnetka became one of the most influential centers for research on reading during the 1920-1930 years, being a stronghold for individualization in the midst of a strengthening push for increased structuring. Washburne's philosophy contained some of the characteristics of a modern individualized program, as he favored a highly individualized reading program, and recognized that teachers needed information about children's interest and reading preferences in order to conduct such a program successfully. [16]

Parkhurst, [17] also at this time, started the Dalton plan in which the basic philosophy was to have students function as individual members of a social community.

Although most of the psychological research verifying the importance of individualization had not yet been accomplished, the committee of the Twenty-fourth Yearbook of the National Society for the Study of Education distinguished itself in its 1925 publication by recognizing the need for differentiating instruction at all levels. Stauffer, [18] reviewing the material presented in this publication, found that it indicated clearly many of the principles of the current individualization reading approach: (1) no group has yet been found in which the individuals composing it possess equal amounts of any one ability, (2) performances vary so greatly as to indicate that no single requirement is adequate as a stimulus to the majority of the group, and (3) to provide for the development of a learning process, it is absurd to set up a standard of a definite quantity of performance and expect each member of the group to accomplish just that amount and no other. [19] Perhaps most forceful is the statement:

> All in all, the hierarchy of individuality sets as the first task for education the discovery of the amount of development that had occurred in each student, and as a second task the discovery of a means whereby greater ability may be developed. [20]

According to Stauffer, [21] the yearbook also fosters the practice of self-selection, indicating that varying tastes and interests are the bases for the selection of varied materials,
and points to the need for an organization of classroom procedures which permits a reasonable amount of choice in the
selection of materials. Stauffer[22] also notes that the yearbook recommends the use of small groups, spontaneously
formed, since individualized teaching and learning was not,
they believed, to be considered as meaning that it was to be
solitary. Both Part I and Part II of this yearbook accented
the values of wide personal reading.

Stauffer[23] evaluated the message of this yearbook:

> The seed is sown for individualization of instruc-
> tion by (1) repeated referral to the need for in-
> struction in reading with all classroom activities,
> and (2) for independent and directed reading to
> stimulate personal interests and develop permanent
> habits of reading. The facts cannot be emphasized
> too vigorously that the essential aims of instruc-
> tion are attained primarily through wide reading.

Stauffer continued to point out that the committee
leveled the same charges at traditional methods as are now
being leveled, and also emphasized that one of the measures
of how effective reading instruction has been is the amount
of time which each pupil devotes to his own purposeful reading. Only the seed was being sown, however, for the spe-
cifics in the later part of the yearbook were concerned with
grouping. This is, possibly, not to be unexpected, for to
many at this time, grouping was thought of as a means of
providing for individual differences.

Two early studies concerning individualized reading
were reported in this yearbook. According to Sperry, [24]
Courtis and Washburne[25] both reported the results of studies, in Detroit and Winnetka, in 1920, comparing pupils in
schools where individualized instruction was practiced with
those in a school organized on a group instructional plan.
Both found much greater gains for their individualized methods.

The success of these experiments was followed by a
surge of individualized teaching, so that by 1948, according
to a National Education Association Research Bulletin, [26]
forty percent of the cities had adopted some form of indi-

vidualized instruction.

Butts and Cremin[27] indicate, however, that many communities which found it unwise or politically impossible to commit themselves completely to this concept introduced a compromise between the Winnetka plan and the traditional organization. Most frequently this took the form of dividing the students in each grade into sections of slow, average, and rapid learners on the basis of group intelligence tests. In this manner the movement for individualization contained the beginnings of its own decline.

This modification of individualization into grouping procedures was indicative of the events and situations of the time, for the pressure of class size, due to a rising birth rate, and the general acceptance of John Dewey's emphasis on the importance of shared social experiences and goals to learning in the classroom resulted in lessening or abandonment of the movement to true individualized reading during the period between 1925-1950.

An often quoted study by Gates, et al.[28] was damaging to the individualized movement, for he strongly indicated negative findings for what was termed "an opportunisitic method," although he did not report that evidence indicated the opportunistic method was advantageous in respect to development of interest, initiative, determination, and other personal and social traits.

When the concept of individualization came to be interpreted as a modification of large single groups into a series of three smaller groups, the learning problems encountered were considered as problems of methodology; studies, research, and discussion centered around word method versus phonics, controlled vocabulary, and sequential skill development, all tending toward tighter structuring. Objective tests to measure reading achievement were developed, practice exercises and workbooks were widely used. The result of this was the development of several series of basal reading texts, planned to provide for these reading needs, as they were seen at that time.

In 1940 a concerted effort was made to foster the dividing of classes into subgroups, supposedly to accommodate the various levels of abilities. By 1950 ability grouping within the classroom was firmly established in most elementary schools. This, in effect, eliminated a more complete form of individualization from general concern and attention.   As West[29] noted

> Important to the success of the basal reading program is the unity of oneness that must characterize the daily progression of each of the reading groups; there is little room in such a program, in practice, for gearing its direction and program to the interests, pace, and unique needs of each individual number of the group.

Stauffer described the situation, "What was happening was merely the replacement of a whole class lock-step with a three-group lock-step.   This was particularly true in primary grades, and for the teaching of reading."[30]

Although the three-group pattern held generally unchallenged until the 1950's, a few researchers continued working quietly in the interests of individualization.   Leadership was supplied by Olson and his co-workers, who adopted an individualized approach to reading at the University of Michigan.   Experimental programs involving various forms of individualized, developmental, and recreational reading were tried in a number of progressive schools during the 1930's.   Studies reporting the results of these investigations were published, infrequently, but steadily, indicating a firm core of interest and belief in the principles of individualization of teaching.   Sibley[31] reported good results for an individualized reading program in 1929.   In 1930, W. D. Anderson, [32] Field, [33] and Meriam[34] found in separate studies that individualized programs were effective.   O'Brian, [35] however, found negative results comparing intensive training and wide reading.

LaBrant, [36] in 1936, wrote a highly favorable report on a program of completely free reading at the Ohio State University School.   Among the advocates of such plans at the elementary school level at this time were Paul Witty, E. W. Dolch, and C. DeWitt Boney. [37]

This activity and these publications had relatively little effect on reading instruction in general, however, and the National Society for the Study of Education issued in 1937 a second report on the teaching of reading in which very little was said about individualizing reading.

The Seventeenth Annual Yearbook of the National Ele-

mentary Principal, of 1938, however, contained brief descriptions of a few programs that were essentially individualized programs, [38] and during the same year Luella Cole
published The Improvement of Reading which advocated essentially an individualized study skills method of teaching
reading. [39]

In 1937 Boney and Agnew[40] presented a study that indicated the less advanced group appeared to do better with
individualized reading.   Ray B. Dean's "A Plan for Individualized Reading in the Intermediate Grades"[41] was published
in 1938, and C. DeWitt Boney[42] published his report that in
his schools using individualized reading, the standardized test
scores were equal to or above those using basal programs.
A similar report came from Boney and Lehman[43] at this
time.   Among those studies which appeared in 1939 were
those of Loomis, LaBrant and Heller, Gumlick, and Witty
and Kopel.   Harris[44] summarized several approaches involving "free reading" as a major part of reading instruction in
1940.

It was in the early 1940's that Olson first published
the ideas about individualized reading which have since become the bases for much work in this area.   In 1941 a report appeared which, according to Harris, [45] did much to
build interest in individualized reading.   This was Teaching
Reading in the Elementary School, [46] a description of a highly informal, largely individualized reading program, using
children's experiences, and not dependent on ability groups
or basic readers, in the Maury School in Richmond, Virginia.

Emmett Betts, in 1946, made a plea for differentiated instruction in a chapter entitled, "Levels of Differentiation," in Foundations of Reading Instruction. [47]

Walter W. Cooke's study published in 1948 in the
Journal of Educational Psychology[48] clearly stated the grouping principles which were to become a part of individualized
reading as it is currently perceived, when he indicated that
there should be grouping within classes on the basis of
status and needs in specific learning areas.   These groups,
he held, should be flexible as to size and duration and specific purpose.   He further found that the grade levels at
which certain knowledge, skills, and abilities should be
learned cannot be determined with any degree of specificity.

Daisy Jones, [49] in 1948 contributed a controlled study, and Melva Harris[50] published an uncontrolled one in 1949, citing the advantages of individualized reading.   According to A. J. Harris, [51] the Forty-eighth Yearbook of the National Society for the Study of Education, Reading in the Elementary School, was published in 1949 with a description of the Maury School reading program as one of the kinds that were in harmony with desirable objectives.   Harris also points out, however, that in the chapter on adjusting instruction to individual needs, Betts stressed a combination of systematic instructional sequences with differentiated guidance, and some individual attention, a recommendation to which some writers are still adhering.

About 1950, widespread reaction to the basals erupted. According to Witty[52] the influence leading to the resurgence of interest in individualized reading was dissatisfaction with some of the outcomes of what was then the current reading instruction.   He believed unjustifiably high incidence of very poor reading was to be found among pupils in the schools. Witty considered the second factor to be the failure of many to develop a personal interest in reading.

Many writers have stressed the growing interest in, and knowledge of, psychological and sociological factors, as another important aspect in the impetus toward individualized reading.

A. J. Harris[53] notes several factors which seemed to have paved the way for this movement.

First and most important is our democratic emphasis on the value and worth of the individual... one of the major contributing factors has been the growing awareness of individual differences as studied systematically by psychologists... the third contributing factor was the growing interest in dynamic psychology.

West[54] considered the movement toward individualized reading to be the expression of dissatisfaction with lock-step inefficiency, neglect of individual differences, tastes, and abilities, and failure to stimulate ongoing reading interests. He noted that there also began to appear what he considered a forceful and appealing argument that ability grouping for reading instruction is basically an undemocratic practice in that it encourages the creation of a social caste system and

is a form of social stratification.   Summing these factors,
he stated:

> Undoubtedly this trend is the result of a number
> of factors.   Among these are the increased inter-
> est of educators in the kind of quality education
> that can only be achieved through some degree of
> individualization of instruction... and the encour-
> aging results of carefully controlled experimental
> studies that individualized reading instruction is,
> in terms of the reading achievement of children,
> at least equal to ability grouped basal reading in-
> struction. [55]

Without doubt the rallying point for all these developing forces was the writing of Willard Olson, who had carried on longitudinal studies of children's growth patterns.
Although his major research findings were published in the
early 1940's, his conclusions, which he interpreted as favor-
ing a highly individualized, highly permissive reading program, did not attract a great amount of attention until they
appeared in a little pamphlet, published in 1952.   It was
this pamphlet, "Seeking, Self-Selection and Pacing in the Use
of Books by Children,"[56] explaining his now widely influential theories of the nature of child development and principles
of learning, which provided the psychological rationale for a
thoroughly individualized reading program.

During the 1950's, interest in individualized reading
steadily increased.   Leaders in developing the movement
were Roma Gans, Leland Jacobs, Alice Miel and Irene Vite
at Teachers' College; May Lazar and the staff of the Bureau
of Educational Research, of New York City; Alvina Burrows
of New York University; Gertrude Hildreth of Brooklyn College; Jeannette Veatch of Pennsylvania State University; and
Frances Maib of the University of Idaho.   Many articles explaining the principles, delineating objectives, describing
methods and citing examples were written about individualized reading, and considerable attention was given to it at
several of the more influential reading conferences.   A large
number of reports, descriptions of programs, and studies,
both controlled and uncontrolled, meaningful and meaningless,
have since appeared in the literature on individualized reading.   It is these studies published after 1952, which will be
considered next.

Characteristics of Current Individualized
Reading Programs

A synthesis of the literature on individualized reading in the past fifteen years would indicate an increasingly clear description of the qualities considered essential to an individualized approach to teaching reading. The basis would be a clear recognition of the essential individuality of the human race, in all traits, and an acceptance of Olson's findings on child development. [57] It means making full use of his seeking, self-selection, and pacing theories, as applied to teaching of reading. [58] The essential knowledge and understanding of each child's needs, abilities, and interests is utilized to provide a functional skills program, adapted to each individual. Grouping is practiced on a flexible, short term basis, for needs and purposes other than ability ranking. Materials used are many and varied, including the child's own experiences. There is no basal text, no minimum, no limitations, no set sequences of learning. Diagnosis and evaluation are constant. An important facet of this approach is that it leaves open the opportunity to use any technique, or apply any methods or concepts of learning procedure from any discipline which may be developed and found valuable in the process of learning to read.

Although there is evidence that any teacher, without special training, can apply this approach successfully, with any size class, the growing use of individualized reading does have special implications for our teacher training programs, since it makes the teacher responsible for the reading program, and in this respect is particularly responsive and sensitive to the influence of a well-trained, creative teacher. It is a noteworthy aspect of the method that its use seems to come from the personal concern and interest of the teacher, and is spread within the level of the practicing members of the profession rather than from the recommendations of training institutions or the urging of commercial interests.

Current Research

Consideration of studies presented in the literature on individualized reading reveals a great amount of conflict and considerable variance, both in conclusions and in interpretations of findings. A portion of the difficulty lies in the nature of the reading act, for it is a complex process, which

has many variables and qualities which seem to defy measurement. Staiger points out:

> It is extremely difficult to measure in an objective
> fashion the amount of reading done, and the attitude
> toward reading. Yet these are important areas. [59]

Vite advises, "Yet to be carefully assessed are many values
in terms of attitudes and human relations... which seem to
defy measurement. "[60]

Another major problem has been lack of clear definitions and agreement as to what constitutes a basal program,
and what are essential characteristics of an individualized
program. Both those who favor the individualized approach,
and those who adhere to the basal system object to what is
considered improper, or too vague a delineation of procedures, believing that many studies fail to include the essential qualities of one or both of the programs, and so fail to
present an accurate evaluation. In some studies there has
been such a blending of characteristics in the programs as
to make a clear differentiation of approaches almost impossible, and to result in inevitably neutral findings. In other
studies differences found have been small, or applicable to
a limited portion of the population only. Other researchers
have reported neutral findings, but indicated strong trends
they believed important.

Technical problems involved in such a study are many
and varied. Sartain[61] lists (1) inadequate sampling, (2) lack
of replication, (3) failure to control "the all important factor
of difference in teacher capability." Dolch[62] points out that
even using the same teacher does not eliminate teacher variables, as teacher attitude is still an important and uncontrolled factor. Sartain[63] feels that the strong teachers are
the first to test a new approach, while Austin believes, as
a result of her Carnegie-supported "Field Study of Content
and Conduct of Reading Courses," that most college courses
on teaching of reading fail to prepare teachers for the teaching of individualized reading. Austin found:

> College instructors interviewed were reluctant to
> adopt what amounts to a revolutionary practice be-
> fore it has been supported by adequate research
> evidence. Until controlled experimental research
> proves that the individualized reading program can
> be implemented with ease and security by the class-

room teacher, and does in fact produce a more mature and interested reader, the college instructors
in reading will continue to ground their students in
the principles and procedures of a systematic program of reading instruction, centered on the basal
reading series. [64]

This would seem to have the inhibiting effect of an im-
passe on the development of much adequate and fair research,
since any method should have teachers equally and adequately trained in its use, if accurate evaluation is to be made.
In this situation, as it currently exists, longitudinal research
is especially difficult to obtain, since a series of consecutive
years of individualized reading, taught by adequately trained
teachers is not easily provided, until the method is more
widespread.

Adequate controls have been conspicuously absent in
some studies in regard to matching children in ability, back-
grounds, sex, and extent of help provided in skills areas.
Sufficient length of time, equality of sequence of time, and
artificial ceilings and limitations have also proven to be
problems in achievement of good research.

Some authors feel there is undue prejudice in published discussions and evaluation of research. West says,

Some of the most forceful objections come from
nationally recognized experts in the field of reading instruction, many of whom are editors or con-
sultants of basic reading series. [65]

Lazar challenges,

Critics seem worried about the lack of scientifically conducted experimental evidence regarding individualized reading.   My question is, why have they
not expressed the same fears about the basic reader systems?   What scientifically controlled experiments have proved that any one basic reader is
best? [66]

Austin advises,

Because basal reading materials dominate the
scene, authors and publishers should conduct additional studies to determine whether the content and

suggested methodology of their books are appropriate for today's youth. [67]

McCullough, however expressed her opinion of the research
of the time, 1957,

> Measurements of the success of the individualized
> experiment has been limited to cheerful miens,
> numbers of books read, and the scores on survey
> tests in reading. [68]

Objective consideration of the literature, therefore,
would seem to indicate the value of the following recommendation made by Sartain.

> Confronted with these inconsistent views and find-
> ings, the teacher should weigh carefully the evi-
> dence already in, and be alert to note new evi-
> dence, especially of an experimental and unbiased
> nature. [69]

In view of this situation, and so that evaluation may
be made by reference to the study itself, a chronological
listing of studies following in time those included in the discussion of the development of the movement toward individualized reading will include those studies presented from 1950
to 1964.   Indication has been made as to whether the study
was controlled or uncontrolled, and whether it was favorable
toward individualized reading approach, the basal method, or
considered neutral in its conclusions.   Adequacy of controls
or significance of study is not evaluated.

Burrows, 64.   Uncontrolled; individualized.
Johnson, 288.   Uncontrolled; individualized.
Schmidt, 490.   Uncontrolled; individualized.
Evans, 156.   Uncontrolled; individualized.
Palmer, 412.   Controlled; neutral, individualized.
Criqui, 107.   Uncontrolled; individualized.
Kaar, 295.   Controlled, basal.
Parker, 415.   Uncontrolled; individualized.
Jenkins, 281.   Uncontrolled; individualized.
Anderson, 7.   Controlled; first basal, later individual-
  ized; neutral.
Thompson, 557.   Uncontrolled; individualized.
Oser, 411.   Uncontrolled; individualized.
Parkin, 416.   Uncontrolled; individualized.
Bohnhorst, 39.   Controlled; individualized.

Bruce, 57.   Uncontrolled; individualized.
Carson, 83.   Uncontrolled; individualized.
Duker, 142.   Controlled; individualized.
McChristy, 333.   Controlled; individualized.
Walker, 599.   Controlled; neutral.
Wood, 638.   Uncontrolled; individualized.
Young, 644.   Uncontrolled; individualized.
Carr, 81.   Uncontrolled; individualized.
Derbyshire, 132.   Controlled; individualized.
Dickhart, 135.   Uncontrolled; individualized.
Fay, Leo C.   "Improving the Teaching of Reading by
    Teacher Experimentation." Bulletin of the School of
    Education, Indiana University, 34:1-101, September
    1958.   Uncontrolled; individualized.
Kingsley, 303.   Uncontrolled; individualized
Picozzi, 422.   Uncontrolled; individualized.
Sharpe, 504.   Uncontrolled; individualized.
Vite, 594.   Uncontrolled; individualized.
Sperber, 524.   Controlled; individualized.
Wiggins, 617.   Controlled; neutral.
Acinapuro, 2.   Controlled; individualized.
Crossley, 109.   Uncontrolled; individualized.
Cyrog, 116.   Uncontrolled; individualized.
Dickinson, 137.   Uncontrolled; individualized.
Edwards, 149.   Uncontrolled; neutral.
Greenman, 200.   Controlled; individualized.
Hart, 239.   Uncontrolled; individualized.
Hilson, 253.   Controlled; individualized.
Largent, 310.   Uncontrolled; individualized.
Patterson, 418.   Controlled; individualized.
Pirsig, 423.   Controlled; individualized.
Pollach, 425.   Controlled; individualized.
Steiner, 535.   Uncontrolled; individualized.
Braidford, 53.   Controlled; neutral.
Carline, 76.   Controlled, neutral.
Carlisle, 78.   Controlled; neutral.
Crosby, 108.   Uncontrolled; individualized.
Gresham, 202.   Controlled; individualized.
Ingram, Vivian.   "Flint Evaluates Its Primary Cycle."
    Elementary School Journal, 61:76-80, November 1960.
    Uncontrolled; individualized.
Izzo, 277.   Controlled; neutral.
McVey, 351.   Uncontrolled; individualized.
Marcatante, 357.   Uncontrolled; individualized.

Robinson, 447.   Uncontrolled; individualized.
Safford, 464.   Controlled; basal.
Sartain, 483.   Controlled; neutral.
Senderling, 499.   Uncontrolled; neutral.
Skapski, Mary.   "Ungraded Primary Reading Program:
   An Objective Evaluation." Elementary School Journal,
   61:41-5, October 1960.   Controlled; individualized.
Smith, 510.   Uncontrolled; individualized.
Warford, 602.   Uncontrolled; individualized.
Wells, 611.   Controlled; basal.
Williamson, 618.   Controlled; basal.
Arkley, 13.   Uncontrolled; individualized.
Aronow, 15.   Controlled; individualized.
Bailey, 21.   Controlled; individualized.
Donahue, 141.   Controlled; neutral.
Garment, 186.   Uncontrolled; individualized.
Gordon, 195.   Controlled; individualized.
Rollins, 450.   Uncontrolled; individualized.
Rothrock, 485.   Controlled; neutral.
Schnitzer, 491.   Uncontrolled; individualized.
Sperry, 525.   Controlled; individualized.   Longitudinal.
Willis, Margaret.   The Guinea Pigs After Twenty Years.
   Columbus, Ohio: Ohio State University Press, 1961,
   p. 127-64.   Controlled; individualized; longitudinal.
Adams, 3.   Controlled; neutral.
Cyrog, 115.   Controlled; individualized; longitudinal.
Ellingson, 152.   Controlled; individualized.
Hostetler, 261.   Uncontrolled; individualized.   Compila-
   tion of responses.
Rohm, 449.   Uncontrolled; individualized.
Roston, 456.   Uncontrolled; neutral.
Wilson, 625.   Controlled; neutral.

Table 1

Summary of Findings of Studies, 1950-1964

Study		Controlled			Uncontrolled	
		Favor Individualized	Neutral	Favor Basal	Favor Individualized	Neutral	Favor Basal
Burrows	1950				X		
Johnson	1951				X		
Schmidt	1951				X		
Palmer	1953		X				
Evans	1953				X		
Criqui	1954				X		
Karr	1954			X			
Parker	1954				X		
Jenkins	1955				X		
Anderson	1956		X				
Thompson	1956				X		
Oser	1956				X		
Parkin	1956				X		
Bohnhorst, Sellers	1957	X					
Bruce	1957				X		
Carson	1957				X		
Duker	1957	X					
McChristy	1957	X					
Walker	1957		X				
Wood	1957				X		
Young	1957				X		

Table 1 (cont.)

Study		Controlled			Uncontrolled		
		Favor Individualized	Neutral	Favor Basal	Favor Individualized	Neutral	Favor Basal
Burdette	1958						
Carr	1958		x		x		
Derbyshire	1958	x					
Dickhart	1958				x		
Fay	1958				x		
Kingsley	1958				x		
McNabb	1958				x		
Picozzi	1958				x		
Sharpe	1958				x		
Vite	1958				x		
Sperber	1958	x					
Wiggins	1958		x				
Acinapuro	1959	x					
Crossley and Kniley	1959				x		
Cyrog	1959				x		
Dickinson	1959				x		
Edward	1959					x	
Greenman, Kapilian	1959	x					
Hart	1959				x		
Hilson and Thomas	1959	x					
Largent	1959				x		

Author	Year	(1)	(2)	(3)	(4)	(5)
Patterson	1959					X
Persig	1959					X
Pollack	1959					X
Steiner	1959		X			
Braidford	1960				X	
Carline	1960				X	
Carlisle	1960				X	
Crosby	1960		X			
Gresham	1960					X
Ingram	1960		X			
Izzo	1960					
McVey	1960				X	
Marcatante	1960		X			
Robinson	1960		X			
Safford	1960		X	X		
Sartain	1960				X	
Senderling	1960	X				
Skapski	1960					
Smith and Belcher	1960		X			X
Warford	1960		X			
Wells	1960			X		
Williamson	1960			X		
Arkley	1961					
Aronow	1961		X			X
Bailey	1961					X
Donahue	1961				X	
Garment	1961		X			
Gordon	1961					X

Table 1 (cont.)

Study		Controlled			Uncontrolled		
		Favor Individualized	Neutral	Favor Basal	Favor Individualized	Neutral	Favor Basal
Rollins	1961						
Rothrock	1961		x				
Schnitzer	1961				x		
Sperry (longtid.)	1961	x					
Willis (longtid.)	1961	x					
Adams	1962	x					
Cyrog (longtid.)	1962	x					
Ellingson	1962	x					
Hostetler	1962				x		
Rohm	1962				x		
Roston	1962					x	
Wilson	1962		x				
Lane	1963		x				
Skolnick	1963		x				
Totals		21	15	4	41	3	0

Notes

1. Eby, Frederick and Arrowood, C. F. The History and
   Philosophy of Education, Ancient and Medieval. New
   York: Prentice-Hall, 1942, p. 926.

2. Harris, A. J. 233.

3. Peterson, A. D. C. A Hundred Years of Education New
   York: MacMillan, 1952, p. 209.

4. Harris, W. T. "The Early Withdrawal of Pupils from
   School: Its Causes and Its Remedies." The Ad-
   dresses and Journal of Proceedings of the National
   Education Association for the Year 1872. National
   Education Association, 1873, p. 266.

5. Stauffer, R. G. 531.

6. Search, Preston An Ideal School New York: Appleton,
   1901.

7. Stauffer, R. G. 530.

8. National Society for the Study of Education Adapting the
   School to Individual Differences Twenty-fourth Yearbook, 1925, Part II, p. 59-77.

9. Darwin, Charles Origin of Species New York: New
   America Library, 1958.

10. Galton, Francis "Classification of Men According to
    Their Natural Gifts" Hereditary Genius: An Inquiry
    into its Laws and Consequences New York: Appleton,
    1870, Chapter 3.

11. Binet, Alfred and Simon, Theophile The Development
    of Intelligence in Children Publication No. 11. Vine-
    land, N. J. : Training School at Vineland, N. J. 1916.

12. Thorndike, Robert L. and Hagen, Elizabeth Measure-
    ment and Evaluation in Psychology and Education.
    New York: Wiley, 1962, p. 4.

13. Zirbes, Laura 647

14. LaBrant, Lou "An Evaluation of Free Reading in Grades
    Ten, Eleven, and Twelve, for the Class of 1925, the
    Ohio State University School" Columbus, Ohio: Ohio
    State University Press, 1936.

15. Washburne, Carleton "Burk's Individual System, as De-
    veloped at Winnetka" Adapting the School to Individu-
    al Differences Twenty-fourth Yearbook, National So-
    ciety for the Study of Education, Part II, 1925, p.
    198-200.

16. Stauffer, R. G.   531.

17. Parkhurst, Helen Education of the Dalton Plan   New
    York: E. P. Dutton Company, 1922.

18. Stauffer, R. G.   531.

19. National Society for the Study of Education op. cit. p. 6.

20. Ibid. p. 30.

21. Stauffer, R. G.   531.

22. Ibid.

23. Ibid.

24. Sperry, Florence "What Research Says About Individu-
    alized Reading" Twenty-fifth Yearbook, Claremont
    Reading Conference. Claremont: Claremont Univer-
    sity College, 1961, p. 73-91.

25. Washburne, Carleton "Is Individualized Instruction More
    or is it Less Effective Than Class Instruction in
    Teaching School Subjects?" Adapting the School to
    Individual Differences Twenty-fourth Yearbook, Na-
    tional Society for the Study of Education, Part II,
    1925, p. 198-200.

26. National Education Association "Trend in City School
    Organization, 1938-1948" Research Bulletin 27:4-39,
    February 1949.

27. Butts, R. Freeman, and Cremin, Lawrence A. A His-
    tory of Education in American Culture New York:
    Holt and Company, 1953, p. 298.

28. Gates, Arthur, et al "A Modern Systematic versus an
    Opportunistic Method of Teaching: An Experimental
    Study" Teachers' College Record 27:679-700, April
    1926.

29. West, Roland. 612.

30. Stauffer, R. G. "Individual and Group Type Directed
    Reading Instruction" Elementary English 37:375-82,
    October 1960.

31. Sibley, Martha "Individualized Reading Method Adapted
    to the Grade Readers for Work Type Reading" Edu-
    cational Administration and Supervision 15:441-7,
    September 1929.

32. Anderson, Will D. An Experimental Study of Free Read-
    ing Versus Directed Reading Master's thesis. Chi-
    cago: University of Chicago, 1930.

33. Field, Helen A. 163.

34. Meriam, J. L. "Avoiding Difficulties in Learning to
    Read" Educational Methods 9:413-9, April 1930.

35. O'Brian, Ida "A Comparison of the Use of Intensive
    Training and of Wide Reading in the Improvement of
    Reading" Educational Methods 10:346-9, March 1931.

36. LaBrant, Lou "An Evaluation of Free Reading in Grades
    Ten, Eleven, and Twelve, for the Class of 1925, the
    Ohio State University School" Columbus, Ohio: Ohio
    State University Press, 1936.

37. Harris, A. J. "Progressive Education and Reading In-
    struction" Reading Teacher 18:128-38, November
    1964.

38. Harris, A. J. 233.

39. Ibid.

40. Boney, C. DeWitt, and Agnew, Kate "Periods of A-
    wakening or Reading Readiness" Elementary English
    Review 14:183-7, 1937.

41. Dean, Ray B. 124.

42. Boney, C. DeWitt, 46.

43. Boney, C. DeWitt, and Lehman, Edna, 47.

44. Harris, A. J. 231.

45. Harris, A. J. "Progressive Education and Reading In-
     struction" Reading Teacher 18:128-38, November
     1964.

46. Maury School Staff, 362.

47. Betts, E. A. "Levels of Differentiation" Foundations of
     Reading Instruction New York: American Book Com-
     pany, 1954, p. 713-28.

48. Cooke, W. W. "Individual Differences and Curriculum
     Practices" Journal of Educational Psychology 39:
     257, March 1948.

49. Jones, Daisy M. 291.

50. Harris, Melva 237.

51. Harris, A. J. op. cit.

52. Witty, Paul 631.

53. Harris, A. J. 233.

54. West, Roland 612.

55. Ibid.

56. Olson, Willard C. 402.

57. Olson, Willard C. 403.

58. Ibid.

59. Staiger, Ralph 527.

60. Vite, Irene 591.

61. Sartain, Harry 482.

62. Dolch, E. W. "Unsolved Problems in Reading" Ele-

mentary English 31:329-31, October 1954.

63. Sartain, Harry 475.

64. Austin, Mary, et al. 19.

65. West, Roland 612.

66. Lazar, May 317.

67. Austin, Mary C. "Reading Instruction in the Public Schools of the U. S. A." Reading an an Intellectual Activity, ed. by J. Allen Figurel. International Reading Association Conference Proceedings. New York: Scholastic, 1963. p. 245.

68. McCullough, Constance "What Does Research Reveal About Practices in Teaching Reading?" English Journal 46:475-90, 1957.

69. Sartain, Harry, 472.

History of the Teaching of Reading

by

Jane Anderson Goode

(This material is excerpted from the author's 1965
Baylor University master's thesis, A Historical
Study of Reading Instruction in the Elementary
Schools of the United States, 1880-1963.)

In general the methods of teaching reading applied to
group instruction of a whole class by a single teacher except
for some differentiated assignments and individual help. The
existence of wide differences in achievement and rate of
progress among pupils was well known by this time as many
scientific investigations had already been made in this area.
Thus far, however, educators had not been able to solve the
problems of providing adequately for these variations within
the classroom.

Although a final solution to this problem would not be
found during this period, two significant innovations were to
prove of permanent usefulness in future attempts to meet
this dilemma. The first was applied to the traditional classroom organization with its uniform pace and annual promo-
tions. In this situation the teacher usually met the problem
in two ways: by ability grouping, using suitable materials
for each group; and by providing extra attention for the bright
and dull pupils. [1] Actually this plan received widespread acceptance and was soon thought of as a very effective means
of meeting individual needs with a minimum of change in curriculum necessary.

The second plan for meeting individual needs in reading was not received so favorably as the first; yet, in recent
years, it has become more accepted and has been the center
of much discussion in educational circles. Presently referred to as "individualized reading, " this procedure had its
beginning in 1912 in the elementary school of San Francisco

State Normal School.   Later, a similar plan was tried in a
public school in Winnetka, Illinois, at which time the idea of
individualized instruction first received widespread attention.

The well-known "Winnetka Plan" was organized by the
superintendent of the school system, Carleton W. Washburne.
Basically it was simply individualized instruction in all subjects of the school program. [2]   Washburne found that beginning reading was the most difficult aspect of the curriculum
to individualize.   The procedure decided upon was the same
sequence as that found in many methods of teaching reading.
Initial sight words were taught first; then followed individual
work in phonics.   The chief differences between this plan and
conventional methods were that the first-grade pupil used
self-help materials (picture dictionary, printed rhymes) in
order to read by himself, and the child began independent
reading in the second grade rather than working with the
whole class or even a particular group.   After the initial
work on mechanical skills, he was tested and given books on
his reading level.   Each child read at his own rate, making
individual reports to the teacher. [3]   In defending this plan,
Washburne gave comparative test results from the Winnetka
school and a group of other schools studied.   The reading
achievement of Winnetka pupils was not only above the national norms but also above the average of other schools. [4]

Many other plans of individualized instruction, including the widely-known Dalton Laboratory Plan, developed
throughout the country.   None of these made as significant
a contribution to future reading programs as the Winnetka
Plan.   They either were modeled on this basic idea or, as
was true of the Dalton Plan, did not include individualized
work in the primary grades.   Although the present concept
of individualized reading is much broader in scope than it
was forty years ago, this early experimentation provided a
basis from which this new type of instruction would be developed.

A discussion of meeting individual needs in the classroom would be incomplete without reference to the beginnings
of remedial reading work in the early twenties.   About this
time a few books and articles on this subject made their appearance.   This initial interest in reading difficulties was
the result of scientific studies of achievement in which new
standardized reading tests were applied.   These test results,
along with school records of pupil progress, gave evidence
of the great need for remedial work in the public schools.

The early experimentation by educators centered around several areas: techniques for diagnosing individual cases, types of remedial cases in reading, causes of difficulty, and methods used in remedial work. The significance of these studies was readily recognized, bibliographies were compiled by several educators, and further studies in the general area multiplied rapidly. Over the years remedial reading has probably received more experimentation than any other aspect of the reading program. For this reason there is almost an overabundance of material on the subject. Of greatest interest to the educator and retarded reader is the fact that much valuable material in the way of aids for both teacher and pupil has been made available; and as a result, the educational future of disabled readers has become more optimistic with each year since the early 1920's.

This beginning of attention to needs in remedial reading was the third of the significant contributions of this short period in the history of reading instruction. Of primary importance was the emphasis on silent reading involving both speed and comprehension; and the emergence of the new concept regarding instruction according to individual abilities and needs marked the other important emphasis. In the reading era from 1880 to 1918 initial work in the application of scientific principles to education had been begun; but it was not until this later period that some results of this experimentation began to be applied in the school programs.

Another plan for meeting individual needs in the 1930's was through individualized reading instruction. [5] Usually each pupil participated in a reading group and then received additional attention as needed. The most common procedure used with the advanced pupils was to challenge them by encouraging extra work such as individual assignments related to classroom projects or content subjects, voluntary reading in free periods, and reading at home. The poorer students were helped by remedial instruction. Special classes and teachers were not available in the early part of the century; hence corrective instruction had to be given by the regular teacher. Means for discovering pupils in need of help had improved with the advent of intelligence and standardized tests. Still, the teacher's observations and informal tests were also considered valuable in diagnosing problem cases.

The responsibilities of the primary and intermediate teachers with regard to remedial instruction became clear

in the 1920's as the result of scientific studies conducted at
this time.   These studies revealed that many cases of reading disability could have been prevented by the use of better
teaching techniques such as those used in ability grouping and
individualized instruction; it was also found that the early discovery and quick treatment of deficiencies in reading is very
important because bad habits become easily fixed.   The responsibility of the primary teacher was to prevent reading
difficulties if possible, or to discover and to correct them
promptly if they had already developed.   The intermediate
teacher could only detect problems and try to overcome them,
as most were already ingrained by the time the pupil reached
these grades.

The teacher who worked with several reading groups
and also gave individualized instruction had a heavy teaching
load.   This factor plus the fact that these teachers must be
well trained and abundant materials must be available probably caused this method to receive limited use at this time.

During the 1940's the reading curriculum began to
feel the influence of research in child development.   Accordingly curriculum makers and teachers in planning the reading program emphasized more and more the characteristics
and needs of children rather than subject matter.   This new
focus on the child had been in the making for several dec-
ades.   By the late 1940's it had made an impact on the public schools, and in the 1950's resulted in the program referred to as the "child-centered curriculum." Briefly, the
ideas behind this curriculum were as follows: the child
should want to learn for himself according to his present and
future needs and interests; since he is in contact with other
people, he should acquire happy and wholesome ways of dealing with them; the school should foster both mental and emotional growth; adequate attention should be given to all aspects of the child's nature so that his mental ability could
be fully realized. [6]

Although educators recognized the child study movement and its implications for education as one of the outstanding events in educational history, the resulting curriculum changes did not meet with widespread acceptance, particularly among laymen.   Even the most caustic critics of
the child-centered curriculum would not discount completely
the value of studies in child development, but many were
highly opposed to what they believed to be an elimination of
the three R's in this new program.   In discussions and writ-

ings about the new curriculum, the specific subjects such as
reading were not given prominence, as they were now considered as a means rather than the end in itself. Because
of this latter fact there was much misunderstanding, and
many felt that these subjects were not being taught adequately.

Criticism was forthcoming from both laymen and educators, but the discontent was of a different nature. Laymen felt that children were not being given sufficient direct
instruction in reading. They were quick to suggest that pupils under this system were engaged in much irrelevant activity at school and that this time could be put to better use
by basic instruction in the three R's. The use of phonetic
instruction was frequently suggested.

The outspoken advocate of phonics was Rudolf Flesch[7]
whose well-known book, Why Johnny Can't Read, aroused
much furor over the methods of reading instruction. In the
early pages of his book Flesch states that the teaching of
reading all over the United States is totally wrong; he then
elaborates on the erroneous conceptions of reading instruction. [8] His caustic criticism, directed not only at methods
of instruction but at professional educators in general, did
not go unanswered. Betts' reaction is perhaps typical: he
states that Flesch gives rash, extravagant statements and is
a master of histrionics. [9]

There was general agreement among school personnel
that although some of Flesch's criticisms have been justified,
he did not give adequate study to the problem and as a result was not qualified to draw authoritative conclusions. With
the publication of this book, public interest in methods of
teaching reading reached a new high; and educators were
forced to examine teaching methods closely and critically as
they defended the school programs.

Many educational authorities expressed dissatisfaction
with the reading achievement of pupils under the child-centered curriculum, but they saw the fault from a point of
view different from that of the laymen. Few would agree
with Flesch and Walcutt that a revival of phonics was the
complete answer to the problem, for a number of investigations comparing reading achievement currently with that of
prior years indicated that instruction was as successful now
as it had been in the past. [10] These affirmative results
caused educators to be less critical of specific methods for

teaching reading. Their criticism centered on other phases
of the reading program such as a lack of adequate provision
for the needs of each individual pupil (the retarded, average,
and gifted), and the failure of students to acquire a permanent interest in reading. Curriculum makers could not answer all the criticism received. The fact that they were influenced by the reaction of the public and by the views of
other educators is evident in the aims for reading instruction formulated during this period.

Of the aims adopted at this time two were of primary
significance. The first, an emphasis on the development of
the whole child, had been devised in the 1940's; but its influence was not fully manifested until the 1950's. In relation
to reading, this aim meant continued attention to the pupil's
personal and social growth through his reading experiences.
Emphasis was placed on fostering good mental health, creating a wholesome classroom atmosphere, and securing a desirable teacher-pupil relationship.

The second aim--of even more paramount importance
than the first--was the recognition that the school must allow for individual differences. This concept also was an
outgrowth of the child study movement and may be considered
the foremost influence on reading instruction during this period. Attempts to meet this aim were centered in three areas:
aiding the retarded reader, challenging the gifted pupil, and
meeting individual differences of all pupils through a program utilizing individualized reading.

In addition to these main objectives for the reading
program, several lesser aims were stressed. A suggestion
relating to the curriculum organization called for an integration of reading with the language arts program. It was felt
that through such a plan the teacher could more nearly aid
the child in all-round personal development and meet his
needs as an individual. Another emphasis at this time (also
suggested in the previous decade) was attention to critical
reading and reading in the content fields. Many educators
urged that pupils be directed in critical reading and thinking
in order to be prepared as adults to read discriminatingly,
weigh and consider, distinguish fact from opinion and reason
from emotional opinion. A further aim recommended by
educators was the wider use of books from school and public libraries and an increased use of audio-visual aids for
instructional purposes in the classroom.

After these aims of reading instruction were set up, it again remained the task of individual schools or school systems to determine how their particular programs would be modified in an effort to meet these goals. Two procedures for instruction were generally followed in the primary grades. The more common approach was the use of a developmental program in which ability groups formed the classroom organization. According to one educator this procedure was the prevailing method in 1958 in 99 per cent of the elementary school classrooms. Advocates of this basal reading approach usually encouraged the use of supplementary work for whole class participation, small group projects, and independent reading.

Until recent years there had been no attempt to replace the regular developmental reading program with another plan as the former was believed to be adequate. Now this attempt is being made by educational leaders who feel that individualized reading is an even more effective approach to reading instruction. Although the present concept of individualized reading instruction is new, [11] a similar approach was used under the Winnetka and Dalton plans in the twenties and thirties. At that time the primary purpose was simply to permit children to progress at their own rates. With the reappearance of the idea in the 1950's, the concept had changed to include a concern for the child's "interest in reading, his attitude toward reading, and his personal self-esteem and satisfaction in being able to read." [12] Individualized reading today may be characterized further as a way of thinking about reading or

> an attitude toward the place of reading in the total curriculum, toward the materials and methods used, and toward the child's developmental needs. It is not a single method or technique but a broader way of thinking about reading which involves newer concepts concerned with class organization, materials, and the approach to the individual child. [13]

This plan, which is specifically an outgrowth of Willard Olson's psychology of "seeking, self-selection, and pacing" is based on sound psychological principles.

Briefly, the procedure that would be followed by teacher and pupil under the individualized reading program is as follows: each child selects a book he wants to read.

During the daily conference period of about forty-five minutes, the pupils go to the teacher for individual conferences
of two to ten minutes. (Everyone would not have a conference with the teacher every day.) This conference is a very
important part of the program because at this time "the
teacher checks, diagnoses, teaches, evaluates, and extends
the pupil's interests and activities."[14] A written record is
kept by the teacher of the child's needs, interests, attitudes,
and progress. The pupil keeps a record of books read,
date of completion, and comments on the books. If it is
found that several children need help on the same skills, a
small group may be formed temporarily for this instruction.
Varied supplementary activities may be used as outgrowths
of the reading.

Because individualized reading is relatively new, there
is much debate as to its merits. Advantages and disadvantages have been pointed out by educators and observed by
teachers actually engaged in this program. The advantages
generally agreed upon are as follows: the psychological effect on the pupil is good in that he is relieved of group pressure as to achievement; individual differences and needs are
provided for more effectively than under other programs;
children read more, read faster, and comprehend better; un-
desirable attitudes toward reading tend to be eliminated and
more permanent interests acquired;[15] because reading and
the language arts are closely integrated, greater growth is
evidenced in oral and written expression and critical thinking; the child takes more initiative, demonstrates self-man-
agement, and gains more independence; more creative teaching is possible under this plan.[16] The above if obtained
would represent the ultimate in achievement for the program; but actual practice will fall much below the level of
the ideal.

More realistic critics of the program have singled
out a number of problems or disadvantages that have been
met on an operational level: hindrance of overcrowded classrooms, increased demands on the teacher such as keeping
of additional records, lack of sufficient knowledge on the
part of many teachers for conducting such a program, difficulty in teaching basic skills, and need for participation in
group activities by the pupils. Even the strongest proponents of individualized reading recognize problems of this
program and realize that much more experimentation is necessary. Certainly the program has merit. Whether its
greatest contribution to reading instruction will be as the

sole method of teaching reading in a classroom or as a
method to be used in combination with other plans will be
seen.

The basic plan of individualized reading as outlined
above was also followed in the intermediate grades. Many
educators were more amenable to its use in these higher
grades than in the primary years. [17] From reports of such
programs in action it may be concluded that no teachers conducted the reading activities in the same way although they
followed the same basic procedure. In their direction of the
program they expressed their own individualities in a number of ways. For instance, some preferred to exercise
much control over what the children read, some used pre-
structured practice material for development of skills, and
some incorporated small group and total class activities as
appropriate.

Although individualized reading has been the most significant new plan for reading instruction proposed in the last
decade, the most popular means for teaching reading in the
intermediate grades has continued to be through some form
of grouping. Flexible ability grouping for basal reading instruction was the most common procedure used in 1959.
In spite of its popularity this developmental plan is still very
difficult to put into practice in the intermediate grades. Because of the wide range of reading ability several sets of
readers, workbooks, and manuals are usually needed. In
classrooms which do not use the basal reader, a number of
grouping plans have been utilized. The entire class might
occasionally become a reading group while making plans for
a class trip or while hearing a report of a smaller group.
Small groups might be formed on the basis of mutual interests or social choice. Need for help in reading skills by
several pupils might prompt the teacher to form a group for
temporary instruction.

Even though some school systems adhered rigidly to
one procedure for teaching reading in the intermediate grades,
others used a combination of plans. For example, a teacher
might use a developmental program with all pupils except the
superior ones. These would be allowed to follow an individualized plan. Some educators suggested that the reading time
be equally divided between basic reading instruction and individualized reading for all pupils with possibly alternate
weeks devoted to each. A combination of whole-class activities, group reading, individualized reading, and committee

assignments was also recommended, partially as a safeguard against children becoming overly conscious of belonging to a particular group placement.

Notes

1. Suggested ways to provide for individual differences were given by Samuel C. Parker, General Methods of Teaching in Elementary Schools, 2nd ed. rev.; Boston: Ginn and Co., 1922, p. 269-320 and W. W. Theisen, "Provisions for Individual Differences in the Teaching of Reading," Journal of Educational Research 2:560-71, 1920. Theisen based his recommendations on the methods used by 118 successful teachers. Included were the following ideas: ability grouping, use of graded materials, silent reading for good pupils and oral reading for poor pupils, development of individual interests through the reading materials, supplementary assignments for proficient pupils, emphasis on thought-getting, drill of specific defects, and voluntary reading at school and home.

2. For a report on the Winnetka Plan, see Carleton W. Washburne, Mabel Vogel and William S. Gray, A Survey of the Winnetka Public Schools. Bloomington, Ind.: Public School Publishing Co., 1926.

3. Modifications had been made in this basic reading plan by the 1940's, with the teacher being relieved of pressure with regard to pupil academic achievement in the first two grades. There were no fixed standards of sight words, phonics, or reading skills to be achieved during this period; each teacher was the judge as to when a child was ready for systematic instruction. When several children were ready, he formed a small group and taught according to the standard procedures: use of experience charts and pre-primers, practice on recognition of sentences, phrases, word and phonetic elements. The groups were flexible, and transfer from one to another was frequent. In these early grades the chief aim of reading was the development of enjoyment and fluency. If testing in the fifth grade revealed deficiencies, appropriate practice was given. As a result of this plan there were few cases in remedial reading. Carleton W. Washburne, "Individualized Plan of Instruction in Winnetka." 232, p. 107-109.

4. Washburne, Vogel, and Gray, p. 50-56.

5. A more accurate term here would be "individual read-
    ing." Technically, "individualized reading" is a meth-
    od of teaching reading which did not achieve promi-
    nence until the 1960's.

6. Brownell, William A. "Are We Neglecting the 3 R's?"
    National Parent-Teacher, 47:11, 1952.

7. Charles C. Walcutt also believed phonics to be an answer
    to reading problems in the schools.   For his evalua-
    tion of the phonic systems in present use, see Charles
    C. Walcutt (ed.), Tomorrow's Illiterates Boston:
    Little Brown, 1961, p. 141-63.

8. Flesch, Rudolph Why Johnny Can't Read New York:
    Harper, 1955, p. 2.

9. Betts, Emmett A. "Is Phonics a Cure-All?" High Points
    38:40, 1956.

10. Spache, George D. "Are We Teaching Reading?" 232,
    p. 25-28.

11. For a practical guide to individualized reading see Helen
    Fisher Darrow and Virgil M. Howes Approaches to
    Individualized Reading, 120.

12. Smith, Nila B. Reading Instruction for Today's Chil-
    dren, 515, p. 134.

13. Ibid.

14. Smith, Nila B. 515, p. 143.

15. Evans, N. Dean, 156

16. Lazar, May, 232, p. 130-35.

17. The success of individualized reading in the first grade
    has been doubted.   An experiment conducted in 1955-
    56 revealed above-average scores for pupils learning
    under this type of program. Frances Cyrog, 116.

Chapter 14

Research

Several excerpts from the San Diego study have been included in this book. Finally, as the first selection in this chapter, an excerpt describing the research project on which the monograph series was based, is included.

The second and final item in this chapter is a reprint of an article which I wrote for Elementary English on research that is needed.

A Plan for Research

by

San Diego County Department of Education

(This material is excerpted from Analysis of Pupil
Data. Improving Reading Instruction, Monograph
No. 5, 1965.)

Treatment of Data

The specific statistical procedures which were followed
in the treatment of the data derived from the various instruments administered to teachers and pupils are indicated below.

Determination of Teacher Approaches

Data derived from the instrument, "Teacher Inventory
of Approaches to the Teaching of Reading," consisted of the
following:

1. Three descriptions of teaching accuracy scores.
   These scores were derived by taking the sum of
   ratings given by each teacher to each set of eleven
   items representing each of the three approaches.
   A five-point scale starting with one: "entirely inaccurate" to five: "entirely accurate" was used. It
   should be noted that each of the three sets of eleven
   items were placed at random in the instrument and
   in no way identified as a set.

2. Three average accuracy scores derived by dividing
   the sums by eleven and rounding to the nearest
   whole number.

3. A consistency index number derived by adding the

highest average accuracy score to the opposite values of the two lower average accuracy scores. Opposite values on the five-point scale were as follows: one equals five, two equals four, three equals three, four equals two, five equals one.

4. A consistency index score composed of the index number described above plus a prefix consisting of the three average accuracy scores and a suffix consisting of a capital letter standing as the symbol for the approach receiving the highest accuracy score and a capital letter enclosed in parentheses standing as the symbol for the approach receiving the second highest accuracy score. When both of the lower two accuracy scores are equal, the suffix consists of the capital letter symbolizing the highest accuracy score only. The capital letters standing for the approach are B for Basic, I for Individualized, and LE for Language Experience.

To clarify the use of accuracy scores, average accuracy scores, consistency index numbers, and consistency index scores, examples are given in the next paragraph of three teachers who participated in the study. The five-point scale of accuracy has already been discussed. The consistency index numbers have the following values: index numbers 14 and 15 represent a degree of consistency stated as "Approach is consistently implemented;" index numbers 12 and 13, "Approach tends to be consistently implemented;" index numbers 10 and 11, "Approach is identifiable but eclectic in implementation;" index numbers 8 and 9, "Approach tends to be inconsistently implemented;" index numbers 3 through 7, "Approach is inconsistently implemented." The following accuracy scores were made by three different teachers, one from each approach group, and during both control and experimental periods. In addition, the consistency index scores are shown for each of the examples. The consistency index scores are then analyzed and interpreted.

A teacher from the Basic Approach group made the following accuracy scores during the control period: basic approach score, 48; individualized approach score, 37; language experience approach score, 23. Converting the accuracy scores to average accuracy scores (accuracy score divided by 11) and then computing the consistency index number as described above, the consistency index score is as follows: 432 11 B(I). This index score is interpreted as follows:

The teacher implemented an approach during the control period characterized as an eclectic (11) basic (B) approach
drawing more heavily on elements of the individualized [(I)]
approach than upon the language experience (43$\underline{2}$) approach.
This same teacher made the following accuracy scores during the experimental period: B = 43, I = 41, LE = 25.
The consistency index score is 442 10 B(I). This index
score is interpreted as follows: The teacher implemented
an approach during the experimental period characterized as
an eclectic (10) Basic (B) Approach drawing more heavily
on elements of the Individualized Approach [(I)] than the Language Experience (44$\underline{2}$) Approach. Comparing the consistency index scores for the two periods (control and experimental) it can be noted that no significant change in approach
was made. In fact, the experimental approach tended to be
more eclectic and more oriented to the Individualized Approach than was the case during the control period. With
regard to this teacher, the individual teacher approach implemented during the in-service (control) phase was not different from the approach implemented during the implementation period (experimental). Since this teacher chose the
Basic Approach as her experimental approach, and since her
individual approach was also characterized as the Basic Approach, no comparison of approaches is possible. However,
a comparison of teaching the approach as individually conceived with teaching the approach as theoretically conceived
is possible. For purposes of assessing consequences by
groups of teachers and classes, this teacher was placed in
a group of teachers who demonstrated a similar consistency
pattern for both control and experimental periods.

A second example comes from a teacher who chose
the Individualized Approach as the one she wished to implement during the experimental period. Her scores for the
control period were B = 39, I = 34, LE = 24. Experimental period accuracy scores were B = 29, I = 54, LE = 29.
Consistency index scores would thus be: Control, 432 11
B(I); Experimental, 533 11 I. The control period index
score is identical to the control period score for the teacher
in the first example. However, the experimental index score
indicates that the teacher has shifted from an eclectic Basic
Approach to an eclectic Individualized Approach. The consequences of implementing the theoretical approach can thus be
compared with the teacher's own approach during the control
period.

The third teacher was a member of the Language

Experience group.   Control period accuracy scores were
B = 26, I = 54, LE = 49.   Experimental period accuracy
scores were B = 27, I = 53, LE = 54.   The respective consistency index scores were thus 542 11 I(LE) and 552 11
LE(I).   The analysis of these scores indicates that this
teacher shifted from an eclectic Individualized Approach drawing heavily on elements of the Language Experience Approach
to an eclectic Language Experience Approach drawing heavily
on the Individualized Approach during the experimental period.   A contrast of approaches is possible in this case.

    The consistency index score thus makes it possible to
describe accurately the contrasts in approaches employed by
a given teacher during each of the two periods.   Groups of
teachers can be described also in terms of consistency of
implementation.

Individualized Reading Approach

    The total number of teachers originally selecting this
group was thirty-six.   However, two teachers and classroom
groups were eliminated from inclusion in most of the tables
presented since student data for these two classroom groups
were incomplete.

    For clarity and ease of use, all data presented in the
following tables are in terms of three subgroups.   These
subgroups contain the teachers whose control period individual approaches are common as defined by their consistency
index scores.   Again teachers are listed in order of degree
of consistency in implementing the theoretical Individualized
Approach with highest consistency first.   This determination
is also based upon consistency index scores.

    Subgroup III reported in Tables VII through XI may
be described as follows: Nineteen teachers whose implementation of their individual approaches was characterized as a
basic approach during the control period implemented the
theoretical Individualized Approach during the experimental
period.

    In the nineteen classes there were 414 pupils.   Aver-
age class size was 21.95 after screening incomplete pupil
data cards.   The mean intelligence quotient and chronological age for pupils in Subgroup III were 110 and 101 months

respectively.

Nineteen teachers are represented in Table VIII. The first nine implemented the Individualized Approach in a consistent manner during the experimental period, eight were eclectic, and the last two teachers tended to be inconsistent in their implementation. All of these teachers employed, to some degree of consistency, an approach characterized as a basic approach during the control period. It is, therefore, possible to compare the theoretical Individualized Approach with individual teacher versions of the basic approach.

Tables IX, X, and XI present pupil data for Subgroup III. Table IX summarizes the achievement data for Subgroup III. For thirteen of the nineteen cases, there were no significant differences in gains for the two periods. In five cases, the differences were significant and favored the control period. In one case, the difference was significant and favored the experimental period. For the group as a whole, the difference was significant at the 0.1 per cent level and favored the control period.

Total gain in months of achievement for both periods combined for Subgroup III was 12.7 months or nearly a year and four months' mean gain. The mean gain for this subgroup during the control period was 8.5 months while the mean gain for the experimental period was 5.1 months. This is impressive since normal mean expectancy for a four-month period has been established as 4.0 months of gain. The mean intelligence quotient of 110 might account, to some degree, for this group's higher-than-expected achievement results.

No significant differences in gains on the attitude inventory (Table X) are reported for Subgroup III. One of the classroom groups reported a difference (MnD) of 24.1 points of gain which favored the experimental period and is significant at the 1.0 per cent level.

Personal/social adjustment (Table XI) differences are significant for two of the nineteen classes in Subgroup III and for Subgroup III as a whole. These differences favor the experimental period.

Table VII

Individualized Approach Group: Subgroup III
Description of Teachers and Classes

Teacher Code No.	District Code Number	Total Years of Teaching	Years in Present Grade	Grade Taught	Number of Pupils	Mean Intelligence Quotient	Mean Chronological Age (Months)
19	3	--	--	3	15	95	103
22	3	21	--	4	26	113	112
24	3	17	10	1	15	---	75
51	8	20	9	5	15	110	124
25	3	6	6	4	29	121	111
23	3	7	1	2	16	107	91
3	1	15	9	2	19	132	88
21	3	28	3	5	18	129	126
30	3	22	4	2/3	29	107	93
1	1	3	3	3	25	111	102
35	4	4	1	3	24	107	101
36	4	8	8	1/2	22	126	82
53	10	--	--	2	21	107	90
65	12	18	6	5	28	105	126
28	3	4	3	3/4	25	113	105
62	12	3	3	3	23	110	102
64	12	13	7	3	23	107	101
63	12	8	8	2	26	102	88
40	6	12	7	1	15	---	76

Table VIII

Analysis of Approaches Employed by Teachers
in Subgroup III Individualized Group

Sub-group	Teacher Number	Consistency Index Score Control Period	Consistency Index Score: Exptl. Period
III	19	522 13 B	522 13 I
III	22	522 13 B	522 13 I
III	24	432 11 B(LE)	522 13 I
III	51	521 14 B(LE)	522 13 I
III	25	422 12 B	531 13 I(B)
III	23	442 8 B(I)	532 12 I(LE)
III	3	433 10 B	422 12 I
III	21	433 11B(I)	422 12 I
III	30	421 13 B(I)	422 12 I
III	1	432 11 B(I)	533 11 I
III	35	522 13 B	533 11 I
III	36	433 10 B	533 11 I
III	53	433 10 B	533 11 I
III	65	442 10 B(I)	533 11 I
III	28	433 10 B	432 11 I(LE)
III	62	432 11 B(I)	432 11 I(LE)
III	64	433 10 B	543 10 I(LE)
III	63	544 9 B	443 9 I(LE)
III	40	432 11 B(LE)	442 8 I(LE)

Table IX

Reading Achievement Test Data: Individualized Group
Subgroup III

Teacher Number and Subgroup	Mean T_1	Mean T_2	Mean T_3	Mean of $T_3 - T_1$ Total Gains	Mean of Differences (E-C=D): MnD	Standard Error of the Mean: σ_M	Significance Ratio: S. R.	Level of Significance (%)
19	27. 8	34. 3	41. 8	14. 0	+1. 1	2. 440	+4. 63	---
22	50. 8	64. 5	70. 3	19. 5	-7. 9	2. 090	-3. 790	0. 1
24	13. 8	13. 6	22. 3	8. 5	+8. 9	1. 951	+4. 577	0. 1
51	57. 9	67. 9	74. 3	16. 4	-3. 5	2. 360	-1. 500	---
25	53. 5	65. 4	70. 1	16. 6	-7. 1	2. 403	-2. 970	1. 0
23	22. 5	33. 9	37. 2	14. 7	-8. 1	2. 330	-3. 489	1. 0
3	33. 9	38. 3	42. 6	8. 7	- . 1	1. 195	- . 042	---
21	54. 9	63. 1	68. 4	13. 5	-2. 9	2. 640	-1. 091	---
30	26. 8	39. 6	43. 4	16. 6	-8. 9	. 968	-9. 191	0. 1
1	38. 3	46. 5	51. 7	13. 4	-3. 0	1. 850	-1. 600	---
35	36. 7	44. 8	49. 7	13. 0	-3. 3	1. 790	-1. 816	---
36	24. 0	30. 0	32. 7	8. 7	-3. 2	1. 484	-2. 144	---
53	26. 6	33. 6	37. 6	11. 0	-3. 0	1. 446	-2. 041	---
65	59. 2	67. 0	70. 3	11. 1	-4. 4	2. 450	-1. 793	---
28	44. 9	56. 7	60. 4	15. 5	-8. 1	1. 777	-4. 565	0. 1
62	47. 6	54. 3	61. 6	14. 0	+ . 7	2. 171	+ . 300	---
64	43. 4	49. 7	56. 0	12. 6	+ . 04	1. 716	+ . 025	---
63	31. 2	39. 8	49. 0	17. 8	+ . 6	1. 790	+ . 344	---
40	14. 5	19. 3	24. 4	9. 9	+ . 3	2. 693	+ . 099	---
III	38. 6	47. 1	52. 3	13. 7	-3. 2	. 496	-6. 450	0. 1

Table X

Pupil Attitude Data: Individualized Group
Subgroup III

Teacher Number & Subgroup	Mean T_1	Mean T_2	Mean T_3	Mean of T_3-T_1 Total Gains	Mean of Differences (E-C = D): MnD	Standard Error of the Mean σ_M	Significance Ratio: S. R.	Level of Significance (%)
19	95	78	85	-10	+24. 1	6. 450	+3. 740	1. 0
22	91	96	104	13	+ 1. 7	4. 530	+ . 364	---
24	69	78	79	10	- 8. 1	6. 681	-1. 217	---
51	97	96	98	1	+ 2. 7	3. 300	+ . 809	---
25	91	98	98	7	- 6. 6	4. 757	-1. 377	---
23	87	97	99	12	- 8. 2	3. 390	-2. 413	---
3	98	100	109	11	+ 6. 6	4. 516	+1. 468	---
21	97	99	103	6	+ 2. 9	4. 320	+ . 671	---
30	81	87	85	4	- 8. 4	3. 564	-2. 351	---
1	90	94	95	5	- 3. 5	3. 770	- . 923	---
35	91	95	95	4	- 3. 8	4. 349	- . 872	---
36	77	84	91	14	- . 5	4. 158	- . 109	---
53	82	88	81	- 1	-13. 7	5. 449	-2. 517	---
65	101	101	103	2	+ 2. 9	1. 984	+1. 458	---
28	85	87	94	9	+ 5. 1	3. 891	+1. 306	---
62	99	102	104	5	- 2. 0	1. 966	-1. 039	---
64	86	92	102	16	+ 3. 8	4. 543	+ . 842	---
63	86	95	99	13	- 4. 8	6. 407	- . 750	---
40	83	86	99	16	+ 8. 9	5. 497	+1. 613	---
III	89	93	97	8	- . 6	1. 073	- . 585	---

Table XI

Personal/Social Adjustment Data: Individualized Group
Subgroup III

Teacher Number & Subgroup Mean T_1	Mean T_2	Mean T_3	Mean of $T_3 - T_1$ Total Gains	Mean Differences (E-C = D): MnD	Standard Error of the Mean: σ_M	Significance Ratio: S. R.	Level of Significance (%)
19 63	66	66	3	- 3. 6	4. 100	- . 885	---
22 107	113	117	10	- 2. 9	5. 360	- . 545	---
24 59	59	69	10	+11. 0	5. 924	+1. 857	---
51 117	121	123	6	- 1. 0	2. 840	- . 327	---
25 113	111	111	-2	+ 1. 9	5. 558	+ . 335	---
23 71	75	81	10	+ 1. 6	2. 430	+ . 642	---
3 74	72	83	9	+14. 2	2. 750	+5. 149	0. 1
21 108	113	123	15	+ 4. 2	5. 150	+ . 816	---
30 69	69	69	0	- . 6	3. 467	- . 179	---
1 73	75	80	7	+ 2. 8	3. 990	+ . 702	---
35 73	77	79	6	- 3. 0	3. 368	- . 891	---
36 67	71	79	12	+ 4. 5	5. 014	+ . 906	---
53 72	64	71	1	+14. 6	6. 129	+2. 385	---
65 108	113	121	13	+ 4. 2	5. 391	+ . 775	---
28 90	93	101	11	+ 4. 2	4. 673	+ . 899	---
62 78	76	79	1	+ 5. 6	3. 284	+1. 708	---
64 69	74	88	19	+ 8. 7	4. 314	+2. 026	---
63 70	75	78	8	- 4. 9	3. 691	-1. 313	---
40 73	69	78	5	+13. 2	3. 888	+3. 395	1. 0
III 83	85	90	7	+ 3. 5	1. 067	+3. 281	1. 0

Table XII

Individualized Approach Group: Subgroup IV
Description of Teachers and Classes

Teacher Code Number	District Code Number	Total Years of Teaching	Years in Present Grade	Grade Taught	Number of Pupils	Mean Intelligence Quotient	Mean Chronological Age (Months)
20	3	15	12	3	20	107	101
50	8	5	5	3	19	109	102
13	2	16	1	3	23	116	100
45	7	15	9	5	21	105	125
41	6	13	5	4	29	104	112
2	1	9	4	6	17	114	136
29	3	8	5	5/6	13	95	131
44	6	3	3	6	28	106	137
42	6	7	4	4	31	107	111
54	10	--	--	2	12	105	93

Table XIII

Analysis of Approaches Employed by Teachers
in Subgroup IV Individualized Group

Sub-group	Teacher Number	Consistency Index Score Control Period	Consistency Index Score: Exptl. Period
IV	20	532 12 I(B)	522 13 I
IV	50	322 11 I	522 13 I
IV	13	443 9 I(LE)	422 12 I
IV	45	443 9 I(B)	532 12 I(LE)
IV	41	433 10 I	533 11 I
IV	2	433 10 I	432 11 I(LE)
IV	29	432 11 I(B)	432 11 I(B)
IV	44	533 11 I	432 11 I(LE)
IV	42	442 8 I(B)	433 10 I
IV	54	543 10 I(LE)	443 9 I(B)

Table XIV

Reading Achievement Test Data: Individualized Group
Subgroup IV

Teacher Number & Subgroup	Mean T_1	Mean T_2	Mean T_3	Mean of $T_3 - T_1$ Total Gains	Mean of Differences (E-C=D): MnD	Standard Error of the Mean: σ_M	Significance Ratio: S.R.	Level of Significance (%)
20	38.5	52.3	56.9	18.4	-9.3	1.570	-5.920	0.1
50	36.6	43.2	48.6	12.0	-1.1	1.270	-.827	---
13	49.1	54.6	57.3	8.2	-2.7	2.160	-1.270	---
45	61.3	66.4	71.6	10.3	-.1	1.038	-.046	---
41	49.0	57.6	62.2	13.2	-3.9	1.903	-2.029	---
2	80.7	85.3	87.1	6.4	-2.8	1.832	-1.541	---
29	41.7	43.4	49.5	7.8	+4.5	3.005	+1.485	---
44	68.2	71.5	78.1	9.9	+3.3	1.538	+2.113	---
42	47.8	61.4	65.1	17.3	-9.9	2.448	-4.058	0.1
54	25.6	32.9	36.5	10.9	-3.8	2.160	-1.736	---
IV	51.2	58.7	63.2	12.0	-3.0	.697	-4.271	0.1

Table XV

Pupil Attitude Data: Individualized Group
Subgroup IV

Teacher Number & Subgroup	Mean T_1	Mean T_2	Mean T_3	Mean of T_3-T_1 Total Gains	Mean of Differences (E-C=D): MnD	Standard Error of the Mean: σ_M	Significance Ratio: S. R.	Level of Significance (%)
20	106	111	111	5	-3.5	1.400	-2.460	---
50	79	88	93	14	-3.7	8.790	-.425	---
13	95	95	99	4	+5.6	2.640	+2.110	---
45	95	102	102	7	-5.4	3.046	-1.782	---
41	93	97	101	8	-.9	3.213	-.290	---
2	92	97	101	9	-2.3	1.994	-1.150	---
29	75	70	68	-7	+2.5	5.288	+.466	---
44	82	95	98	16	-9.5	4.296	-2.211	---
42	91	100	100	9	-8.8	3.506	-2.503	---
54	95	99	99	4	-4.4	3.371	-1.310	---
IV	91	96	99	8	-3.5	1.329	-2.653	1.0

Table XVI

Personal/Social Adjustment Data: Individualized Group
Subgroup IV

Teacher Number & Subgroup	Mean T_1	Mean T_2	Mean T_3	Mean of $T_3 - T_1$ Total Gains	Mean of Differences (E−C=D): MnD	Standard Error of the Mean: σ_M	Significance Ratio: S.R.	Level of Significance (%)
20	83	88	94	11	+ 1.1	2.350	+ .447	---
50	75	76	78	3	+ 1.2	3.610	+ .335	---
13	76	78	82	6	+ 1.7	3.370	+ .504	---
45	112	115	119	7	+ .6	4.717	+ .131	---
41	110	114	120	10	+ .7	3.906	+ .177	---
2	114	122	122	8	- 8.1	5.186	-1.554	---
29	---	---	---	---	---	---	---	---
44	108	120	127	19	- 5.3	5.142	-1.021	---
42	100	114	117	17	-10.6	4.715	-2.237	---
54	70	74	78	8	- .3	4.718	- .071	---
IV	96	103	107	11	- 2.5	1.497	-1.667	---

Table XVII
Individualized Approach Group: Subgroup V
Description of Teachers and Classes

Teacher Code Number	District Code Number	Total Years of Teaching	Years in Present Grade	Grade Taught	Number of Pupils	Mean Intelli-gence Quo-tient	Mean Chrono-logical Age (Months)
46	7	2	1	6	24	109	137
11	1	14	14	2	21	100	90
27	3	2	2	2	15	109	88
43	6	2	1	4	21	104	106
26	3	19	19	2	21	115	87

Table XVIII
Analysis of Approaches Employed by Teachers
in Subgroup V Individualized Group

Sub group	Teacher Number	Consistency Index Score Control Period	Consistency Index Score: Exptl. Period
V	46	222 8 I (LE)	521 14 I(LE)
V	11	443 9 B (I)	522 13 I
V	27	444 8 B (LE)	532 12 I (LE)
V	43	442 8 LE (I)	532 12 I(LE)
V	26	444 8 B (I)	542 9 I

Table **XIX**
Reading Achievement Test Data: Individualized Group
Subgroup V

Teacher Number & Subgroup	Mean T_1	Mean T_2	Mean T_3	Mean $T_3 - T_1$ Total Gains	Mean of Differences (E=C=D): MnD	Standard Error of the Mean: σ_M	Significance Ratio: S. R.	Level of Significance (%)
46	71. 4	76. 0	80. 0	8. 6	-1. 0	1. 930	- . 539	---
11	21. 7	31. 8	35. 7	14. 0	-6. 3	1. 530	-4. 110	0. 1
27	27. 5	28. 5	31. 4	3. 9	+2. 0	1. 807	+1. 107	---
43	48. 3	57. 6	61. 9	13. 6	-5. 1	2. 535	-2. 010	---
26	26. 1	37. 6	43. 1	17. 0	-6. 1	1. 777	-3. 430	1. 0
V	40. 6	48. 2	52. 3	11. 7	-3. 6	. 919	-3. 862	1. 0
All Ind.	42. 6	50. 6	55. 5	12. 9	-3. 2	. 370	-8. 602	0. 1

Table **XX**
Pupil Attitude Data: Individualized Group
Subgroup V

Teacher Number & Subgroup	Mean T_1	Mean T_2	Mean T_3	Mean of $T_3 - T_1$ Tot. Gains	Mean of Diff. (E=C=D): MnD	Standard Error of the Mean: σ_M	Significance Ratio: S. R.	Level of Significance (%)
46	86	79	84	-2	+12. 2	3. 860	+3. 160	1. 0
11	77	92	86	9	-20. 1	5. 970	-3. 370	1. 0
27	84	90	94	10	- 2. 6	7. 121	- . 365	---
43	84	94	97	13	- 7. 5	4. 269	-1. 751	---
26	87	98	102	15	- 8. 4	2. 550	-3. 305	1. 0
V	84	90	92	8	- 4. 9	2. 344	-2. 104	---
All Ind.	89	94	97	8	- 2. 1	. 795	-2. 605	1. 0

Table XXI

Personal/Social Adjustment Data: Individualized Group
Subgroup V

Teacher Number & Subgroup	Mean T_1	Mean T_2	Mean T_3	Mean of T_3-T_1 Total Gains	Mean of Differences (E-C=D): MnD	Standard Error of the Mean: σ_M	Significance Ratio: S.R.	Level of Significance (%)
46	111	105	114	3	+15.0	3.860	+3.880	0.1
11	66	69	73	7	+ 1.1	3.720	+ .296	---
27	72	70	73	1	+ 4.2	3.531	+1.189	---
43	109	102	114	5	+20.0	7.883	+2.531	---
26	74	71	83	9	+16.1	3.177	+5.051	0.1
V	88	85	93	5	+11.8	2.253	+5.226	0.1
All Ind.	87	90	95	8	+ 3.0	.829	+3.626	0.1

Table XXII

Correlation Matrix: Individualized Group*

Variable	(1) Intelligence Quotient	(2) Vocabulary T₁	(3) Comprehension T₁	(4) Total Achievement T₁	(5) Attitude T₁	(6) Personal T₁	(7) Social T₁	(8) Total Personality T₁	(9) Total Achievement T₂	(10) Attitude T₂	(11) Total Personality T₂	(12) Total Achievement T₃	(13) Attitude T₃	(14) Total Personality T₃
(2)	33	.	91	96	24	60	61	63	90	20	64	90	24	65
(3)	34		.	97	22	61	63	65	90	17	66	89	24	67
(4)	34			.	23	61	63	65	92	19	66	92	23	68
(5)	18				.	27	35	32	26	63	30	27	50	24
(6)	20					.	83	96	63	26	91	63	24	79
(7)	16						.	96	65	30	79	64	31	79
(8)	19							.	67	29	83	67	29	82
(9)	37								.	25	70	93	28	69
(10)	22									.	37	26	64	29
(11)	22										.	70	35	87
(12)	37											.	31	70
(13)	23												.	36
(14)	21													.

*Diagonal elements and decimals are omitted.

Conclusions and Recommendations

The following statements relate to the findings regarding all aspects of the project and also represent the conclusions and recommendations presented in the dissertation upon which this monograph is based.

Conclusions

1. Three different approaches to the teaching of reading have been identified, analyzed, and described in the form of operational definitions which can be used by classroom teachers as a guide to implementation. These approaches are the Basic, the Individualized, and the Language Experience.

2. In-service education programs designed to assist teachers prepare for implementation of any one of these approaches were valuable to the teachers involved.

3. Teachers generally employed their own version of one of the three described approaches, but some employed a mixture of the elements of the three approaches, when given the opportunity to employ whatever teaching approach they wished during the in-service phase.

4. Teachers, after studying the description and operation definitions of a particular approach chosen from among the three approaches, were generally able to implement to some acceptable degree of consistency any one of the three approaches.

5. After study and experimental implementation, teachers ranked the elements of the approach they chose as workable, practical, and significant. Therefore, they ranked the definitions and analysis of each of the three approaches as educationally sound and useful to the classroom teacher.

6. With regard to all three aspects of pupil behavior changes as measured by three instruments, it must be concluded that in most instances the differences calculated for classroom groups did not constitute significant differences. However, the following conclusions regarding certain tendencies are useful:

a. Individual teacher approaches implemented during the control period in the fall months, in which teachers used their own versions of all three theoretical approaches as well as a mixture of approaches, tended to provide for greater pupil gain than was achieved by pupils when their teachers implemented any one of the three theoretical approaches (experimental period).

b. Gains in pupil attitude tended to remain stable, with no tendency to favor either the individual teacher versions (control period) or the three theoretical approaches (experimental period).

c. Greater gain in personal/social growth was made by pupils in the three theoretical approaches implemented during the spring months (experimental period) than during the period when their teachers implemented their own versions of one of the three theoretical approaches or a mixture of approaches.

7. When teachers take part in a project such as this one, pupils may be expected to exceed expectancies in achievement gains. Expected gains in achievement at the norm over the eight-month period of the study was eight to eight and one-half months. However, pupils in the Basic group achieved 12.5 months, pupils in the Individualized group achieved 12.9 months, and pupils in the Language Experience group achieved 12.9 months. These approaches and combinations of these approaches may produce better than average results in pupil achievement when implemented under conditions such as those employed in this project.

8. No clear-cut superiority of any one of the approaches (when compared with either of the other two approaches) is indicated by the findings of this study. When individual teachers employed their version of the basic approach (Subgroup III) versus the theoretical Individualized Approach a difference in mean achievement gains favored the basic approach. A difference in personal/social growth, on the other hand, favored the theoretical Individualized Approach. It should be noted, however, that the pupils in this subgroup achieved the greatest over-all achievement --13.7 months--of any subgroup in the study.

A similar result for Subgroup V (a mixture versus theo-

retical Individualized) occurred. The over-all mean
gain in this case, however, was 11.7 months. The only subgroups yielding differences that were significant
for two of the three measures, and were also subgroups
that contained contrasting approaches, were Subgroups
II and V.

9. There are positive relationships between pupil achievement scores and pupil attitude inventory scores, pupil
achievement scores and pupil personal/social adjustment
scores, and pupil attitudent inventory scores and pupil
personal/social adjustment scores. The degree of relationship is greater for achievement and personal/social
adjustment (from .50 to .77) than for the other two
pairs of relationships (range for both about .20 to .40).

Recommendations

1. School districts should consider utilizing the descriptions
of the approaches as bases for in-service education in
the area of reading instruction.

2. Teachers should be encouraged to study the three approaches with a view of implementing one or more of
them in their own classrooms.

3. Instruments should be developed which measure more accurately the reading achievement of pupils, pupils' attitudes toward reading, and pupil self-concept.

Needed Research

by

Sam Duker

(The article reproduced here appeared in Elementary English in March, 1966.)

Individualized reading has attracted much attention
during the last five or six years. While the idea is by no
means new, it probably has never had as much consideration before. Much has been written about this approach.
A good deal of this writing is exhortative material tinged
with the authors' missionary zeal. Some research has been
done[1] but many issues remain unsettled. It is the purpose
of this article to suggest some significant questions concerning individualized reading where research might yield useful
answers.

Before listing specific research needs, three general
principles that should govern any study in this area will be
discussed briefly.

1. The desirability of an individualized approach to
the teaching of reading cannot be established by showing that
results obtained are as good as, or even better than they
would be if obtained by some other method. The real question is whether individualization leads to accomplishment of
the aims of reading instruction. Despite the millions of
words devoted to the subject of reading, it is not easy to
determine just what these aims are. It is not possible to
obtain any satisfactory research finding concerning the effectiveness of any way of teaching reading unless such findings may be measured against a set of aims for reading instruction. A prerequisite to any effective research in reading is, therefore, the preparation of a set of aims. In
passing, I note that I am not aware of any extended research
of this kind in support of the basal reader approach.

2. It is often assumed that only research which has
a control group built into its design is valid. This is certainly a mistaken concept. As Brownell pointed out in an ad-
dress to the American Educational Research Association,
much of the most elaborately designed educational research
has tended to be sterile. Brownell suggests that we need
to take a rather large sample and,

> we would then note carefully what occurs from day
> to day--which children progress rapidly, and which
> slowly, and why; at what points in the sequence
> learning difficulties arise; what they are, and why
> they appear, which instructional devices or aides
> are successful, which unsuccessful, and why. Our
> procedures would be those of testing, interviewing,
> and observing. [2]

Quite likely research of this kind will require the creation of
new tests. Developing satisfactory tests may be one of the
most difficult tasks facing the research worker.

3. Much educational research deals only with immediate, short-term results. This in my opinion is a major de-
fect especially in research involving reading. We are not
particularly concerned with results obtained at the end of a
six-week or even at the end of a two-year period. We are
much more interested in the effect of a particular mode of
teaching reading on a long-term basis.

There is, of course, a very good explanation for the
fact that short-term results have been reported so persist-
ently. Doctoral and masters' candidates have only a limited
period at their disposal in which to complete their research.
I have long contended that graduate research should be on a
continuing basis and that theses should be based on a particular segment of such research. It is not reasonable to
expect theses to cover a six-year period, and yet, such a
period or even a longer one would give us the significant
answers we are seeking. The "recommendations for further
research," which have become a traditional feature of the last
chapter of theses, serve no real purpose. Only seldom in
very exceptional cases is anything done about them, either by
the writer himself or by anyone else. In the continuing type
of research I have proposed, such recommendations would
have real meaning since gaps would be filled in by those who
write on subsequent segments of a continuing research project.

In the light of these three general statements, I shall now list and briefly comment on twenty-five of the specific unanswered questions having to do with the effectiveness of individualized reading which could usefully be made the focus of research studies. This does not purport to be an exhaustive list. It does give a clue, I believe, to rich opportunities open to those wishing to do research on this topic.

1. Is individualized reading equally effective at all grade levels? No longer can there be any question about the possibility of using this approach at all grade levels. The relative degree of effectiveness, however, has not been established.

2. What is the relationship between varying levels of mental ability and the success of individualized instruction in reading? Here again, it is not a question of whether this approach can be used. That has been established for almost the full range of mental abilities. The question, once more, is one of relative effectiveness.

3. How many books are needed to assure a successful program? Arbitrary statements calling for from three to ten books per pupil are frequently made. Is that enough or do we need more? Or less? Should a classroom library provide for the omniverous reader? To what extent?

4. What is the effect of a successful individualized reading program on pupils' achievement in other subject areas? Many general statements have been made about this relationship but I have not seen any substantial evidence to support these statements.

5. What is the effect of a successful elementary school individualized reading program on pupils' achievement in secondary school?

This is typical of those projects requiring a long-term study. It is obvious that unless the individualized approach is used throughout the elementary school years, no portion of high school success or failure may be attributed to this type of instruction.

6. What is the nature of the most effective teacher-pupil conference? Such conferences, by whatever name they may be called, are at the very root of the individualized approach. We need to know more about them. We can re-

cord what happens by use of tape recorders. New measures must be developed to evaluate what goes on and to determine why it is effective or otherwise. Research findings should not, of course, be used in order to standardize these conferences, since that would defeat the very purpose of this approach. On the other hand, research, skillfully carried on, could shed much light on the desirability of various procedures and techniques.

7. What is the nature and extent of desirable formal instruction in the so-called "basic skills" of reading under the individualized plan? We need to know the optimum time and extent of such instruction. The way it can most effectively take place is not defined by current research. Other questions that arise are:

What are these "basic skills?"

Is there a sequence in which these skills can be taught most effectively?

Should all or some of these skills be taught to all children regardless of any need arising from their reading?

What teaching tools are most useful in the teaching of such skills?

What is the role of exercise material?

Do special workbooks or other types of material for this purpose need to be developed?

8. What are the most effective ways in which a child shares his reading with his class group? It is not sufficient to make long lists of possible ways of doing this. We need to find out through well-structured research and searching analysis which ways are best for the individual and for the group, and why.

9. What is the value of reading tests in assessing a program of individualized reading? An examination needs to be made as to the adequacy of existing reading tests. The possibility of developing new tests needs to be explored. Gray[3] has reported the reading characteristics of what he called the "mature reader." Tests are needed that will measure the degree to which children are making progress toward

the goal of maturity in reading.

10. <u>What are reasonable expectancies for growth in</u> <u>reading?</u> Very little is really known about the potential extent of the growth in reading that could be expected as a result of a truly efficient instructional program. We read of phenomenal improvements. It is, however, never made quite clear whether such unusual degrees of progress can or should be attained again. We also need to know what degree of progress can reasonably be expected in the period following one of such abnormal progress.

11. <u>To what extent are children of various age groups</u> <u>capable of selecting material of a degree of reading difficulty</u> <u>appropriate to their abilities?</u> Is it true, as often asserted, that children will find their own level if self-selection is employed? Is there any real danger that children will choose materials that are too easy or too difficult? In an individualized reading program what satisfactory way is there to measure the relative difficulty of books? Is this a purely individual matter that varies from reader to reader, as some writers state? Or, is there a standard progression in degree of difficulty that has universal application? What value do the various readability formulae have for the teacher of individualized reading? What legitimate use can be made of various graded lists? It seems to me that we need an investigation of the criteria used in developing such lists. I suspect that the compilation of many of these lists is based on rather subjective criteria. Is it desirable to label books in the classroom library as to degree of difficulty? What effect does labeling have on children's choices of books?

12. <u>What is the optimum extent and nature of record</u> <u>keeping in an individualized reading program?</u> Reports of individualized reading contain a plethora of forms for use by pupils and teachers in recording books read, reading difficulties, and a variety of other matters. Definitive research is needed to determine the value of these records. To what extent are records necessary? What actual use is made of them? Is there danger that keeping lists of books read may place an undue emphasis on the supposed value of making claims that large numbers of books have been read? To what extent has record keeping become a fetish rather than a necessary, useful activity?

13. <u>What are the values of the case study approach in</u> <u>an individualized reading program?</u> Does recording "what

happens," even in the greatest detail, serve any useful purpose unless there is a subsequent analysis and evaluation?
What guidelines are there for such analysis and evaluation?
What should be included in a case study? How long a period should be covered? Is it desirable or even possible to
make a case study of each of the children in a class? If
only a selected number of children in a class can be studied
in this way, which children should be selected? I am under
the impression that the study of children close to the norm
might prove to be more valuable than the usual selection for
study of those farthest removed from the norm. The validity of this impression needs to be investigated. Research
is needed on what is done with the data after they are gathered. Does the value, perhaps, lie in merely gathering the
data? What are the values of a case study approach in terms
of the child? of the teacher?

14. What is the effect of an individualized reading approach on speed of reading? How fast one should read is a
subject lending itself to bitter controversy. There are those
who seriously suggest that phenomenal reading rates of ten
or even twenty or thirty thousand words per minute are possible. Others urge that very slow, deliberate reading is
most desirable. The truth very likely lies somewhere between these viewpoints. No satisfactory research findings
exist on this matter. Cuomo in a recent article sums up the
problem in what I think is an extraordinarily fair way:

> Probably the most common and groundless miscon-
> ception about reading is the one that equates even
> moderate speed with sloppiness. Actually, the
> slow readers are the sloppy ones. They read aim-
> lessly and passively and have more trouble in con-
> centrating than do faster readers. In addition,
> they do not understand as much, do not evaluate
> as well, and do not remember as effectively. The
> person who says he always reads slowly because he
> is being careful is just fooling himself. He is
> neither as careful nor as diligent as he likes to
> think. He is simply inefficient. He's driving a-
> long a smooth, clear highway in the same low gear
> he uses to get his car out of the mud. The fast
> reader is fast because he is alert and skillful. He
> has been trained--or has trained himself--to use
> his ability and his intelligence effectively. Thou-
> sands of persons... have proved that such training is
> both possible and practical. [4]

Making the assumption (please remember that this assumption is not based on adequate research findings) that some degree of rapid reading is desirable, we need to know what the effect of individualized reading is on the development of whatever speed is considered to have optimum merit.

15. To what extent are the principles of individualization of instruction adaptable to other subjects in the curriculum? There is a constantly increasing emphasis at the college level on independent study and honors work. This is in effect often individualized instruction and has much in common with the approach to reading which concerns us in this article. To what extent are these principles applicable in the elementary school, for instance, to the teaching of foreign languages? The possibilities in other curricular areas also need to be explored. The role of an individualized approach in teaching English to non-English-speaking children, which is a major task in many of our large cities today, lends itself to useful research activities.

16. What is the role of the individualized approach in remedial reading? To what extent can this approach be effective in helping remedial cases of various kinds? The motivational merits of individualized reading are generally recognized as the strongest features of the program. Creating motivation is one of the most urgent problems facing the remedial reading teacher. These two statements lead to the conclusion that it may be well worthwhile to explore the value of the individualized approach with remedial reading cases. It must, of course, be remembered that no general conclusions should be drawn about all types of remedial reading cases on the basis of a study of cases with one particular type of reading difficulty.

17. In using the individualized approach, is there danger of failing to identify children with severe reading handicaps? An analysis needs to be made of cases of children, taught reading through an individualized approach, who subsequently turned out to be so emotionally, physically, or otherwise handicapped that special remedial work was necessary. We need to know what the extent of recognition of such problems was by the teacher of individualized reading. Care must be taken by the research worker not to fall into the trap of merely comparing the number of unrecognized cases of this sort in one type of reading class with those found in another class. A satisfactory reading program must provide for the discovery of such cases with reasonable dispatch.

18. To what degree is "self-selection" of reading materials essential to the individualized approach to reading instruction? I feel that children's freedom to choose their own
reading matter is one of the most appealing features of individualized reading. I am certain that I am far from alone
in this feeling. On the other hand, I have observed in many
classrooms where all the features of individualized reading
were in use except that children used the same materials in
a fixed sequence at their own rate. (The Science Research
Associates' kits[5] can be and are used in this way and, for
that matter, so can a series of basal readers be used.) Research is needed to determine whether an individualized approach is just as effective in attaining the aims of reading
instruction when "self-selection" is not employed.

19. How is this approach best explained to children?
to parents? to administrators? to the public? and to
teachers? No educational program can be successful unless
it is appropriately "sold" to all concerned. Many of the articles and theses dealing with individualized reading tell of
ways in which it was introduced to various groups but I have
been unable to find any study investigating the effectiveness
of any of these methods of explanation.

20. Is it possible for any teacher assigned to the
teaching of individualized reading to be successful? Is it
necessary that a teacher believe in the effectiveness of this
approach? Are there certain personality types among teachers who are ill-adapted to this kind of teaching?

21. To what extent is the success claimed for various individualized reading programs attributable to the fact
that more time was spent than would ordinarily be devoted
to reading instruction? Due to the fact that many of the
teachers using this approach have been zealously enthusiastic,
larger blocks of time have been allotted to reading than is
usually the case. We need to know what role this factor
played in making programs productive of good reading. This
question is closely related to that of the so-called "Hawthorne
Effect." Many experimental programs appear to succeed only because of unusual enthusiasm on the part of pupils and
teachers.

22. Is the individualized reading approach equally successful with all children? In this question the term "equally
efficient" should not be equated with "equal performance."
What we know about individual differences makes it certain

that all children will not learn with equal increments. The
research question posed here refers to relative performance
of children. We need to know whether certain personality
patterns found among children may make the self-directed,
pacing approach of individualized reading ineffective in some
cases. We all know children who seem to need the security
of close and continuous step-by-step direction. It seems a
plausible hypothesis, worthy of being tested, that some children may find it very difficult to adjust to individualized
reading.

23. Does the individualized reading approach cultivate
habits of carelessness and lack of thoroughness in reading?
Is there danger that children will become skimmers rather
than readers? How can this be controlled? What degree of
comprehension and recall is necessary and desirable in reading? This, of course, relates to the question of aims discussed above. Since it is such a sticky question with all
sorts of implications, I re-emphasize it here. Obviously
the very best of readers does not have either total comprehension or total recall. How far do we compromise? Does
the drive to read more and more books lead to an unaccept-
able level of reading? This drive, of course, can arise
either from a competitive desire to excel or from misguided
enthusiasm.

24. What emphasis should be given to individualized
reading in teacher training courses? Even the most ardent
enthusiast about individualized reading will have to concede
that the chances of a beginning teacher being assigned to an
individualized reading program are less than even. To what
extent are college teachers of prospective teachers justified
in going beyond those methods and skills that are most likely
to be used by their students in a school situation? To what
extent are they obligated to open new pathways toward improved methods of instruction? Being in this position myself, I am painfully aware of the time pressures that impinge
on those engaged in teacher-training. How does one avoid
shortchanging the prospective teacher?

25. What is the most effective way of training teachers in service to teach individualized reading? What methods
should be used? What materials are desirable? (Obviously
in regard to individualized reading the "cook-book approach"
with specific recipes á la teaching manual is inappropriate.)
Do such materials exist? How long a period of preparation
should be allowed for such training? Who can most effec-

tively conduct this training?

It is easier to pose questions than it is to find answers. Research on most of the vital questions listed in this article will not be easy, especially if it is rigidly performed. Unless, however, the research is carefully planned and an appropriate experimental design is set up, results will be neither definitive nor reliable. Who is going to engage in this research? A great deal of it can be done by masters' and doctoral candidates, especially if the type of continuing research advocated in the beginning of this article should become commonly accepted. It may be that a major research project, which would seek to determine many of the answers, could be designed to attract financial support from governmental or private sources. The classroom teacher with an adequate background of knowledge about research design and techniques could also make a significant contribution.

Until these and other questions are definitely answered by researchers it will be impossible to properly evaluate the desirability of the individualized approach to the teaching of reading.

Notes

1. Thirty-four master's theses were listed in an article in Elementary English, 40 (March, 1963) 280-83. Since that date there have been a number of additional master's theses, but doctoral dissertations on this subject are very few in number. Other major research on this topic is very sparse.

2. Brownell, William A. "Educational Research in the Decade Ahead" Washington: American Educational Research Association, 1960, Mimeo.

3. Gray, William S. and Rogers, Bernice Maturity in Reading Chicago: University of Chicago Press, 1956.

4. Cuomo, George "How Fast Should a Person Read?" Saturday Review 45 (April 21, 1962) 13-14.

5. S. R. A. Elementary Reading Laboratory Chicago: Science Research Associates, 1960.

Chapter 15

Summary

The preceding pages have touched on many of the issues involved in the use of the individualized approach to the teaching of reading. Obviously, in the space allotted not all matters could be discussed nor could those issues that were dealt with be considered as thoroughly as they might have been.

It has been pointed out, notably by Groff, that individualized reading is a grass roots movement. The classroom teacher is the one most engaged by this approach whereas in general the authorities on reading are less enthusiastic. It, therefore, seems appropriate to me that selections should be included to the extent that they have been in this book from masters' theses. Such theses are more often than not written by classroom teachers.

It also seemed desirable to use material that with a few exceptions was written in the decade of the sixties. This was done for two reasons: first, because such material is less likely to have been read previously by the users of this book and secondly, in order to dispel the idea that individualized reading reached its hey-day in the fifties. Certainly this material was not used because of a lack of suitable articles that were written before 1960. Great contributions have been made by the earlier writers and these should not in any way be deprecated.

Unfortunately, there has been a great amount of controversy about individualized reading which sometimes has resulted in a degree of shrillness on both sides. The omission of all such material in this book has not been accidental. It seems to me that very little can be gained by reproducing these arguments once again.

It is a matter of keen regret that space could not be found for a more complete treatment of some of the fine research projects that have been carried out in this field.

456

True, more research is needed, but there have been a number of studies that meet the highest criteria for good research.

The philosophical and psychological bases supporting the soundness of the individualized approach to the teaching of reading have also regretfully been largely omitted in this book.   This was a hard choice and there certainly would be some validity to an opinion that this omission is not justifiable.

In ending this book, I must express the hope that reading it will induce teachers to try this approach and thus to unshackle the pupils they teach.   Learning to read is indeed an unshackling experience especially when it is not at the expense of learning how to read as well.

Acinapuro, Philip Joseph 401, 404
Adams, Phyllis Stevens 14, 161, 169-206, 341, 352-358, 402, 406
Agnew, Kate 393, 394
Allen, R. Van 41, 55, 174
Anderson, Irving H. 400, 403
Anderson, Marjorie R. 16, 341, 348-351
Anderson, Will D. 393
Archer, Marguerite P. 16, 297, 302-306
Arbuthnot, May Hill 163
Arkley, Rose Adatto 16, 313, 323-324, 341, 365-369, 402, 405
Aronow, Miriam S. 402, 405
Arrowood, C. F. 387
Austin, Mary C. 398-399

Bailey, Auline Lowery 15, 208, 229-231, 313, 325-326, 336-338, 402, 405
Barbe, Walter B. 86
Beattie, Willard W. 384, 389
Belcher, Jane 402, 405
Betts, Emmett Albert 394, 395, 416
Binet, Alfred 389
Bohnhorst, Ben A. 400, 403
Bollinger, Janie Keith 12, 40, 67-71
Boney, C. De Witt 393, 394
Braidford, Margaret 401, 405
Brownell, William A. 415, 447
Bruce, Percy W. 401, 403
Burdette, Eunice E. 404
Burk, Frederic 16, 376, 377-382, 383-386, 389

Burrows, Alvina Truet 396, 400, 403
Butts, R. Freeman 392

Caliver, Marguerite Pittman 13, 72, 85-93
Carline, Donald Eugene 401, 405
Carlisle, DonEtta June 401, 405
Cattell, James McKeen 389
Carr, Constance 401, 404
Carson, Louise G. 401, 403
Clark, Christine H. 402, 405
Cole, Luella 394
Cooke, Walter W. 394
Cordt, Anna B. 49
Courtis, Stuart Appleton 391
Cremin, Lawrence A. 392
Crique, Orvell Anthony 400, 403
Crosby, Muriel 401, 405
Crossley, Ruth 401, 404
Cuomo, George 451
Cyrog, Frances Vanderhoof 13, 99, 101, 104, 342, 372-373, 401, 402, 404, 406, 420

Darrow, Helen Fisher 174
Darwin, Charles 389
Dean, Ray B. 394
Dees, Margaret 249
DeLisle, Robert G. 15, 16, 249, 258-266
Delph, Donna 13, 99, 118-135
Derbyshire, Maurice A. 401, 404
Dernbach, Beverly M. 13, 99, 105-117

Dewey, John 392
Dickhart, Audrey 401, 404
Dickinson, Marie 196, 401, 404
Disney, Walt 91
Dixon, W. Robert 400, 403
Dolch, Edward W. 86, 299, 393, 398
Donahue, Dorothy L. 15, 202, 207, 232-234, 402, 405
Duker Sam 17, 401, 403, 423, 446-455

Eby, Frederick 387
Edwards, Edith 401, 404
Ellard, Mary 249
Ellingson, Ruby 402, 406
Evans, N. Dean 400, 403, 419

Farley, Edgar S. 15, 237, 238-241
Fay, Leo C. 401, 404
Field, Helen A. 393
Flesch, Rudolph 416
Fox, Gudella 15, 208, 235-236
Fox, Raymond B. 15, 208, 235-236
Frazier, Alexander 12, 19, 29-32

Galton, Francis 389
Gans, Roma 396
Garment, Sylvia 402, 405
Gates, Arthur I. 51, 56, 392
Goode, Jane Anderson 17, 376, 412-422
Gordon, Ira J. 402, 405
Gray, Glenda Arlene 12, 14, 72, 76-79, 161, 167-168, 313, 330-332
Gray, William S. 178, 403, 449
Greenman, Ruth 401, 404
Gresham, LaVerne P. 401, 405
Groff, Patrick J. 13, 14, 16,

99, 150-154, 161, 162-166, 297, 298-301
Gumlick, Helen R. 394
Gunderson, Agnes G. 249

Hagen, Elizabeth 389
Harris, Albert J. 388, 393, 394, 395
Harris, Melva 395
Harris, W. T. 388
Harrison, M. Lucille 193
Hart, John Douglas 401, 404
Heller, Frieda M. 394
Hildreth, Gertrude 44, 52, 56, 193, 396
Hilson, Helen Heacock 401, 404
Hostetler, Beverly 402, 406
Huck, Charlotte S. 15, 163, 249, 250-257
Hughes, Byron O. 400, 403
Hune, Anna Marie Hess 14, 207, 218-220, 313, 327-329, 342, 370-371
Hunt, Lyman C., Jr. 12, 16, 19, 33, 267, 288-296

Ingram, Vivian 401, 405
Izzo, Ruth Kelly 401, 405

Jacobs, Leland B. 396
Jenkins, Marian 400, 403
Jensen, Amy Elizabeth 14, 208, 221-228, 313, 314, 339-340, 342, 374-375
Johnson, Mabel L. 400, 403
Jones, Daisy Marvel 395

Kaar, Harold Wright 400, 403
Kapilian, Sharon 401, 404
Karp, Etta E. 86, 174
Keener, Beverly M. 15, 237, 246-248
Kingsley, Marjorie 401, 404
Kniley, Mildred 401, 404
Kopel, David 394
Kozol, Jonathan 11, 19, 21-23
Krone, B. P. 163

LaBrant, Lou Le Vanche 390, 393, 394
Lane, Kenneth Boyd 406
Largent, Mary 401, 404
Larrick, Nancy 163, 249
Lazar, May 249, 399, 419
Lehman, Edna 394
Loken, Olga 249
Loomis, Mary Jane 394
Lowrie, Jean E. 16, 297, 307-312
Luther, Martin 388

McChristy, Antoinette 401, 403
McCloskey, Robert 91
McCullough, Constance 400
McKay, Beverly Lee 13, 99, 100, 155-160
McNabb, Isabel 404
McVey, Marcia 401, 405
Maib, Frances 396
Marcatante, John 401, 405
Meriam, J. L. 393
Michalek, Goldie Katherine 249
Miel, Alice 396
Monroe, Marion 193
Moore, Annie E. 298

Nulton, Lucy 55

O'Brian, Ida 393
Olson, Willard C. 252, 303, 393, 394, 396, 397, 418
Oser, William Howard 400, 403

Palmer, Delores Cooper 400, 403
Parker, Samuel C. 412
Parker, Ethel T. 400, 403
Parkhurst, Helen 389, 391
Parkin, Phyllis 400, 403
Patterson, Agnes MacLachlan 401, 405
Picozzi, Adelaide 401, 404
Pirsig, Elsie A. 401, 405

Peters, Carol Huenink 12, 72, 73-75
Peterson, A. D. C. 388
Pollach, Samuel 401, 405

Reeve, Olive R. 194
Renick, Marion 91
Rix, Anna Marie 13, 99, 146-149
Robinson, Ruth 402, 405
Roettger, Doris Dornfeld 14, 207, 217, 313, 321-322, 341, 343-347, 359-363
Rogers, Bernice 449
Rohm, Emma L. 402, 406
Rollins, Kay 402, 406
Roston, Sylvia Willner 12, 14, 40, 58-66, 207, 215-216, 313, 333-335, 402
Rothrock, Dayton, G. 402, 406
Russell, David H. 86, 174

Safford, Alton Lugton 402, 405
Sartain, Harry W. 398, 400, 402, 405
Schmidt, Ethel M. 400, 403
Schnitzer, Eunice E. 402, 406
Search, Preston W. 383, 388
Seeber, Frances Mangelsdorf 16, 376, 387-411
Sellars, Sophia N. 400, 403
Senderling, Elizabeth Allen 12, 40, 41-57, 402, 405
Sharpe, Maida Wood 401, 404
Sibley, Martha 393
Simon, Theophile 389
Skapski, Mary 402, 405
Skolnick, Sidney 406
Smith, Lois 402, 405
Smith, Nila Blanton 303, 402, 418, 419
Spache, George D. 416
Sperber, Robert 401, 404
Sperry, Florence Bond 391, 402, 406
Staiger, Ralph 398

Stauffer, Russell G. 235, 388,
390, 391, 393
Steiner, Barbara A. 400, 401,
405
Sullivan, Gertrude M. 14, 207,
209-214

Theisen, W. W. 412
Thomas, Glenn G. 401, 404
Thompson, Mildred E. 400,
403
Thorndike, Robert L. 389
Tooze, Ruth A. 163

Utz, Floy 12, 72, 80-84

Veatch, Jeannette 46, 56,
196, 201, 202, 235, 396
Virgil 387
Vite, Irene Williams 396,
398, 401, 404
Vogel, Mabel 413
Vorontosov, Anna 299

Wahle, Roy Patrick 15, 237,
242-245
Walcutt, Charles C. 416
Walker, Clare Connoly 401,
403
Warford, Phyllis 402, 405
Washburne Carleton W. 384,
389, 390, 391, 413
Webb, Hazel Sparks 13, 72,
94-98
Wells, Mary Maloney 402, 405
West, Roland 297, 393, 395,
396, 399
Wiggins, Evelyn L. 401, 404
Williamson, John 402, 405
Willis, Margaret 402, 406
Wilson, Ruth L. 402, 406
Witty, Paul A. 393, 394, 395
Wood, Ruth V. 401, 403
Wundt, Wilhelm Max 389

Young, Doris A. 163
Young, Elizabeth 401, 403

Zirbes, Laura 389

Subject Index

Administrators 134-135
  Reaction of, to individual-
    ized reading 115
Aims to individualized read-
  ing (See Individualized
  reading.)
American Library Associa-
  tion 304-305
Attitude Toward Reading
  Scale 315-322

Baltimore County Schools 13,
  136-149
Basal reading
  Basal reader manuals 174
  Basal readers 21-22, 42,
    43, 45, 48-49, 50, 63,
    80, 87, 95, 101, 111,
    138, 151, 173, 289, 305,
    358
  Combined with individual-
    ized reading 63, 77, 235-
    236, 352-358
Bibliography 9

Case studies 450-451
Charts (See Experience
  charts.)
Child study movement 415-
  416
Children's literature 250-257
Class size 55, 116, 146
Classroom organization (See
  Teaching procedures.)
Classroom, physical arrange-
  ment of (See Teaching
  procedures.)
Conferences 29, 46-48, 60-61,
  77, 80, 81, 82-83, 88-
  89, 96, 97, 98, 102,

  104, 113, 142, 148,
  158, 201-202, 209-220,
  288, 291, 294, 419, 488
  Activities 212
  Contribution 212-213
  Duration 211
  Frequency 211
  Records 183-185, 218-220
  Scale for measuring pupil
    attitude toward 215-216
  Weaknesses 213
Creativity 289
Curriculum
  Child centered 415-416

Dalton Plan 303, 390, 413,
  418
Discipline 116

Evaluation 84, 87, 93, 115,
  205, 268, 294, 315-322,
  352-358
  By pupils 22, 43-44, 98,
    127, 315-322, 323-324,
    327-329, 330, 336-338
  California Reading Tests
    371
  Discussion of books 293
  Gates Advanced Primary
    Reading Test 366-369
  Independent work 204
  Iowa Silent Reading Test
    360-361
  List of reading 183
  Metropolitan Achievement
    Test 353
  Metropolitan Readiness Test
    353
  Teacher-made tests 353
  Tests 449

462

Need for development 447
Results 360, 361, 366-369, 371, 372-373
Expectancy of reading growth 450
Experience charts 171, 191, 291, 292, 294

Games 86
Word games 293
Grade levels, programs in 448
Grade 1 41, 57-66, 169-206, 291, 292, 294, 295, 352, 358
Grade 2 57-66, 290, 291, 293, 294
Grade 3 67-71, 291, 292, 294, 295, 366-369
Grade 4 73-79, 103-104, 291, 293, 295
Grade 5 21-23, 76-79, 80-84, 85-93, 167, 291, 292, 293, 295
Grade 6 94-98, 291, 293, 294
Grades 3-6 372-373
Primary Grades 101ff
Grouping 27, 58-60, 74, 77, 83, 113, 143, 153, 159, 175, 203, 288, 290-291, 292, 302, 304, 316, 392-393

Ability 392-393, 414-415
Flexible 244, 394

Independent work 27, 200, 209, 389
Individual differences 238-245, 302, 389, 417
Individual instruction 376
Individualization of instruction
Marks of 243-244
Resistance to 392

Spread of 391-392
Individualized reading
Aims 24, 160, 303, 374-375, 446
Characteristics 288-289
Combined with basal reading (See Basal reading)
Criteria 24-28
Effectiveness 169-206
Essentials 162
Integration with language arts program 417
Objections 165-166, 419-420
Other teachers' reactions 115, 134-135
Outcomes 447
Problems 76
Rationale 24-28
Reading interests 153-154
Types 149
(See also Reading, Orientation to individualized reading.)
Initiation of individualized reading programs (See Orientation to individualized reading.)
Instructional materials (See Materials.)
Interaction with individualized reading
Mental ability 448
School Achievement 448
Spelling 39
Writing 290, 295

Learning theory 24
Librarians 300, 308-309, 311
Role 297-312
Library 244, 417
Classroom library 74-75, 77, 80-81, 85, 95, 101, 104, 149
Curriculum development 308
Instructional program 308
Public library 75, 80, 85-

463

Library (cont.)
        86, 92, 103, 124
    School library 81, 310
        Insufficiency 300
        Professional books 164
    Services 144

    Materials 24-25, 29, 30,
        108-109, 157, 170-171,
        303, 307, 310
        Audio-visual aids 91-92
        Films 288-296
        Filmstrips 173
        Books 172-173, 371, 448
            Easy to read 299
            Reading guides 258, 265
            Sources 156
        Children's magazines 173
        Dictionaries, picture 191
        Diversification 305
        Free materials 173
        Obtaining, problems of
            124-125
        Paperbacks 21-23
        S. R. A. Reading laboratory
            78
        School newspapers 173
        Selection 124+
        Sources 209
        Tradebooks 21-23, 305
        Workbooks 86, 110-111,
            174
    Maturity in reading 449

National Council of Teachers
        of English 304

Objections to individualized
        reading (See Individual-
        ized reading.)
Orientation to individualized
        reading 106, 118-122,
        161+, 196-197
    By teacher 162-166
    Class visitation 162
    Of administrators 163, 167,
        453

    Of parents 86-87, 94, 167,
        288-296, 453
    Of public 453
    Of pupils 167, 193, 453
    Of teachers 453
Outcomes (See Individualized
        reading.)

Pacing 26, 61, 101-102, 288
Parents
    Attitudes 114, 134-135,
        325-326
    Conferences with teachers
        318
    Role 339-340
    School visits 93, 94
    (See also Orientation.)
Phonics 49-50, 293, 357, 416
Poetry 59, 65
Problems in individualized
        reading (See Individual-
        ized reading.)
Pupil teacher conferences (See
        Conferences.)
Pupils
    Books read 362-363
    Disadvantaged 246-248
    Interests 357
        Extending 29
    Personality 453
    Reading attitudes 352, 357
    Reading Preference Scale
        333-335

Reading
    By adults in United States
        250
    Experiences and 293
    Habits 352
    Outcomes of program 374-
        375
    Purposes 30
    (See also Individualized
        reading, Skills, Remedial
        reading.)
Reading Inventory Record 186-
        189

Reading readiness 41, 152
  Check-list 179-182
Reading skills (see Skills)
Reading, teaching of
  Basal approach 268-287
  Language experience approach 268-287
  (See also Skills.)
Record keeping 38, 73, 86,
  95-96, 107-108, 116,
  131-132, 139-140, 157,
  178, 232-234, 303-304,
  450
  By pupil 74, 75, 81, 232-
  233
  By teacher 27, 81-82,
  233-234
Recreational reading 66, 117,
  300, 308
Remedial reading 112, 414,
  452
Research
  Basal reading and individualized reading compared 169-206, 304
  Child development 415
  Control groups 447
  Coordination needed 447
  Longitudinal 372-373
  Studies after 1950 396-406
  Studies before 1950 393-
  395

San Diego County Department
  of Education 12, 24, 268-
  287, 315-322
San Diego County Reading
  Study Project 268-287
San Francisco State Normal
  School 376, 412
Self selection 28, 30-31, 58-
  59, 73, 83-84, 85, 90-
  91, 96-97, 114, 203-204,
  221-231, 289, 290, 292,
  295, 309, 449
Sharing 28, 30-31, 58-59, 73,
  83-84, 85, 90-91, 96-97,
  114, 203-204, 221-231,

  289, 290, 292, 295,
  309, 449
Skills 26, 31-32, 33-39, 49,
  62, 74, 89-90, 110, 111-
  112, 117, 132-134, 151,
  175, 288, 290, 352, 449
  Chart for recording progress
  348-351
  Comprehension 176-177,
  292, 302, 357
  Critical reading 177, 417
  Oral reading 34, 112, 357
  Sequential development 35
  Sight vocabulary 42, 357
  Silent reading 34, 357
  Speed of reading 451-452
  Vocabulary development 34,
  74, 293
  Word recognition 36-37, 51-
  52, 176, 190-191, 293,
  357
  Word study 34
    word analysis 150-151
  Work study habits 153-154,
  177, 352, 357
Surveys, reports of 67-71,
  105-117, 118-135, 136-
  145, 146-149, 150-154,
  155-159, 330

Teacher inventory of Approaches to the Teaching
  of Reading 424-427
  Scoring 424-427
  Use of, described 427-442
Teacher-pupil conferences
  (See Conferences.)
Teachers
  Difficulties 150ff
  Function 24
  In-service training 443
    By open circuit television 288-296
  Inventory 268-287
    Uses of 269
  Personality 453
  Requirements 304
  Role 24, 37-38

465

Teachers (cont.)

Scale for evaluation of pu-
pil performance 343-
347
Time spent 140
Training 288-296
Teaching materials (See Ma-
terials.)
Teaching procedures 128-131
Activities during reading
period 106
Busy work 54
Classroom
Appearance and physical
arrangement 57-58, 87-
88, 95, 168, 191-192
Organization 128-131,
292
Corresponding with authors
58, 91
Diagnosis of reading diffi-
culties 452
Free reading programs 390
Length of period 106
Routines, establishment of
189
Schedule 197-199
Storytelling 294
Tests and testing (See Evalu-
ation.)

Vocabulary
Controlled 36

Weekly Reader 58
Whittier, California 372-373
Whole child theory 417
Winnetka, Illinois 303, 384,
413, 418